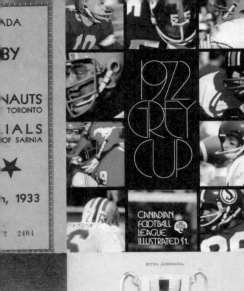

'88 COUPE GREY CUP

WINNIPEG — B.C./C.-B.

GREY CUP 1997

GREY CUP 1966

GREY CUP 1979

CANADIAN FOOTBALL LEAGUE ILLUSTRATED $1.

37th ANNUAL

GREY CUP

39TH ANNUAL
GREY CUP

OFFICIAL SOUVENIR PROGRAM

HAMILTON WINNIPEG

B.C. LIONS × HAMILTON
SATURDAY, NOVEMBER 30, 1963 — EMPIRE STADIUM, VANCOUVER, CANADA
OFFICIAL SOUVENIR PROGRAM
AND TELEVISION GUIDE — 50c INCLUDING TAX

OFFICIAL SOUVENIR PROGRAM
GREY CUP '64
HAMILTON vs B.C. LIONS

OTTAWA
FIFTY CENTS

LE MATCH DE LA COUPE GREY
THE GREY CUP CHAMPIONSHIP

CALGARY   MONTRÉAL

GREY CUP '74

GREY CUP '95
SOUVENIR MAGAZINE

CFL ILLUSTRATED
COUPE GREY CUP
1984

COUPE GREY CUP 1982

THE GREY CUP 1993

THE CANADIAN PROFESSIONAL FOOTBALL CHAMPIONSHIP

EAST WEST

GREY CUP '71

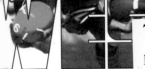
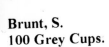

STEPHEN BRUNT

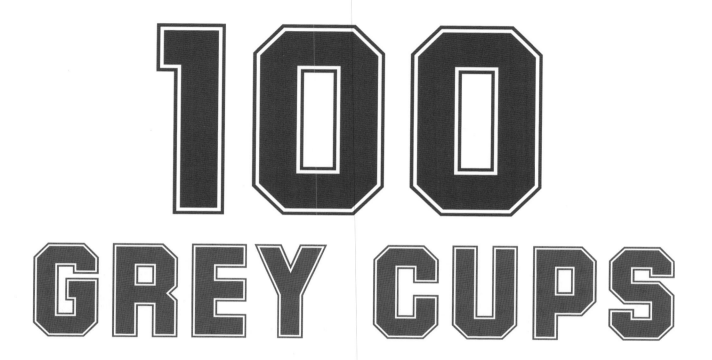

100 GREY CUPS

THIS IS OUR GAME

McClelland & Stewart

Library and Archives Canada Cataloguing in Publication

Brunt, Stephen
    100 Grey Cups : this is our game / Stephen Brunt.

ISBN 978-0-7710-1744-5

    1. Grey Cup (Football)–History. 2. Canadian Football League–History. 3. Canadian football–History.
I. Title.
II. Title: One hundred Grey Cups.

GV948.B78 2012   796.335'648   C2012-900975-X

We acknowledge the financial support of the Government of Canada through the Canada Book Fund and that of the Government of Ontario through the Ontario Media Development Corporation's Ontario Book Initiative. We further acknowledge the support of the Canada Council for the Arts and the Ontario Arts Council for our publishing program.

Published simultaneously in the United States of America by McClelland & Stewart, a division of Random House of Canada Limited, P.O. Box 1030, Plattsburgh, New York 12901

Library of Congress Control Number: 2012932354

All photos courtesy of the Canadian Football Hall of Fame except pages 72, 136, 148 courtesy of the Canadian Football League; page i courtesy of Ryan Enn Hughes.

Typeset in Electra by M&S, Toronto
Printed and bound in Canada

McClelland & Stewart,
a division of Random House of Canada Limited
One Toronto Street
Toronto, Ontario
M5C 2V6
www.mcclelland.com

1   2   3   4   5   16 15 14 13 12

CONTENTS

THE GREY CUP REFLECTS US ALL

We Canadians are proud of our heritage, and the Grey Cup is one of our country's most enduring icons.

We celebrate excellence, and so, too, does the Grey Cup, for only the names of champions can grace it.

We are sometimes defined by our weather, and Grey Cup lore is thick with snow and mud and ice and fog.

We are all shaped by our past, and the history of the Grey Cup is very much our history.

We are confident about Canada's future, and the Grey Cup mirrors that confidence, as it is about to boldly launch into its second century.

But above all, the Grey Cup reflects our ability to come together, as Canadians.

The Grey Cup has been called the nation's glue, for it has joined us together – whether we be Canadians by birth or Canadians by choice, young or old, easterners or westerners – for as long as any of us can remember.

So the 100th Grey Cup is not only a chance to celebrate the great game of Canadian football, tremendous championship contests, and our own league, the Canadian Football League.

It's an opportunity to celebrate something that is uniquely, passionately, and unapologetically *ours*.

It's a time to celebrate Canada.

And Stephen Brunt is distinctly qualified to help us do just that.

An accomplished author and award-winning journalist, Stephen is one of our country's pre-eminent storytellers. What's more, he's a diehard fan – a Hamilton kid who grew up idolizing the Tiger-Cats at what was then Civic Stadium, and a columnist whose coverage of every major sporting event in the world has confirmed his deep-seated conviction that the Grey Cup championships are second to none, and truly something special.

We at the Canadian Football League will cherish this book. And we will proudly share it with our fellow Canadians for years to come, because this celebration is as much a renewal as it is a retrospective. This is not the end. It's just the start of the next chapter.

Today, the Grey Cup is attended by tens of thousands, watched by millions, and revered by Canadians from coast to coast to coast, as well as by Canadians living abroad.

It is bigger and better and stronger than ever, giving us every reason to be confident that our Grey Cup, like our Canada, has a future even brighter than its past.

MARK COHON
Commissioner
Canadian Football League

ACKNOWLEDGEMENTS

This book would not have been possible without the assistance of the outstanding researcher Paul Patskou, who unearthed a treasure trove of contemporary newspaper accounts, and also allowed me access to his vast collection of historic film.

Larry Robertson also provided help filling in some very specific details.

The two most significant works on the history of Canadian football were invaluable resources. They are: *The Grey Cup Story: The Dramatic History of Football's Most Coveted Award* by Jack Sullivan (Greywood Publishing, 1972); and *100 Years of Canadian Football* by Gordon Currie (Pagurian Press, 1972). Also consulted was *Heroes of the Game: A History of the Grey Cup* by Stephen Thiele (Moulin Publishing, 1997).

Thanks to everyone at McClelland & Stewart, to the folks at the Canadian Football League offices, and to the staff of the Canadian Football Hall of Fame.

EARL GREY

INTRODUCTION:
OUR GAME, OUR STORIES

Albert Henry George Grey, the fourth Earl Grey, liked to stroll through the streets of Ottawa, or at least that's how legend would have it. He was anything but narrow in his outlook, especially in the context of those early days of the twentieth century. In fact, he was a bit of a Renaissance man who, during his tenure as Canada's governor general, greatly expanded the role of the Crown's representative in the Dominion. He travelled the whole of the vast country at a time when that was no simple proposition, and visited the colony of Newfoundland as well. He became friends with the American president, Theodore Roosevelt. He promoted the idea of a national culture, was a patron of the arts, set up awards for music and drama, and was a champion of social reform. Appalled by anti-Asian rioting in Vancouver, he arranged for Prince Fushima of Japan to come to Canada, the nation's first important foreign royal visit. And his wife, Lady Grey, the first governor general's better half to be granted the title Her Excellency, sponsored competitions for the most beautiful gardens in her adopted hometown. Any one of these achievements would have made him a notable figure, and collectively they certainly left their mark in the Canadian history books. But it is almost by accident that Lord Grey lives on as a household name.

The story is that during his walks in the nation's capital, Earl Grey would occasionally pass the Varsity Oval, where he sometimes saw a game being played that must have seemed familiar. As a product of England's "public" school system – he was educated at Harrow and at Trinity College – Earl Grey would have known of the type of football invented at the Rugby School in Rugby, Warwickshire. Rugby was a sport that had evolved from the myriad brands of organized and not-so-organized "football" whose roots reached back to ancient times when warriors kicked around the heads of vanquished opponents. Two distinct styles would emerge: one in which handling the ball was forbidden, which would become the passion of the working classes, and one in which players were allowed to pick up the ball and run with it, which would become the sport of England's privileged elite.

The game played in Ottawa looked very much like rugby football, with fourteen or fifteen men a side, with scrums and lateral passes. But the truth was, it was actually a New World variant, already evolving into something distinct from its English antecedents, though still a long way from resembling what we now know as Canadian football. In 1909, Earl Grey decided that it would be a service to the nation to donate a trophy in his name, and so he commissioned a silver bowl to be made by Canadian jeweller, Birks, with an inscription composed by Rev. Dr. D. B. Macdonald of Toronto, one of those chosen as the new trophy's trustees: "Presented by His Excellency Earl Grey, for the Amateur Rugby Football Championship of Canada."

More than a hundred years later, that battered old mug is still being passed from team to team. The plates attached to its base bear the names of the champions of a game that has transformed into one distinctly Canadian.

OPPOSITE: A portrait of Earl Grey which resides in the Canadian Football League Hall of Fame.

These inscriptions trace a nearly unbroken line that reaches deep into the nation's sporting past. The trophy has come to symbolize a long-standing rivalry between the eastern and western halves of the country. The game and the festival surrounding it have evolved into a kind of national sporting holiday, a moment when the country stands still and, in many ways, celebrates itself. One day, the popular story continues, Lord Grey had a bright idea, and the next, somebody was riding a horse through a hotel lobby, Mud Bowls and Fog Bowls were entering national sporting lore, Pierre Trudeau was performing a ceremonial kickoff, Doug Flutie and Anthony Calvillo were working their magic, and 'Rider Pride was painting the Grey Cup green. Just like that.

It is a neat and tidy pocket history, but as anyone who follows the twists and turns of Canadian football can tell you, its story rarely moves in a straight narrative line. And that was true even at the game's very origins, even in the time of Earl Grey, who may well have walked by rugby matches at the Varsity Oval in Ottawa, and who did indeed donate a trophy for the national champion of the game.

But it seems that was not his original intention. Apparently, during his travels, during his strolls, he also saw another sport being played. Following the lead of Lord Stanley of Preston, one of his predecessors as governor general, who in 1892 had had the bright idea of donating a challenge cup that would be symbolic of hockey supremacy in Canada, Earl Grey decided that he would donate a prize, too – also for hockey. The Stanley Cup was by now being presented to the best professional team in the land. Perhaps Grey could put his name on a cup that would be awarded to the best pure amateurs in Canadian hockey.

Problem was, Lord Grey wasn't the only one to have that particular bright idea at that particular time.

As the *Toronto Star* reported on January 14, 1909:

Sir H. Montagu Allan, who is [honorary] president of the M.A.A.A., has taken a great deal of interest in the amateur hockey question and the formation of the Inter-provincial Hockey Union. The latter so far has been without an emblem of championship. This Sir Montagu has offered to supply.

It is also reported that his Excellency the Governor-General Earl Grey may give a cup to be competed for by amateur clubs of the whole Dominion to stand to the amateur clubs as the Stanley Cup does at present to the professionals.

The associations qualified for the Grey Cup award would be the O.H.A., the largest amateur hockey association in the world, the Inter-Provincial, the Inter-Collegiate, the Manitoba, and the Maritime Province amateur teams.

There is no record of how that presumably embarrassing convergence of like-minded generosity was resolved. But we do know that the Allan Cup, which once nearly rivalled the Stanley Cup in importance, is still presented to Canada's best senior amateur hockey team. Meanwhile, Earl Grey had a change of heart, or had one forced upon him: perhaps a football trophy would be the way to go. He commissioned a cup that would be presented to the champion of Canadian amateur football – though in a sport that was mired in ongoing jurisdictional disputes, even deciding who that was would prove to be a bit of a challenge. The president of the *Journal* newspaper in Ottawa, P. D. Ross, was asked by the governor general's representative to figure that out, but he demurred, suggesting instead the establishment of a board of trustees. That three-man group included Rev. Macdonald, author of the famous inscription, and Percival Molson, scion of the great Montreal brewing and sports family, along with H. B. McGiverin, a member of Parliament, a former football and cricket player of some renown, and the president of the Ottawa Football Club. In the spring of 1909, they decided that the trophy would be presented to the champions of the Canadian Rugby Union and, after that, would be a challenge trophy – as was the Stanley Cup.

But by the autumn of that year, with the football season drawing to a close, the trustees faced one minor problem: the promised trophy had not yet turned up. How do you tell a governor general – with the utmost respect, of course – that perhaps he ought to keep his promise? It would take three gentle nudges from the trustees before the eighteen-inch-tall sterling silver mug – valued at $48 – finally arrived in Toronto.

That wasn't the end of it, though. The base of the trophy had to be replaced with one more appropriate to the purpose, and the inscription composed and engraved. And then there was the small matter of the bill for those changes. Just whose responsibility might that be? The trustees again sent out a carefully worded note to Earl Grey, which included a photograph of the trophy, and the jeweller's invoice. They offered to foot the bill themselves "if there is the slightest disposition on the part of His Excellency against it," Rev. Macdonald wrote. Lost to history is the answer as to who finally anted up. Only in the spring of 1910 did the first Grey

SAT'Y. OCT. 6, 1907
TIGERS vs MONTREAL A.A.A.

HAMILTON FOOTBALL TEAM, 1898.

Cup champions from the University of Toronto finally receive their prize – presumably having had no real idea they were playing for it the previous December.

But still, the match at Rosedale Field, in what is today one of the oldest and wealthiest neighbourhoods in the City of Toronto, is remembered and recorded as the moment when a great Canadian tradition was born.

And now to 2012, back to Toronto – today a great, vital cosmopolitan city – and to a place just a short distance from the site of that first championship game. The Grey Cup will be presented for the 100th time at Rogers Centre, and that humble trophy has become emblematic of a game, of a truly national event, and of a country its donor could never have imagined.

The story of the Grey Cup, from its origins through to the twenty-first century, is firmly lodged in our collective memory, and in many ways reflects some of the great themes of our history. Individual games really can seem like signposts along the road of our evolution as a nation.

It is telling that the Grey Cup's power as a symbol of and rallying point for Canadian identity seems even more significant today, at a time when we can connect with anyone, anywhere, anytime, with the push of a button, and in a world in which so many cultural lines of demarcation have been erased, than it did back in the days when horses were first – reportedly – being ridden into hotel lobbies.

No other sporting event in this country has such lineage, such history. On no other day on the calendar do so many Canadians pause to celebrate something that is absolutely, 100 per cent their own.

This selective and subjective history of the Grey Cup touches on just a handful of those 100 games. Rather than approach the history chronologically, or focus on the familiar milestones – the Mud Bowl, the Fog Bowl, etc. – the years and games chronicled here were chosen because each seemed to represent a particular moment in time for Canadian football, for one of its teams, or for Canada.

One of these moments came in 1935, when the Winnipeg Football Club made the long train trip east and came home with the Grey Cup, the first time a western team captured the national football championship, ending years of futility, knocking central Canadian arrogance down a notch – and hasn't western alienation been a long-running theme in our national conversation?

Another emblematic moment in the game's history took place during the Second World War, when service teams competed for the Grey Cup. Some of the players who took the field later died on foreign battlegrounds fighting under Canada's flag.

After the war, in 1948, Calgary fans took over downtown Toronto, effectively creating what is now known as the Grey Cup festival, before they bore the trophy home to Alberta. In the 1950s and early 1960s, Canada's burgeoning industrial might was embodied by those tough Tiger-Cat teams from Hamilton, whose grit on the field was inextricably linked to Steeltown's own working-class identity. In 1969, Prime Minister Trudeau's ceremonial kickoff in swinging Montreal – and the victory of an Ottawa Rough Rider team quarterbacked by homegrown Russ Jackson – played directly into the themes of Canadian cultural independence and confidence that were so much a part of the times. And, in 1995, our great push/pull relationship with the United States, and the long-running struggle to define and preserve what makes us Canadian, was played out on a football field in Regina as, for the first and only time, a U.S.-based team took Earl Grey's trophy back across the great unguarded border.

The Grey Cup made Edmonton the City of Champions years before Wayne Gretzky came along. The Grey Cup – and especially those 31 years between Argos victories – made all-powerful Toronto the butt of at least one long-running, unifying joke for the rest of Canada. The Grey Cup brought Vancouver fully into the national sporting life when the Lions won their first in 1964, and returned French Canada to the fold when the reborn Montreal Alouettes claimed their first championship in 2000. And back in the days when Regina teams came east to mount hopeless challenges for the Grey Cup, or even in more modern times when the

THE FIRST CANADIAN CHAMPIONSHIPS

THOUGH THE 1909 GAME was the first to be played with the newly donated Grey Cup on the line, it was not the first time that teams had competed for the championship of Canadian football. On the morning of November 6, 1884 – Thanksgiving Day – the Montreal Football Club, having won the Quebec championship, arrived in Toronto to play their Ontario counterparts, the Argonauts.

The teams met on the University Lawn of the University of Toronto, Montreal clad in black-and-red jerseys while the Argonauts, who would later gain fame as the Double Blue, wore maroon. According to *The Globe*, the Argonauts, "though they played a good and plucky game . . . were overmatched in the scrummages, and their backing proved powerless against the brilliant attacks of the Montrealers." Montreal racked up a 14–0 lead in the first half, and was just as dominant in the second, as the final score of 30–0 would indicate.

An item in the next day's Montreal *Gazette* noted that the Argos subsequently "'dined' the visitors," who boarded a train for Montreal that very night. Remarkably, the Argonauts weren't done for the season just yet – they were due to visit Montreal themselves the next day for a game against the Britannias.

In 1892, with the establishment of the Canadian Rugby Union, the "Dominion championship" finally became (with a few exceptions) an annual affair. That year, Toronto's Osgoode Hall met the Montreal Winged Wheelers at Rosedale Field – which would be the site of the inaugural Grey Cup seventeen years later.

The Globe reported that the game took place before a crowd of about two thousand, "including hundreds of ladies," who spent the afternoon "shivering and shouting while 30 brawny young men struggled in the snow for the championship of Canada." The paper estimated that six inches "of a fine sample of snow" covered the field at game time, and while the field was cleared in time for the game, "the sun and frost made the ground slippery and the footing uncertain."

In *The Globe*'s estimation, "Montreal sent up a good fifteen, but . . . Osgoode completely outshone the red and black when the ball was out of the crush." The first half, in which the home side rolled up a 26–5 advantage, "was decidedly the more interesting to the crowd. The play was more open and runs more frequent." Montreal was shut out in the second half, as Osgoode prevailed 45–5.

YEAR	DATE	SITE	SCORE
1892	Nov. 10	Rosedale Field, Toronto	Osgoode Hall 45, Mtl Winged Wheelers 5
1893	Nov. 23	Montreal AAA Grounds	Queen's U. 29, Mtl Winged Wheelers 11
1894	Nov. 17	Rosedale Field, Toronto	Ottawa College 8, Queen's U. 7
1895	Nov. 21	Montreal AAA Grounds	U. of Toronto 20, Mtl Winged Wheelers 5
1896	Nov. 21	Rosedale Field, Toronto	Ottawa College 12, U. of Toronto 8
1897	Nov. 25	Montreal AAA Grounds	Ottawa College 14, Hamilton Tigers 10
1898	Nov. 24	Ottawa College Grounds	Ottawa Rough Riders 11, Ottawa College 1
1900	Nov. 24	Rosedale Field, Toronto	Ottawa Rough Riders 17, Brockville 10
1901	Nov. 23	Montreal AAA Grounds	Ottawa College 12, Toronto Argonauts 12
———	Nov. 28	Montreal AAA Grounds	Ottawa College 18, Toronto Argonauts 3
1902	Nov. 15	Ottawa College Grounds	Ottawa Rough Riders 5, Ottawa College 0
1905	Nov. 25	Rosedale Field, Toronto	U. of Toronto 11, Ottawa Rough Riders 9
1906	Dec. 1	McGill University, Montreal	Hamilton 29, McGill 3
1907	Nov. 30	McGill University, Montreal	Mtl Winged Wheelers 71, Peterborough Quakers 9
1908	Nov. 28	Rosedale Field, Toronto	Hamilton Tigers 21, U. of Toronto 17

No games were played in 1899, 1903, or 1904. The 1901 game was replayed after the teams played to a 12–12 tie.

Opposite: Early Dominion Champions, the Hamilton Tigers, 1906.

Roughriders struggled for survival, who could have imagined that their twenty-first-century incarnation as the beloved obsession of a suddenly booming province, the single greatest economic engine in the entire Canadian Football League, would be even bigger than it had been in the days when Ron Lancaster and George Reed worked their magic at Taylor Field?

There were also times when the Grey Cup seemed less relevant, when the tradition appeared to be petering out, when Canadians' atten-

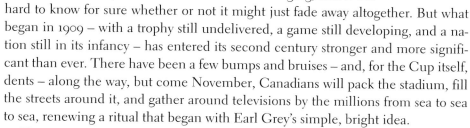

tion seemed to stray and tastes seemed to be changing, and it was hard to know for sure whether or not it might just fade away altogether. But what began in 1909 – with a trophy still undelivered, a game still developing, and a nation still in its infancy – has entered its second century stronger and more significant than ever. There have been a few bumps and bruises – and, for the Cup itself, dents – along the way, but come November, Canadians will pack the stadium, fill the streets around it, and gather around televisions by the millions from sea to sea to sea, renewing a ritual that began with Earl Grey's simple, bright idea.

This is our game.

And these are our stories.

1909

THE BUILDING OF A LEGACY

There was plenty of football talk in Toronto in the fall of 1909. In an era long before hockey gobbled up almost every month of the calendar, it was really the only autumn game in town, and the fans and press were abuzz about the season-ending matches to come.

But the upcoming Grey Cup championship, the first ever staged, was not the focus of the conversation. The local newspapers trained their attention instead on the final match of the Interprovincial Rugby Football Union's season. Formed in 1907, the IRFU consisted of the Hamilton, Montreal, Ottawa, and Toronto clubs, universally known simply as "the Big Four." The Hamilton Tigers and Ottawa Rough Riders finished the 1909 season in a tie and were set to play for the IRFU title on neutral ground in Toronto. The winner of that game would then take on the powerhouse side from the University of Toronto, which had won the highly regarded intercollegiate championship. And the winner of *that* game would move on to challenge Parkdale, champions of the Ontario Rugby Football Union, for the Canadian Rugby Union title and the new "national" championship, symbolized by a trophy that no one had yet seen and that almost no one knew even existed. (The notion that teams from outside Central Canada might be part of the mix was, at that point, hardly considered, though rugby was certainly being played elsewhere in the country.)

Grey Cup action on Rosedale Field, 1909.

Smirle Lawson, one of the standout stars on the University of Toronto team.

The first game was a minor sensation: fans from Ottawa and Hamilton poured into Toronto en masse, the Hamilton crowd arriving on two special trains, with five bands in tow, and with fans wearing yellow chrysanthemums – which, a century later, remain a traditional way of showing home-team loyalty in the Steeltown. Hamilton had won the championship the year before (a victory which would later play into one of the stranger footnotes in Grey Cup history), but on this occasion Ottawa won what seems to have been a less than thrilling match, 14–8 – almost all of the points were singles scored on punts – setting up an even bigger game, to be played against the mighty Varsity side the following weekend, a contest that was billed by at least one Toronto newspaper as being for the "Dominion Championship."

The hoopla surrounding the second game will certainly sound familiar to anyone who has been part of a modern Grey Cup festival. Ottawa's team was coached by Tom "King" Clancy, father of the Hall of Fame hockey player Francis, who later inherited his dad's nickname. Tom Clancy was American-born and had come to Canada to play football, where he was honoured with the name "King" because he was "king of the heelers": a master at the art of "heeling" the ball back to the quarterback (as was the practice before the modern "snap" was incorporated into the sport). The original King Clancy had led Ottawa teams to national titles in the past as a player.

The Ottawa players actually threatened to strike the week before the game, because they believed team officials were hoarding their allotment of what would obviously be scarce tickets for the match, before they relented and agreed to play. Rosedale Field had been designed to accommodate about 3,400 spectators. But when fans started arriving a full twenty-four hours before kickoff, it became obvious that the final number would be far more than that. The Ottawa crowd came in their own fifteen-car train and, the night before the game, joined Toronto supporters in all-night marathon dances. On the morning of November 27 – game day – they began lining up at the gates before dawn.

Tickets were priced between 25 cents and $1.25; a carriage could be driven into the grounds for a dollar, with an additional 50 cents charged for each passenger. In the end, that added up to a remarkable $7,000 take at the box office, and a crowd (including those who climbed trees to get a look at the action) estimated at 12,000. But the game itself was disappointing – no contest, really, as the college boys thumped Ottawa 31–7, keyed by the great open-field running of halfback Smirle Lawson. There

was no serious debate now as to which was the best football team in Canada. The match to follow, against the Parkdale Paddlers, playing for a trophy that wasn't mentioned in any of the pre-game press reports, was viewed as a mere curiosity.

(The University of Toronto and Ottawa teams, by virtue of being considered the best in the land, were invited to New York City that same autumn to stage an exhibition of the Canadian brand of football for an American audience. American football, which had been evolving along a distinct path since the famous first match between Harvard and McGill in 1874, had become notorious for its violent nature, and at one point was on the verge of being banned, so the Americans had some interest in exploring an alternative set of rules. But after some deliberation, the U of T faculty decided that it wouldn't be appropriate for their team to make the trip, given that the players had already had their academic year disrupted by football, and several had important exams in the offing. As *The Globe* reported: "When the matter was first mentioned to Captain Newton, some [faculty] agreed to take the team down 'in the interests of humanity', as he aptly put it, having in view, no doubt the fact that thirty-two American players had been killed or died of injuries sustained in the game. When a canvass for the team was made, however, it was ascertained that only four

of the players were eager to go, but the others signified a willingness to make the trip if called upon." The Hamilton Tigers of the Big Four stepped in to replace Varsity, and took on the Ottawa Rough Riders at Van Cortland Park in the Bronx on December 11

Program for the 1909 semifinal game versus Ottawa.

Rosedale Field as it appeared at the time of the first Grey Cup game, 1909.

in front of 15,000 spectators – a crowd that included Walter Camp, the great rule-maker and innovator regarded as "the Father of American football." The Tigers won 11-6. When asked afterwards, Camp spoke admiringly about several distinctive aspects of the Canadian game.)

The final football match of the 1909 Canadian season was scheduled for December 4, again at Rosedale Field. And though there seemed precious little enthusiasm for the event among those who followed the game, at least one sportswriter tried his best to stir up some excitement.

"An entire new repertoire of songs and yells, in addition to the ones used at the Ottawa game, has been prepared by the Varsity students for the game today," reported *The Globe* in the edition published on the morning of the game.

"With the developments of yesterday and last night there is more confidence than ever at Parkdale and less at Varsity, where the fact is recognized that the Paddlers are going to be worthy opponents of Harry Griffiths' great team. The reserved seat plan is all sold out, and an enormous crowd is a certainty. Last night saw the first of the out-of-town arrivals for the big game. Those who admire high-class football will not neglect the opportunity to see the Varsity wonders and the tricky Parkdale Paddlers in action. The game will be called at 2:30."

What else was going on in the sporting world that week? Baseball's American League had just announced – some time after the season had concluded with the Pittsburgh Pirates' seven-game victory over the Detroit Tigers in the World Series – that Ty Cobb of the Tigers had won the batting title with a .377 average. In the world of big-time hockey – at the time nearly as murky and confusing as the world of Canadian football – the Ottawa team, which had claimed the Stanley Cup at the end of the 1908–09 season, announced that it had accepted a challenge from the

Edmonton Eskimos (Ottawa would win both games against the western challengers the following January). And there was plenty of excitement surrounding the greatest sporting fad of the moment – six-day bicycle races – as the year's biggest event was ongoing in New York City.

Meanwhile, in Toronto, only 3,800 turned up (paying a relatively paltry $2,616.40 at the gate) at Rosedale Field, a tiny fragment of the crowd the week before, their expectations low. Varsity's coronation was surely a *fait accompli*.

The first Grey Cup game, in fact, turned out to be much better contest than advertised, with the underdogs from Parkdale putting up a seriously good scrap, and the University of Toronto team perhaps having read its own press clippings a bit too much. This is how the match was described by the correspondent from *The Star* on Monday, December 6, 1909, an account that gives a real sense of how this early version of the sport was played:

> Varsity defeated Parkdale at Rosedale on Saturday before 4,000 spectators by a score of 29 to 6, and thereby became undisputed Rugby champions of the Dominion.
>
> While the O.R.F.U. champions were decisively beaten, they proved themselves to be a better team than Ottawa, the Interprovincial champions, and gave the College wonders a much harder argument than the team from the Capital. Especially was this the case in the first half, when Parkdale held Varsity to a one-point margin, the score at the half-way station being 6 to 5 in favor of the students. The superior condition of Varsity told in the second half, and they ran up a score, though the last five points came after time was up, Lawson making one of his wonderful 50-yard runs for a touchdown, while the timers were on the field trying to notify the referee.

The first of many Toronto teams to win the Grey Cup, 1909.

THE "AERIAL ATTACK"

EACH ERA OF CANADIAN football has had its stars, those whose talents reflected the most admired skills of their day. Over the years these standouts have ranged from the rough-and-tumble "inside wing" plungers of the 1930s, such as Brian Timmis and Dave Sprague, and the talented two-way players of the 1950s, like Jackie Parker and Hal Patterson, to the more recent passing heroes, including Doug Flutie and Anthony Calvillo. In 1909, the premier gridiron hero was Hugh Gall, renowned for his "aerial" skills.

Today, the concept of an "aerial attack" is easily under-stood as referring to the passing game. But in 1909, the for-ward pass was not yet legal. Instead, punting ability was prized over all other skills – even above running with the ball. In Hugh Gall's era, then, the aerial attack meant the kicking game, and it was his forte. He could kick well with either foot, and would kick on any down in an attempt to gain valuable field position. Scores in football were low in those days, and the "single," or "rouge," was more common than any other scoring method.

As a halfback for the University of Toronto and later for Parkdale, Gall played in three Grey Cups and was twice on the winning team. He was the first player to score a point in a Grey Cup game (after a 65-yard punt and rouge) and added that day's first touchdown as well on a 5-yard end run. Gall's eight singles in 1909 remain the record to this day. So the game we recognize as the first to award the ancient trophy featured a man who – despite the appearance of being much older than his years – probably could not be outkicked by any player of any age or era.

The best way to describe Gall's "game" and persona may be found in 1910 Grey Cup accounts: "As Simpson was the main works on the Tiger back line, so was Gall for Varsity. The young player, with the old man's face . . . booted the pigskin in the style that has given him the reputation of being Canada's greatest." In 1913, after Gall's final Grey Cup appearance, *The Hamilton Spectator* assessed him as follows: "Parkdale was Hugh Gall and a dozen Hugh Galls couldn't beat this team."

No discussion of this great Hall of Famer would be com-plete without pausing to consider an oddity of the Canadian game: the average distance that punts travel has changed little, if any, since Gall's day.

Where Parkdale showed superiority over Ottawa was in the variety of their attack. They had just as good a repertoire of plays as Varsity, and pulled them off just as intelligently, but the wonderful defence of the collegians usually broke up the various attacks just as they were on the verge of completion. Particularly was this the case with trick end runs, the man with the ball being nailed by either Newton or Moulds, or the outside wings by a brilliant tackle when a good gain seemed assured.

Newton played a wonderful defensive game. He seemed to grasp intuitively what was coming off, and instructed his men how best to meet the attack, also performing wonders himself in the thick of the fray. He played up on the line all the time, and his side of the scrimmage was almost impassable.

Parkdale did what Ottawa couldn't do, and that was to buck through the Varsity line for their yards. This they did several times, to the great joy of their supporters. Another feature was the way they marked Smirle Lawson. The great plunging half-back was usually nailed in his tracks by George Barber, who grabbed him high

and held on like a leech. Barber kept Lawson from doing anything spectacular until the very end of the game, when he caught the ball in a broken field and smashed through the whole Parkdale team for his only touchdown.

The crowd enjoyed the match exceedingly, and the Parkdale team were given an ovation at half-time for their fine showing. Most of the people present expected the collegians to "eat 'em up" and at half-time there was some anxiety in the Varsity camp as to the final outcome. However, in the second half the powerful Varsity machine worked irresistibly and gradually forced up the score. The Parkdale team were always a factor in the play, but the defence of the collegians was so strong they could only secure one point in the second half.

The game was clean throughout, only two men were ruled off, both Parkdale players, Brady for tripping and Ross for holding. Both were off at the same time in the third quarter. . . .

The most sensational player on the field was Gage at outside wing for Varsity. He seemed possessed of phenomenal speed and endurance, and though jarred badly in a tackle in the third quarter, played like a fiend to the very end. He made some great catches in a broken field, and if there was a loose ball he was sure to get it. Thomson, the other outside wing, not only followed down splendidly, but was used with great success in carrying the ball. Gall did some great punting and made his kicks effective by booting the ball close to the scrimmage, and giving his outside wings time to get well down the field. His on-side kicks were not so successful, as Parkdale laid for them all the time.

Ritchie played his usual strong game and kept the team on their toes, while his side partner, Jimmy Bell, with the cracked ribs, was always in the midst of the doings, tackling fearlessly despite his injury. Lajoie and Muir also did good work on the line, and Dixon made few mistakes at full back.

The Varsity players were not keyed up like they were in the Ottawa game, but they played a strong game nevertheless and gave Parkdale credit for having a splendid team. "They have a better line than Ottawa," said Ritchie.

Parkdale surprised Varsity several times by working the on-side kick. On one occasion they made a big gain when Cromar got the ball, a beautiful tackle by Foulds, who played a fine game throughout, saving a touchdown. The Parkdale back division played in streaks. Sometimes they couldn't miss anything, while at other times they couldn't catch anything, and Varsity profited by every mistake. Their backs received the very best of protection from their line, and Killaly had all kinds of time to do the kicking. He punted very well, indeed, varying his distance to suit the occasion. Cromar played a very useful game throughout, and Brady made some spectacular catches. The Varsity wings were invariably on them like wolves, and gave them little time to return kicks.

Barber and Brockbank, the Parkdale ends, were usually down under every kick, and the former made quite a name for himself by smothering Lawson's attempted runs. Harper and Meegan were both good on the offence and defence, and Frank Dissette was the best line plunger on the team. Brother Jimmy played a good game at quarter-back, his passing being accurate and nervy. The scrimmage was as solid as a brick.

What beat Parkdale was Gall's fine punting and the unerring tackling of the Varsity wings, and the west-enders' inability to carry their trick plays to a successful completion owing to the magnificent defences of the champions. "You've got to watch them all the time," said Captain Newton of Varsity, and he certainly did. There's a great rugby player, probably the hardest worker and the most effective man on a team of champions. His work is not spectacular, but he has the happy faculty of always being where he is needed and doing the right thing at the right time. He has the "football sense" acutely developed, and his effective playing is best appreciated by those on the inside.

A feature play of the game that was not seen by those in the stands occurred in the first quarter, when Varsity tried to buck over for a try. Lajoie was carrying the ball

Opposite: Souvenir scrapbook for the University of Toronto 1909 Grey Cup win.

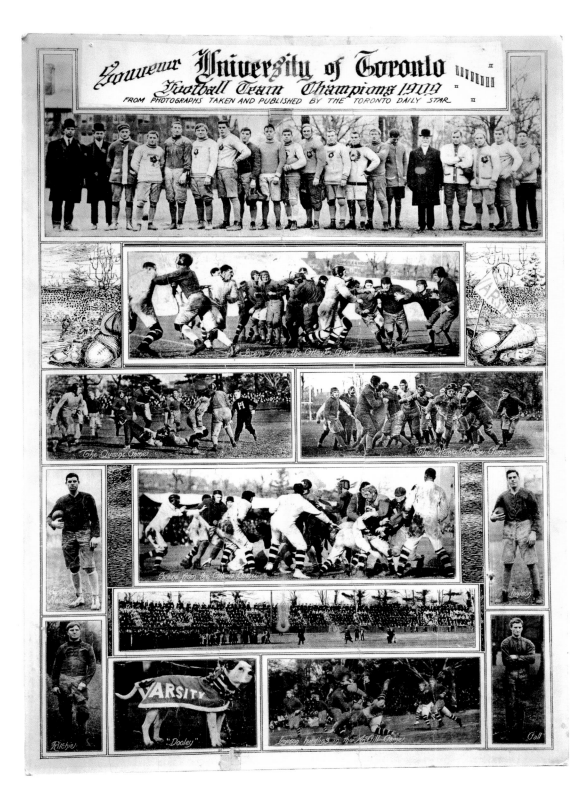

Souvenir *University of Toronto* Football Team Champions 1909
FROM PHOTOGRAPHS TAKEN AND PUBLISHED BY THE TORONTO DAILY STAR

JUST AS CANADIAN FOOTBALL has evolved, there have been many advances in the way news about the on-field action has been relayed to fans across the country. Radio coverage dates back to 1928, and the Grey Cup was first televised – in a limited way – in 1952. Today, fans can follow every play in great detail via the Internet. Each drive is charted using advanced Game Tracker software, with graphics illustrating the movement of the ball up and down the field.

Throughout the history of Canadian football, there has been one constant: then as now, newspaper reporters filed stories on the game. As a result, we have access to wonderfully rich, detailed accounts of every Grey Cup game, allowing us to revisit and verify scoring records and other details. But not even newspaper coverage has escaped the forces of change. From a few reporters at the 1909 Grey Cup game, media coverage has grown to the point where hundreds are transmitting stories about happenings on and off the field. Telegraphs, typewriters, and telephones have given way to laptops connecting sports-

writers, instantly and wirelessly, without having to leave their keyboards. News of the game disseminates in seconds to all points on the globe.

But it was another form of "carrier" that stands out from early Grey Cup accounts. In 1915, the Hamilton Tigers travelled to Varsity Stadium to contest the Grey Cup with the Toronto Rowing Club. *The Globe and Mail* of November 22 provides some insight into how news from the stadium reached anxious fans back in the Steel City: "Hamilton sent down a deputation of several hundred rooters, and they were a silent lot until after half-time. They seemingly could not understand the whys and wherefores of their favourites being beaten so soundly in the first and second periods. Even the homing pigeons, which were released at half-time . . . appeared dazed and loath to take the 4 to 1 adverse score back home."

So, in 1915, we have evidence of the first "wireless carrier" – in the form of the carrier pigeon!

and hit the line hard. Meegan went low to stop the buck and grabbed the ball as the College backs joined in behind Lajoie. Meegan hung on desperately, and the force of the buck tore the ball out of Lajoie's hands. Meegan got the oval, but he turned his ankle painfully, and played under a handicap for the balance of the game.

It wasn't until March 1910 that the champions from Varsity were finally presented with the Grey Cup. The following year, the championship game was played in Hamilton, where a huge, rowdy crowd turned out at the grounds of the Hamilton Amateur Athletic Association (HAAA) to watch the hometown Tigers lose 16–7 to Varsity – a precursor not just of Grey Cup celebrations to come, but of the great, enduring rivalry between a gritty industrial burg and the shiny metropolis down the road. There is no record of Earl Grey having been in attendance. By the time the next championship game rolled around, in 1911, he had returned to the family home, Howick Hall, Alnwick, Northhumberland, his term as governor general, and thus his duties in Canada, having ended. Lord Grey died in 1917, too soon to have seen any hint of what his modest trophy would come to symbolize.

In 1911, the University of Toronto again captured the Dominion championship, this time defeating the Toronto Argonauts. A Hamilton team – the Alerts – finally triumphed in 1912, but they never got their hands on the trophy. Claiming that it was a challenge cup, and that they hadn't been challenged or defeated, the U of T declined to give it up. The champion Hamilton Tigers of 1913 were similarly denied their just reward. Varsity wouldn't allow the Grey Cup back in circulation until 1914, when they lost the championship game to the Toronto Argonauts, and by then the sport, like the country, like much of the planet, had much bigger things on its mind.

The Hamilton boys, though, would find a way to gain a small measure of revenge. After winning the 1915 championship over the Toronto Rowing and Athletic Association, the Tigers players took the trophy to a silversmith in their hometown, whom they asked to add to the base not only an inscription recording their own victory but another commemorating the 1908 national championship team from Hamilton, as though they had been the first Grey Cup winners. The extra inscription wasn't noticed until years later, when the Cup was taken in for repairs in 1951, and at that point the decision was made to leave it, as a permanent record of the Canadian game's idiosyncratic history.

After that 1915 championship game, Canadian football was suspended for the duration of the First World War, and the Grey Cup, still to acquire its iconic status, was locked away in a vault for safekeeping, its future very much uncertain.

Hamilton added their 1908 Dominion Championship win to the Grey Cup after their 1915 victory.

1935

THE YANKS ARE COMING

The revolution began, as most do, in a meeting behind closed doors. In Winnipeg, in the year 1935, the men who operated the local football club, including future Canadian Football League commissioner Sydney Halter, made a decision that would change the course of the sport and finally bring the Grey Cup west.

The Winnipeggers weren't going to take it anymore. They weren't going to make the long trip east and play the patsy, play the role of hopeless, hapless cannon fodder in the national championship game, as western teams had since 1921. Instead, they were going to beat the odds, defy the lessons of history. And to do so, they were going to put their money where their mouth was – no small thing in the depths of the Great Depression.

That group of Winnipeg businessmen pledged $7,500, a considerable sum in those days, to be used to pay for football talent – though, since the game was still technically all amateur, they'd have to be discreet about it. (The truth was, finding the players off-field jobs in a time of sky-high unemployment would have been worth nearly as much to them as whatever they were paid to play.) Those players would, by necessity, come from the much larger talent pool in the United States. The football powers back east wouldn't understand what was being hatched on the

John Bonk being awarded the Grey Cup for the Blue Bombers in 1984.

1958 **WINNIPEG BLUE BOMBERS** **1958**
Grey Cup Champions

Front Row—Leo Lewis, Bob Hobert, Roger Savoie, Garland Warren, James Ausley (Manager), Ralph Parliament (President), Buddy Tinsley, Gordon Rowland, Walter Bilicki, Frank Gilliam.

Second Row—Ken Kovacs, Russ Lecomy (Equipment Men), Tony Kehrer, Ed Kotowich, Ron Latourelle, Ted Mikliechuk, Eugene Wlasiuk, Steve Patrick, Herb Gray, Cornel Piper, Jim Van Pelt, Harry Pop Varnes (Equipment), Bob Jones, (Equipment).

Third Row—Harry Grant (Coach), George Druxman, Barry Roseborough, Ernie Pitts, Frank Rigney, Gerry Vincent, Norm Rauhaus, Cec Luining, Wayne Robinson.

Fourth Row—Joe Zaleski, Dave Burkholder, Charlie Shepard, Jim Tonn, Keith Pearce, Ken Ploen, Ron Meadmore, John Varone, Nick Miller, Rick Potter.

The 1958 Bombers after winning their first of four Grey Cups in five years.

Prairies – and even when they were given a clue, their arrogance prevented them from acknowledging it. They didn't know what was coming until a cold, wet day in December, on a sloppy field in Hamilton, when the sport of Canadian football and the character of the Grey Cup game changed forever, and a whole country learned about a remarkable athlete from Perham, Minnesota, named Fritzy Hanson.

For the first time, the great east-west rivalry that would become the championship's hallmark was not just posturing, but a living, breathing thing, because now both sides understood that the west could win. For the first time, the game was heard across the country on radio, the precursor of television broadcasts that are now routinely among the most-watched sporting events on the Canadian calendar every year.

And, for the first time, the role of American stars in the Canadian game really came to the fore. Two of the great themes in the struggle to define a national identity

GAME BREAKER

A SCAN OF THE list of Dominion rugby football champions, beginning with the inaugural contest in 1892, and well into the Grey Cup era that began in 1909, would lead anyone to conclude that the Canadian game was dominated by eastern clubs. Differing sets of rules of the day made east–west encounters difficult to stage, perhaps explaining why no western team managed to win the Grey Cup until 1935, when Winnipeg's stellar club travelled to Hamilton. The feat was accomplished at last by a great 'Pegs team led by no fewer than eleven future members of the Winnipeg Football Club Hall of Fame, including Canadian Football Hall of Fame members Russ Rebholz, Eddie "Dynamite" James, Greg Kabat, and the star of the 1935 game, Fritz Hanson.

Accounts of the game abound in praise for Hanson's kick-return talents: "The most elusive individual seen on a Canadian gridiron in years was the greatest of them . . . brilliant Tiger tacklers were completely baffled by this tricky little fellow." With the score just 12–10 in favour of Winnipeg late in the third quarter, Hanson caught a punt 78 yards from the Hamilton goal and, surrounded by tacklers, "sprinted to his left, wheeled, reversed his field, and then cut sharply right ahead." Though individual statistics would not be kept in our game for another fifteen years, the best evidence that we have points to some 300 yards of kick returns for Hanson that day, including seven gains between 35 and 50 yards. Hanson and an incredible 'Pegs defence resigned Hamilton to being the first losing eastern team in a truly national final game. On the day, the Tigers managed just three first downs and completed 2 of 15 passes against a western champion side stacked with American stars.

Hanson proved that great kick returners are not limited merely to the modern-day game but may be found throughout our history. Fritz went on to play in six Grey Cups (winning four) and ended his career as a member of the first-ever Calgary Stampeders winning side in 1948. Hanson was elected to the Canadian Football Hall of Fame as a charter member in 1963.

Above: Fritz Hanson led Winnipeg to its first Grey Cup in 1935.

were acted out by football-playing proxies: western alienation and Canada's complicated push-pull relationship with our neighbours to the south. They remain part of the CFL mix – and the Canadian mix – to this day.

Winnipeg football teams have enjoyed a glorious Grey Cup history, playing in the big game twenty-three times – more than any other team – and winning ten times, most recently in 1990.

In all of that, there were three true golden eras. The first began with the championship in 1935, and extended for a full decade, during which Winnipeg teams appeared in eight Grey Cup games and won the trophy three times, in the process becoming the first western teams to win the trophy. In 1936, the Winnipeg team also acquired a nickname – Blue Bombers, coined by a local sportswriter in an echo of Grantland Rice's famous alliterative moniker for Joe Louis, the "Brown Bomber" – that has stuck with it ever since.

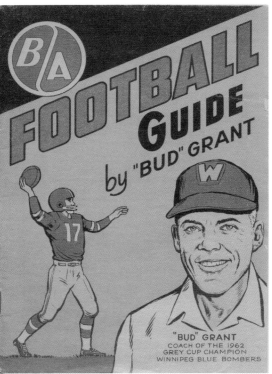

Immediately following that era, and in the wake of two Winnipeg-based RCAF teams who represented the west and lost Grey Cup games during the Second World War, came a series of excellent Bomber sides. They represented the west in the Grey Cup in 1945, 1946, 1947, 1950, and 1953, but never won the trophy, losing all but the last of them to the Toronto Argonauts. Those Winnipeg teams of the early 1950s featured one of the great stars of the era, the fine quarterback from Oklahoma, Jack Jacobs.

The transition from very good to great began with the arrival of Harry "Bud" Grant, who had played for the 1953 Bombers after leaving the Philadelphia Eagles in a pay dispute (Grant also played two seasons in the National *Basketball* Association).

Grant became the Bombers' head coach in 1957 and stayed in the post until taking the same job with the Minnesota Vikings in 1967. In Winnipeg, he assembled the greatest Bomber team of all time, with stars like Ken Ploen and Leo Lewis,

KEN PLOEN

the fabled "Lincoln Locomotive." They won four of the five Grey Cups played between 1958 and 1962 (all over their great rivals of the time, the Hamilton Tiger-Cats), bookending those wins with losses to the Ticats in the 1957 and 1965 Grey Cup games. Grant then went on to become that most rare of species, a Hall of Fame coach in two different leagues.

The last wave of Winnipeg greatness – so far – came in the late 1980s. Cal Murphy was the coach, and then the general manager, as Bomber teams quarterbacked by Tom Clements, Sean Salisbury, and Tom Burgess won championships in 1984, 1988, and 1990, respectively.

But although those other teams earned a special place in the hearts of their fans and had their names engraved on the Grey Cup, it was the very first Winnipeg champions who altered the course of Canadian football history.

The first western side to challenge for the Grey Cup were the 1921 Edmonton Eskimos, who made the journey east by train only to be clobbered by Lionel Conacher and the Toronto Argonauts by a score of 23–0. In succeeding years, the western representative changed, but the story remained much the same:

1922 Queen's University 13, Edmonton Elks 1
1923 Queen's University 54, Regina Roughriders 0
1925 Ottawa Senators 24, Winnipeg Tammany Tigers 1
1928 Hamilton Tigers 30, Regina Roughriders 0
1929 Hamilton Tigers 14, Regina Roughriders 3
1930 Balmy Beach 11, Regina Roughriders 6
1931 Montreal Winged Wheelers 22, Regina Roughriders 0
1932 Hamilton Tigers 25, Regina Roughriders 6
1934 Sarnia Imperials 20, Regina Roughriders 12

That's a cumulative score of 213–29, and that doesn't take into account the four years during that stretch when for one reason or another western teams wouldn't participate in the Grey Cup game. In 1924, the Winnipeg Victorias didn't make it east to challenge Queen's because of a dispute between players and team executives over – you're reading this correctly – which railway they would use. (The players subsequently had

Leo Lewis was one of the many stars of the 1958 team. He is seen here playing in the 1962 Fog Bowl.

Joe Ryan poached American football talent to help bring the Grey Cup west for the first time.

a change of heart but were told not to bother making the trip – on either rail line – because, as the *Toronto Star* reported, "Tickets had been destroyed, Queen's had packed away their football togs for the winter, and the Varsity field had been rented for other purposes.") In 1926, the Regina Roughriders declined to make the trek because the season had run too late for their liking. In 1927, the eastern administrators of the sport decided that no western team would challenge for the Cup. And in 1933, for one year only, a new playoff system was instituted that required the western finalist to play the Big Four champion for a place in the Grey Cup game. The Winnipeg 'Pegs continued a familiar pattern, losing to the eventual champion, the Toronto Argonauts, 13–0.

And the streak of futility wasn't confined to the Grey Cup. Not that the two football solitudes confronted each other on the playing field very often, but in the entire history of the Canadian game, from its nineteenth-century origins all the way through to the 1934 season, no senior team from the west had ever beaten one from the east.

American players had been suiting up with western Canadian teams as far back as 1929, no more than one or two on a squad, normally quarterbacks or halfbacks – "ringers" brought in and paid under the table to give the local boys a boost. Entering the 1935 season, Winnipeg had their two Yanks – quarterback Russ Rebholz and halfback Greg Kabat.

But with that $7,500 to spend, team manager Joe Ryan headed south in search of more, beginning his quest in nearby North Dakota and Minnesota. By the time preparations for the 1935 football season had begun in earnest, the Winnipegs, as the team was known, had nine Americans on their roster, including the holdovers Rebholz and Kabat, plus Bud Marquardt, Joe Perpich, Herb Peschel, Bob Fritz, Bert Oja, a former New York high-school star named Nick Pagones, and Melvin "Fritzy" Hanson, a twenty-two-year-old, 145-pound scatback who had been a star at North Dakota State and signed on with Winnipeg for $125 a game plus room and board. The fans would soon take to calling him "Twinkle Toes," at least when they weren't calling him the "The Golden Ghost."

The recast Winnipegs opened their season on September 14, 1935, beating Concordia College of North Dakota 26–0 in an exhibition game (they had lost 33–27 to the same American school the previous year). A week later, the next challenge would be a formidable one: the 1934 Grey Cup champion Sarnia Imperials were on a western barnstorming tour, taking on the best opposition available, and riding a fourteen-game winning streak. A record Winnipeg football crowd of 3,800 gathered to see the hometown team pull off the upset, defeating Sarnia 3–1. Imperials' coach Art Massucci said the Winnipegs were the best team he'd seen in the previous two years, but that realization didn't spread among the football cognoscenti of Eastern Canada. As the Winnipegs went on to decimate all available competition – without a league in which to compete, they played a series of exhibition games, knocking off two American teams, the Minnesota All-Stars and North Dakota Freshmen, and crushing the local Winnipeg Vics in three successive matches – the traditional football powers in Ontario and Quebec were consumed with what had become a strange Big Four season.

The Toronto Argonauts looked like the obvious Grey Cup favourites after beating their traditional rivals from Hamilton twice, 13–8 and 7–1. It wasn't just Winnipeg that had come to understand the value of imported talent. The Argos had their own American star that year, halfback Tony Rosso from Washington and Jefferson University, while the Tigers employed running back Johnny Ferraro and centre Jerry Brock, both out of Cornell University. And in Ottawa, they had a sensational halfback from Tulsa University named Roy Berry – or at least that's what it said in the program. It turned out he was actually Bohn Hilliard, from the University of Texas, who had borrowed another player's name to cover up the fact that he had played baseball in the low minor leagues, and therefore was a professional, ineligible under Canadian Rugby Union rules.

When Hilliard and another Ottawa import were barred from the team's two remaining games against Toronto, the Argonauts' path to the Big Four championship seemed assured: beat Ottawa twice and it would be all theirs. But they lost both games, 18–13 and 9–5, which allowed Hamilton, by virtue of a 23–0 win over Montreal, to sneak through and claim the Big Four title. In the eastern playoffs, the Tigers humiliated Queen's University 44–4 (it was the last time a Canadian university team would challenge for the Grey Cup), and then knocked off the defending champion Sarnia Imperials, champions of the Ontario Rugby Football Union, 22–3. The Grey Cup game would be played on Hamilton's home field, the HAAA Grounds.

Back in Winnipeg, on November 2, the home team had played its first "real" game of the 1935 season, a playoff against the visiting Regina Roughriders at Osborne Stadium. Local sportswriter Ralph Allen, who would go on to become one of the legends of his profession, predicted a 13–1 Winnipeg victory in his column. He was rather prescient: a last-minute Regina touchdown made the final margin 13–6 for the home side. Lionel Conacher was on hand to watch the match, and

THE VENUES

OF THE 99 GREY Cup games played between 1909 and 2011, only two have been played outside of what may be viewed as a "CFL" city (the nine cities that have had teams since the CFL was formed in 1958, which comprise the current eight plus Ottawa). Today, the Grey Cup moves around the country, with each club that has a viable stadium getting a chance to host the game. Between 2006 and 2011, the Grey Cup was staged in six different cities, and the nine games between 2003 and 2011 were played in eight different stadiums.

But such wasn't always the case. Between 1976 and 1982, for instance, the Grey Cup alternated between Montreal and Toronto. Between 1945 and 1957, Toronto's Varsity Stadium had a virtual lock on the Grey Cup (only in 1955, when the game went to Empire Stadium in Vancouver, was this pattern broken). And for many years prior to the Second World War, the game was usually played at the home of the Interprovincial Rugby Football Union (IRFU) champion.

The Grey Cup was played in a "non-CFL" city for the first time in 1922, when the powerhouse team from Queen's University defeated the Edmonton Elks, 13–1, on their home field, Richardson Stadium in Kingston, Ontario, before 4,700 fans. The only other instance was in 1933, when the Sarnia Imperials, champions of the Ontario Rugby Football Union (ORFU), hosted the Toronto Argonauts at Davis Field.

Founded in 1928, the Imperials were among the best teams of their time, winning the ORFU championship in 1929, and in every season between 1931

and 1939. (They would win again in 1951 and 1952.) In 1933 they were coming off a 5–1 season, en route to their matchup with the Argos. After stumbling out of the gate with back-to-back losses, Toronto won their last four regular-season games, took both ends of the two-game, total-points eastern final, and shut out the Winnipeg 'Pegs, 13–0, in the Grey Cup semifinal.

Conditions in Sarnia on December 9, 1933, were anything but perfect. Amid temperatures of −10°C and a snowstorm, the field was frozen. The final score – 4–3 for Toronto – gives us a hint as to how tough it must have been to move the ball. Only five passes were completed, and Sarnia fumbled the ball nine times. The game was notable for featuring 53 punts, most of which came from the talented legs of two Hall of Fame talents: Toronto's Ab Box kicked the winning single in the fourth quarter, while Hugh "Bummer" Stirling kicked for all three Sarnia points.

The final result hinged on the game's most exciting play, in which a late completion to the Imperials' Norman Perry from Rocky Parsaca that would have put the ball on the Argonauts' 5-yard line was ruled out of bounds back at the 45 instead. Sarnia was unable to punch in a tying score after that close call and Toronto had its third Grey Cup title in hand.

Sarnia reached the Grey Cup again in 1934, defeating the Regina Roughriders, 20–12. Two years later, they prevailed over Ottawa by a 26–20 margin, becoming the last ORFU team to win the national championship.

Sarnia Imperials jersey.

predicted that Winnipeg would beat whichever team came out of the east – but again, it seems no one was listening.

In the western final a week later, the Winnipegs squeaked by the Calgary Bronks 7–0 on a snowy field at home. With a month off before the Grey Cup game, they sent Bert Oja ahead to scout the eastern final. He liked what he saw of the Hamilton Tigers' kicking game but was otherwise unimpressed. "Hamilton tacklers will have trouble bringing down Fritz Hanson and Russ Rebholz," Oja reported.

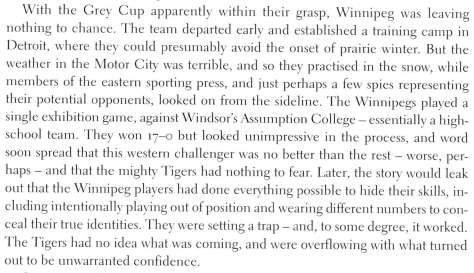

With the Grey Cup apparently within their grasp, Winnipeg was leaving nothing to chance. The team departed early and established a training camp in Detroit, where they could presumably avoid the onset of prairie winter. But the weather in the Motor City was terrible, and so they practised in the snow, while members of the eastern sporting press, and just perhaps a few spies representing their potential opponents, looked on from the sideline. The Winnipegs played a single exhibition game, against Windsor's Assumption College – essentially a high-school team. They won 17–0 but looked unimpressive in the process, and word soon spread that this western challenger was no better than the rest – worse, perhaps – and that the mighty Tigers had nothing to fear. Later, the story would leak out that the Winnipeg players had done everything possible to hide their skills, including intentionally playing out of position and wearing different numbers to conceal their true identities. They were setting a trap – and, to some degree, it worked. The Tigers had no idea what was coming, and were overflowing with what turned out to be unwarranted confidence.

One story, perhaps apocryphal, had Hamilton's Bill Friday, whose day job was as a city cop, sauntering into a local sporting goods store on the night before the big game. He was about to start the night shift, he explained to the guys behind the counter. Off at eight the next morning. Then he'd head home, grab a couple of hours' sleep, and make his way to the HAAA Grounds. Hardly the ideal preparation for a gruelling championship football game, but Friday certainly didn't seem worried.

The football used in the 1935 Grey Cup game.

Neither did the eastern sports press, which was pretty much unanimous in their opinion that the Tigers would win easily. In his pre-game column, Tommy Munns, the sports editor of *The Globe*, listed seven reasons for a Hamilton victory:

1. Tigers should show a definite backfield superiority.
2. Tigers should be as effective as their opponents in tackling – if not better. Their heavy hitting in bringing down opposing ball-carriers has been a feature of their play this season.
3. Granting that Winnipegs possess the expected advantage along the line, it is doubtful if they can make enough gains by plunging to offset the yardage earned by Tigers' backfielders.
4. Tigers' extension plays should equal those of Winnipegs, and perhaps prove better.
5. Home grounds have proved a greater advantage to Tigers than to any other senior team in Canada in the past.
6. The switch to Eastern rules will prove a handicap to Winnipegs, and possibly cost them considerable yardage in penalties.
7. Tigers are at their peak; Winnipegs, who won the Western title several weeks ago, may not be "in form" to the same extent.

Much could be written about the possibilities of the game; many conjectures could be made, but the above reasons back Tigers as this writer's choice. To them may be added the recollection of the defense shown by Tigers against the Sarnia forward passes last week, and the manner in which Johnny Ferraro has adapted himself to Canadian broken-field running without the interference to which he was accustomed in the United States.

What Munns could have added to his list, had he known, was that the Winnipeg players might also be at a disadvantage because of their diet. They had been offered two options for their time on the road: eat at the team hotel for free, or take a dollar-a-meal allowance and look after themselves. To a man, the players opted to take the dollar. At 1935 prices, you could buy a couple of hot dogs, and still have money left over from your buck. So the Winnipegs headed into the 1935 Grey Cup game fuelled almost entirely by tube steaks. Funny, but that didn't seem to slow them down.

It was a nasty, wet, cold day in Hamilton, and the field at the HAAA Grounds was as much mud as grass. Due to the inclement weather, and no doubt because of the anticipated mismatch, only 6,400 fans turned out, paying $1.60 a ticket.

Soon after Winnipeg recovered the opening kickoff, Russ Rebholz hit Bud Marquardt with a touchdown pass, and the visitors took an early 5–0 lead.

Moments later, across Canada, radios tuned to the CRBC – the Canadian Radio Broadcasting Commission, the precursor of the CBC – crackled to life.

"Winnipeg has a touchdown. The score is now 5–0."

It was the voice of Francis "Shag" Shaughnessy, finally coming through after a technical glitch had kept the first five minutes of the first national broadcast of a Grey Cup game off the air. (There had been scattered local broadcasts before that.) Shaughnessy, a Notre Dame grad who became famous as a coach and football innovator at McGill University, was doing his first and only broadcast. He was joined by two others who would call several Grey Cup games during the 1930s and 1940s: Wes McKnight, and the sportsman and philanthropist Harry "Red" Foster.

In the third quarter, the score was 12–10 Winnipeg – shocking to some because it was so close, but still well within reach of the heavily favoured Tigers. And then Hanson took over, turning in one of the most memorable individual performances in any Grey Cup game. Official statistics weren't kept, so there's no way of knowing for sure whether Hanson actually did return punts for an astounding 300 yards, but if that wasn't precisely the number, it was close enough. Playing on the slippery field, and taking advantage of the way Hamilton punter Huck Welch was kicking the ball long and low, Hanson again and again evaded the onrushing tacklers, who were unable to deal with his feints, his quick changes of direction, and his tremendous speed. When the Tigers finally decided to start kicking the ball away from him, a Winnipeg teammate would catch the ball, wait for the Hamilton defenders to be drawn towards him, giving the necessary yards, and then lateral to Hanson, who would immediately head for daylight.

Hanson scored only a single touchdown, which came on a 80-yard return in the third quarter, and the Tigers didn't quit, fighting back to within six points of Winnipeg. But the final score – 18–12 in favour of the new Grey Cup champions – was evidence enough of the seismic shift that had taken place in Canadian sport.

"The Grey Cup, emblematic of the Canadian senior football championship, goes West, and it is in good hands, because this afternoon on the rain-swept H.A.A.A. field a great machine became the titleholder for 1935," wrote M. J. Rodden, the associate sports editor of *The Globe*. "Winnipegs outplayed a courageous Tiger team in nearly every department of the sport, and were full value for their 18-to-12 victory. They had what it takes, and they took it in a bitterly fought engagement, where there was no mercy sought or given.

Shag Shaughnessy was a player, coach, and broadcaster for the CFL. He was inducted into its Hall of Fame in 1963.

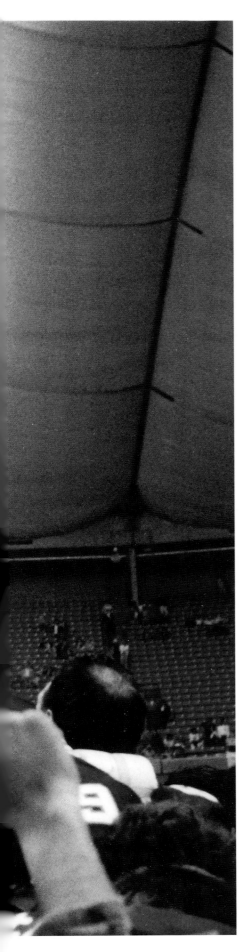

"In the greasy going Bob Fritz, Russ Rebholz, Greg Kabat and Fritz Hanson were the stars, but the 'Pegs all scintillated, and it appeared that they were out there to 'die for dear old Minnesota, Manitoba and the Canadian West,' and possibly also to prove that those who lured them to Winnipeg knew their business."

A western team had won the national football championship for the first time. American professional players had been essential to that victory. There was no turning back now – though, over the next few years, the eastern football establishment would do its best. Tommy Munns wrote:

The result will be in the interest of football. No more will a Canadian final be regarded as a foregone conclusion that another Eastern team is about to win. Finalists henceforth will meet on an equal basis, and the Westerners – they'll be defending champions next time – will command the wholesome respect of their opposition.

From a Western point of view the one regret was that the long-sought victory was scored, not by a team of Western Canada athletes, but by a powerful football machine, principal cogs of which were imported duty-free from the United States market. It was a triumph for Minnesota as well as Manitoba, and in saying that we quote a former Winnipeg resident.

No Interprovincial Union team, despite all the trouble over imports, ever was as 'packed' with U.S. talent as the new Canadian champions. That, of course, doesn't alter the fact that they are a great team. They overcame some very real handicaps to win, and in doing so produced some scintillating football that amazed the onlookers and stamped the Winnipegs as by far the best gridiron squad ever to come out of the West.

And Fritzy Hanson had now entered the Canadian football pantheon.

"He's the fastest thing I ever saw on a Canadian football field . . . and I've seen them all for over thirty years

The Bombers won their last Grey Cup in 1990, at B.C. Place Stadium, Vancouver.

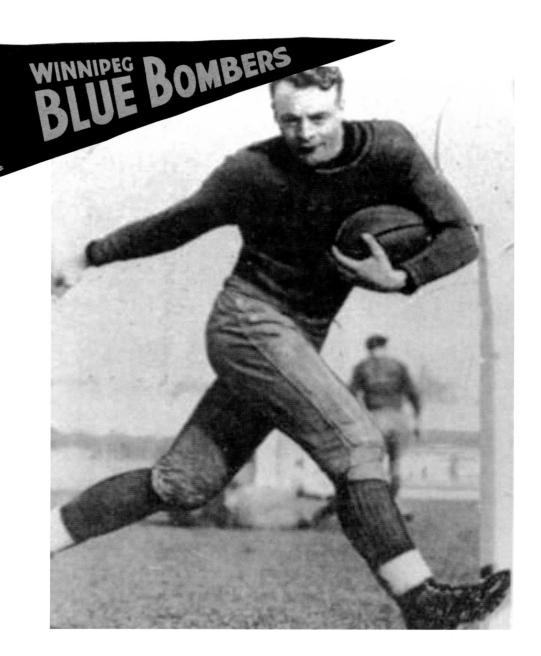

WINNIPEG
BLUE BOMBERS

Russ "The Wisconsin Wraith"
Rebholz, one of the American
imports who helped lead the
Bombers to their first Grey Cup
in 1935.

. . . haven't missed an eastern semi-final or a national final," Lou Marsh wrote in
The Star.

That wasn't quite the end of the adventure for the Winnipeg football team.
There was the embarrassing matter of their Hamilton hotel bill. Because of the
disappointing gate receipts, they didn't have the money to pay it. Fortunately, a
loyal fan and future Blue Bombers' president named Les Isard stepped up to bail
them out.

And then, on the joyous and no doubt rather lubricated train ride back to
Winnipeg, the players learned that another famous "Fritzy" was making the same

trip: violinist Fritz Kreisler, a musical superstar of the day. Some of them decided that the two Fritzes ought to meet each other, and that Kreisler might perhaps be inspired to play something for the newly crowned Grey Cup champions. They found his compartment and started banging on the door.

"Sorry, but I'm too tired to play," Kreisler said.

"Well, then, you don't have to play a real number. Just twang up the fiddle and practise a little," said one of the players.

"I don't practise."

"You don't practise? Mr. Kreisler, how do you expect to amount to anything?"

A story too good to be true? Perhaps. But that's how legends are born.

Following what, for them, was a humiliating Winnipeg victory, the eastern football powers tried desperately to put the genie back in the bottle. The Canadian Rugby Union quickly passed a rule that it claimed was designed to protect domestic talent, but which in reality seemed to have far more to do with preventing any more unpleasant surprises. Players would now be ineligible to compete unless they had lived in Canada for at least a year; in addition, they would have to live in the city in which their team was based from at least October 1.

The new statute would have an immediate impact in 1936, after the Regina Roughriders beat Winnipeg and Calgary in the western playoffs and were told that, under the rule, the five Americans on their roster were ineligible to compete in the Grey Cup game.

The first response from Saskatchewan was one of defiance. If the 'Riders couldn't bring their full roster, they weren't coming east.

"Let them declare their cheese champions," Regina coach Al Ritchie said.

But when the Western Interprovincial Football Union decided that the runners-up from Winnipeg could go instead, the Regina club had second thoughts. *Too late*, said the CRU, *we'll have our championship game without you*.

The Sarnia Imperials beat the Ottawa Rough Riders 26–20, claiming their second Grey Cup in three years (it would be their last – and the last ever won by an ORFU team). Again, in 1940, two eastern teams, Ottawa and Toronto Balmy Beach, played for the Cup – in that single instance, in a two-game, total-points final.

But by the conclusion of the Second World War, aside from two games in the 1990s, when expansion produced an American challenger for the championship game of Canadian football, it would be east versus west from that point hence, national battle lines that would define the Grey Cup and everything it came to represent.

All that was left was for the folks from the west to invent another lasting tradition: the wild Grey Cup party. That was coming, in 1948.

1942

KEEPING THE HOME FIRES BURNING

It is always a difficult decision: to play or not to play. In times of crisis, when real-world concerns make sport seem irrelevant, someone still has to decide whether the games will go on.

Shortly after the First World War began, Canadian football was suspended for the duration. The Grey Cup was contested in 1915, but then would not be lifted by a champion again until 1920. Decades later, in a very different world, in the aftermath of September 11, 2001 – the closest thing to war that North America has experienced in contemporary times – the Canadian Football League decided after some debate to shut down temporarily in midseason, as did the National Football League and Major League Baseball.

In World War II, a different call was made. In the first years of that conflict, Canadian football proceeded with business as usual. The Winnipeg Blue Bombers won the Grey Cup in 1939 and two years later in 1941. In the intervening year, the Ottawa Rough Riders won in an unprecedented two-game championship against Balmy Beach of the Ontario Rugby Football Union, this exceptional contest brought about because, once again, the sport's eastern and western administrators were squabbling with each other.

But by 1942, with war raging in Europe and in the Pacific, it became clear that it would be all but impossible to keep the various leagues running, because so many players were in a different kind of uniform, either already overseas or on their way.

1942 Grey Cup champs, the RCAF Hurricanes.

It was decided that the Grey Cup game should still be played, for the sake of morale on the home front, and for the sake of the troops in faraway places: a little bit of normalcy could only be a comfort. And so for the 1942 season, and the three that followed, teams of servicemen, temporarily thrown together while training to go to war, won the football championship of Canada.

For some of those players, the Grey Cup would be the last game of their lives.

Lew Hayman huddling with the RCAF Hurricanes.

The architect of the first of those wartime champion teams, in 1942, was Lew Hayman, an enormously important figure in the Canadian game. Hayman's influence extended through a remarkable half century, from 1933, when as a twenty-five-year-old

he coached the Toronto Argonauts to the Grey Cup, all the way to 1983, when he still held an executive position with the Toronto team that won its first championship since 1952. Hayman was born in New York City and attended Syracuse University, where he starred on the basketball team. After graduation in 1932, he moved north for a coaching job at the University of Toronto, and also became an

RCAF Hurricanes team photo.

The RCAF Hurricanes practising.

assistant with the Argonauts. Hayman was promoted midway through the Argos' first season when the head coach fell ill. He was given the job full time in 1933 and won a championship that year, and then won the Grey Cup with the Argos again in 1937 and 1938.

After World War II, the Argonaut coaching job was given to Ted Morris, much to Hayman's displeasure, and so he fled to Montreal, where, in partnership with Eric Cradock and Léo Dandurand, he formed the Alouettes football club, taking on the dual role of coach and general manager. Before that, Canadian football had been floundering in the city, but Hayman and company built what would become the dominant team in the east through much of the next decade. The Als won their first Grey Cup with Hayman coaching in 1949. He stepped down as head coach to concentrate on the general manager's duties in 1951, then quit football altogether in 1954 for a new life as a stockbroker. That didn't last long. Hayman was back with the Argos as managing director in 1956, and stayed with the franchise, in one executive position or another, until his death in 1984.

Hayman was a pioneer, an innovator, who is remembered for several firsts. His Als played the first night games and first Sunday games in Canadian football history. He signed one of Canadian football's first black players, Herb Trawick, in 1946. And during the 1946 off-season, he became the general manager of the Toronto Huskies, who played in the first game of what is considered the first season of the National Basketball Association. Hayman also coached the Huskies – for a single game – earning a place in the NBA record books, though his Huskies folded at the end of their only season of existence.

Frequently overlooked is Hayman's role in wartime football. In 1941, with most of

OUTCHARGED AND OUTSMARTED

THE MOST TELLING DESCRIPTION of the 1942 Grey Cup game's final result came from Winnipeg's star lineman and Hall of Famer, Lou Mogul. Mogul had been a member of the Winnipeg club since 1932 (just two years after its inception) and had seen a lot of action in football's "trenches" that day and during the previous decade. In reply to a pestering reporter, he said, "You tell us that we should have won the game when the truth of the matter is that we got the hell kicked out of us. They outcharged us and outsmarted us." The game's final stats don't support that assessment very well, which suggests that a football game isn't decided merely by the numbers. The Hurricanes outgained Winnipeg by just 197 yards to 186, and on the scoreboard led by just 8–5 at the final gun.

Nonetheless, Mogul's "inside" perspective pretty much sums up Canadian football, a game of strength, speed, and, of course, guile. Those attributes went a long way, not only in the service of a football offence or defence, but also in their country's defence. In this game, the entire roster of the winning RCAF Hurricanes were Royal Canadian Air Force personnel, as were fourteen of the Bombers squad. The decision of players to enlist in the war effort necessitated the shutdown of the Big Four and the Western Interprovincial Football Union after 1941, and yet the game carried on among soldiers stationed at home as a much-needed wartime diversion. A scanned copy of the 1942 game program shows that the winning coach, "Flying Officer" Lew Hayman, and many others were committed to the armed services first, and then to football.

The Hurricanes' 1942 roster also included Jake Gaudaur, who played in two Grey Cup games and went on to serve as CFL commissioner from 1968 to 1983. In 2010, three years after Gaudaur's death, the CFL and Veterans Affairs Canada joined forces to recognize players with a new award, the Jake Gaudaur Veterans' Award, given to a player "who best demonstrates the attributes of Canada's veterans."

the leagues opting to suspend operations, Hayman enlisted in the Royal Canadian Air Force. Legend has it that one day Flying Officer Hayman walked into the office of Squadron Leader Ted Kendrick at the No. 1 Training School at the Downsview base in Toronto and announced, "We've got a Grey Cup team at the station."

"Sure we have," Kendrick said. "And we've also got a war on."

It turned out Hayman was right: the squadron included a large number of players who had already made their mark in Canadian football, including Bill Stukus, Don Durno, and a future commissioner of the Canadian Football League, Jake Gaudaur. Hayman was given permission to put together a team, on the condition that its activities not interfere with the men's military training. The Hamilton Tigers, one of several clubs shut down temporarily, offered to loan their equipment. And everyone agreed that morale inside and outside the armed forces could only be boosted by having football continue, even if it was not quite business as usual.

Hayman entered his team, dubbed the RCAF Hurricanes after the famous fighter plane, in the Ontario Rugby Football Union. They went 8–1–1 in a ten-game season, beat Balmy Beach 24–0 for the league title, and then beat another air force team, from the Ottawa Uplands base, in the de facto eastern final.

Their Grey Cup opponents from Winnipeg arrived at a significant disadvantage, having played only a six-game season in a three-team, all-Winnipeg league – the last league still operating in western Canada – before they beat a Regina team in the western final, their only real preparation for the Grey Cup. But Winnipeg's

outspoken coach, Reg Threlfall, whose Bombers had won two of the previous three Grey Cups, was undeterred by those circumstances. He arrived in Toronto for the game, confidently predicting that his team would prevail and suggesting that the Hurricanes were lacking both the necessary talent and the strategic acumen – the latter a direct shot at Hayman.

It was cold and damp on December 5, 1942, and the field conditions were appallingly bad. The day before the game, officials inspected the icy surface at Varsity Stadium – it was so slippery that both teams were forced to relocate their practices – and decided that the best solution was to spread salt on the field to melt it. That only made things worse. On game day, the Hurricanes and Bombers were forced to wear running shoes in the hopes of gaining a little traction.

"On a field that was icy, watery, slippery, sandy – in fact the worst kind of field for the sky-birds style of play – the Hurrys line outcharged and outblocked the vaunted Bombers brigade," Annis Stukus wrote in the *Toronto Star*.

It was a low-scoring contest. The Hurricanes took a 2–0 lead in the first half on two singles, the first of them coming off a 65-yard quick kick by Don Crowe. Winnipeg pulled ahead 5–2 in the second half on Wayne Sheley's short touchdown pass to Lloyd Boivin (the convert was blocked), but then Crowe's 37-yard run set up what would be the winning touchdown for Toronto in a game that finished 8–5.

Despite the lack of scoring, and the Bombers' lack of preparation because of their makeshift season, reviews for the Grey Cup were generally good. As Hal Walker wrote:

> "The crowd of 12,000 which assembled for the seventeenth annual clash of East and West marveled at the fine continuity of play on a gridiron which was dotted with pools of water and has as its foundation a thin, yet dangerous layer of ice. They thrilled at the open offense of both teams, which contributed to a fine football spectacle, and they left

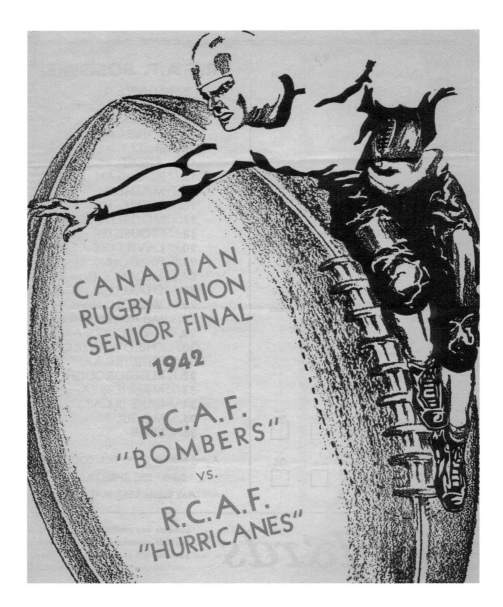

with the impression that Hayman, in accounting for his fourth Canadian title in four trips to the national final, had a team which would stand comparison with any of the great teams he has had in the past."

Winnipeg's coach agreed.
"They had it on us," Threlfall said. "They were a better ball club."

From London, the great Scott Young, working as a correspondent for the Canadian Press, offered a very different perspective on that Grey Cup game – perhaps the one that mattered most:

Gloom hung like pea soup over Western Canada's soldiers, sailors and airmen in Britain today while Easterners celebrated the 8–5 victory of Toronto Hurricanes in the Dominion football final Saturday.

This afternoon, all who were able, clustered around radios in their billets, dispersal huts and auxiliary service canteens to hear a half-hour condensed broadcast account of the game.

Some of the more nostalgic perched themselves on the backs of chairs, which they called "bleachers," eating a variety of food, all of which they nicknamed "peanuts" for the occasion, while others sucked on small bottles which needed no nickname – all trying to create the illusion of a sports atmosphere they have left behind for the duration, but certainly not forgotten.

Dozens listened to the broadcast at London's Beaver Club and in flats all over London civilian Canadians working here – Government officials, radio and newspaper men – were grouped around home radios. Many sentimental bets were placed on the teams the bettors had never seen.

Cheers and groans which roared over the radio when Eddie Thompson made his 62-yard run for the Hurricanes were echoed all over the United Kingdom wherever men listened. As the tide of the game ebbed and flowed, unmerciful kidding was thrown back and forth.

A little bit of Canadianese occurred near the door of the Central Y.M.C.A. in London's Bloomsbury district. Two soldiers from Western units jumped from a moving bus and were running toward the door when three airmen appeared in the doorway, singing: "We don't give a cuss for all the rest of Canada, we're from Toronto."

"What was the score pal?" one of the soldiers asked. "Eight to five for Toronto, pal," was the joyful answer.

There is a photograph that depicts the RCAF Hurricanes celebrating their famous victory: Hayman in dress uniform, and the players wearing jerseys with the RCAF roundel – a red maple leaf inside a blue circle – on the front. Many of them are hoisting a celebratory beer. They played for free that season, though they ate a bit better than their fellow soldiers. They came from different clubs, different places, different countries – there were several Americans among them. They were a team for one year only.

In that crowd are Ed Poscavage (best man at Jake Gaudaur's wedding), Ed Sarvis, Lloyd "Truck" Langley, Ed Burton, Jack Buckmaster, George Oliphant, and Eddie Thompson.

They're the ones who didn't come home.

1948

THE "FIRST" GREY CUP

A man wearing a cowboy hat rides a horse into an elegant hotel lobby in the middle of a stuffy, uptight big city, and suddenly everything changes.

Perhaps it wasn't quite so simple. Perhaps it *could* have happened – and even *should* have happened – but is merely a persistent myth. Maybe there never was a horse in the Royal York Hotel – no independent reports from the time corroborate the oft-told tale. But every story of how the championship of Canadian football was transformed into the country's favourite annual party begins in a particular place, at a particular time: in Toronto, in 1948, when the Calgary Stampeders first played for the Grey Cup. And, whether or not a cowboy actually rode through the doors of the grand old hotel, it's true that the western fans turned staid Hogtown on its ear and transformed a football game into something much bigger.

But first, the game itself.

In the immediate postwar years, Canadian football grew close to its modern form as the final vestiges of amateurism fell away – fully professional, and fully accepting of imported talent. As late as the early 1960s, there wasn't a huge gap between what Canadian and U.S. teams were paying, and so players moved freely back and forth across the border, to wherever they could cut the best deal.

One of these nomadic players was Les Lear, whose biography is particularly unusual. Born in Grafton, North Dakota, Lear moved to Winnipeg at age ten, and

Reggie Holmes talks with a reporter after Calgary's 1971 Grey Cup win.

it was in Canada that he received his football education. He graduated from the Deer Lodge Juniors to the team that became known as the Blue Bombers, and was part of Grey Cup victories in 1939 and 1941, playing offensive guard and linebacker.

In 1944, Lear moved south for a bigger paycheque, where he played four seasons in the National Football League with the Cleveland Rams (winning an NFL championship in 1945), the Los Angeles Rams, and the Detroit Lions, making him the first Canadian-trained player ever to compete in the NFL. Then, in 1948, he was lured back to Canada by the promise of an $8,000 annual salary as a playing coach with the Calgary Stampeders. He arrived in a city with a long, though spotty, football heritage, during which the various home teams had never claimed a championship of any sort.

First there were the Calgary Tigers, a rugby football team founded in 1909 that disbanded a few years later during the First World War. The Canucks came next, playing from 1915 until 1919, and then the 50th Battalion team, in 1923 and 1924. There was no senior football in Calgary at all from the Battalion's demise until the rebirth of the Tigers in 1928 – a side famous for being the first in Canadian football to throw a forward pass. But that strategic innovation wasn't enough to keep them going. In 1931, the Altomahs came into being, and then in 1935 the Calgary Bronks, who finished as western runners-up, behind the great Winnipeg teams of the 1930s, four seasons in a row.

After the Second World War, the Bronks were renamed the Stampeders. In 1948 they adopted the colours red and white, and that same year thirty-year-old Lear arrived in town. He was by all accounts a character, and a tough guy on and off the field (in 1952, he was charged with assaulting a player, though the player later changed his story and the charges were dropped). He also brought the four-man defensive line to Canadian football for the first time.

The Grey Cup-winning 1948 Calgary Stampeders.

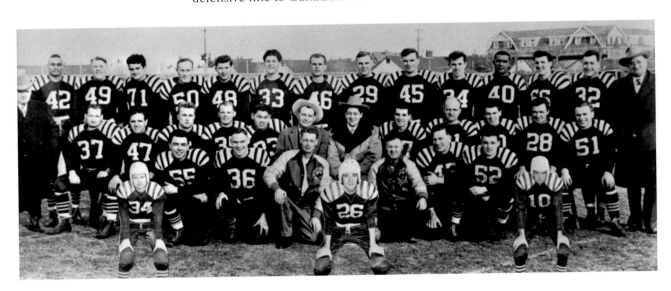

Later in life, after the Stamps let him go in 1952, Lear built a second career training racehorses and became a familiar figure around the Canadian circuit. In 1948, though, his only concern was football, and he assembled a team that would for a short time be one of the best in Canadian history. They were a talented, colourful, and idiosyncratic bunch, including Fritzy Hanson, Lear's old teammate in Winnipeg and the star of the first western Grey Cup victory in 1935; Woody Strode, who after his football career ended would become much more famous as a Hollywood character actor, featured in such films as *Spartacus* and *The Man Who Shot Liberty Valance*; and Normie Kwong, a local teenager, still wet behind the ears who would go on to become one of the CFL's greatest stars with the Edmonton Eskimos, and years later become the lieutenant-governor of Alberta.

In the west that season, no one could touch the Stamps. They finished the year undefeated at 12–0, scoring 218 points and surrendering just 61. Saskatchewan provided a surprisingly stiff test in the two-game, total-points western final, tying the first game in Calgary 4–4. However, the Stampeders took the second 17–6, and booked their trip to Toronto's Varsity Stadium for a Grey Cup date with the Ottawa Rough Riders. The Ottawa team represented the final obstacle between the Stamps and an undefeated season, something no Canadian football team had accomplished before, and no team has accomplished since.

An enterprising local alderman and civic booster named Don Mackay (who later, as mayor of Calgary, began the tradition of giving visiting dignitaries and celebrities white cowboy hats) helped organize the eastbound group of Stampeders supporters – 250 human fans, and 12 horses. On the night of Tuesday, November 23, two trains, one of which was equipped with its own bar car *and* square-dancing car (featuring Jack Friedenberg and his orchestra) *plus* a baggage car adapted to carry the horses, pulled out of Calgary's Canadian Pacific railway station, and chugged towards a city that had no idea what was about to hit it. Two Sarcee chiefs were part of the entourage, and two war veterans from the local convalescent hospital who had won their spots in a draw. The organizers planned to stage pancake breakfasts and hoedowns right in the heart of downtown Toronto, that carnival atmosphere hitherto unheard of at the Grey Cup, which to that date had been merely a football game.

On the Friday morning before Grey Cup Saturday, the train arrived at Toronto's Union Station, and out spilled something spontaneous, unchoreographed, a little

Normie Kwong played thirteen seasons in the CFL before becoming a sports executive and eventually, the lieutenant-governor of Alberta.

bit wild, a little bit inebriated, and a whole lot of fun. At one point, the uninhibited Calgarians crossed paths with the very core of the eastern establishment, who were assembling at the same hotel for a black-tie reception to honour Governor General Viscount Alexander. The Calgarians sang "Home On the Range" as the GG walked to the Royal York elevators, by all accounts with a great big smile on his face.

That party, and its annual return in one form or another wherever the Grey Cup game is held, came to define the event for many Canadians: the one day of the year when they can sit back, watch the big game – their own game – and really let down their hair. Years later, *Globe and Mail* columnist Dick Beddoes would label it the Grand National Drunk.

Jerry Keeling was the Stampeders' quarterback for the 1971 Grey Cup game.

For a city that any Canadian football fan today would identify as one of the game's great hotbeds, Calgary has gone through long stretches with very little to celebrate. After the historic first triumph in 1948, the Stamps would spend twenty years in the wilderness before their next Grey Cup appearance – a losing effort against Russ Jackson and his great Ottawa team in 1968. Calgary was back in 1970 with much the same squad, featuring Wayne Harris, Jerry Keeling, and Herm "Ham Hands" Harrison, but they'd lose the championship game again, this time to the Montreal Alouettes.

STAMPEDERS
ARGONAUTS

50¢

McMAHON STADIUM, SEPT. 29, 1964   NEXT HOME GAME OCTOBER 10

Sandro DeAngelis, the most accurate place kicker in CFL history, with the Grey Cup in 2008.

Finally, Cowtown claimed its second Grey Cup title in 1971, in a game that is better remembered by most CFL devotees for the team that lost – the big-money, star-studded Toronto Argonauts quarterbacked by Joe Theismann – and for two of the great gaffes in Grey Cup history: Leon McQuay's fateful fumble, and Harry Abofs' brain-cramp decision to kick a bouncing punt out of bounds.

The Stampeders spent much of the next two decades playing in the shadow of their great provincial rivals, the Edmonton Eskimos, though when coach Wally Buono arrived in 1990, that began to change – the Stamps represented the west in the 1991 Grey Cup game, losing to Rocket Ismail and the Toronto Argonauts on a frigid day in Winnipeg. Calgary's fortunes changed dramatically in 1992 with the arrival of quarterback Doug Flutie, who had originally been lured to the CFL by the British Columbia Lions, with whom he played for two seasons before the Stamps' colourful owner, Larry Ryckman, enticed him with a million-dollar contract.

A star at Boston College, famous for the original Hail Mary pass that beat the University of Miami, Flutie was small for a quarterback but a great athlete who could run and throw and improvise. During his first years as a professional, in the United States Football League and the National Football League, coaches didn't want to adapt their game to make use of his talents, and he was too short to play the traditional drop-back passer's role that the American game favoured. On the bigger

Canadian field, though, with all receivers in motion and quarterbacks free to wander from the pocket when the situation allowed, Flutie's physical skills and football smarts were a perfect fit.

Though he is regarded by many as the greatest player ever to compete in the CFL, Flutie, at the height of his powers, won only a single Grey Cup during his four seasons in Calgary, a 24–10 win over the Winnipeg Blue Bombers in 1992, his first year as a Stampeder.

It was Flutie's understudy, Jeff Garcia, who took essentially the same supporting cast and delivered Calgary another Cup, in a dramatic 26–24 win – clinched by Mark McLoughlin's field goal on the final play of the game – over the Hamilton Tiger-Cats in 1998.

Calgary's next Grey Cup triumph, in 2001, was the least likely of the bunch, as a team that finished the regular season with a record of 8–10, quarterbacked by the unheralded Marcus Crandell, defeated the Winnipeg Blue Bombers 27–19. The arrival of quarterback Henry Burris in 2005, and coach John Hufnagel in 2008, heralded a new golden era of Calgary football, capped by a 22–14 Grey Cup victory over the Montreal Alouettes in 2008 at Olympic Stadium. By then, the Stampeders had established themselves as perennial contenders and one of the league's best organizations.

Les Lear was only thirty years old in 1948, and a cutting-edge football tactician, but when it came to off-field matters, he was a strict disciplinarian and hidebound traditionalist of the old school. Heading for the championship game, he wanted his players cloistered as far from any fun as possible. During the long train ride to Toronto, they were sequestered in a locked car separate from wives, girlfriends, and the hard-partying fans. When the train stopped along the way, and the supporters dashed off to the closest liquor store, the players got out and did calisthenics – often in the snow. Upon arriving at Toronto's Union Station, the Calgary entourage made the short walk across the street to the Royal York, while Lear took his team to a hotel and roadhouse called the Pig and Whistle in Oakville. Today, the city of Oakville is part of the Greater Toronto Area, but in 1948, it would have seemed like a quiet country village far out in the boondocks, which was just the atmosphere the coach desired. While the Cowtown crowd took over downtown, with their pancake breakfasts,

Fred Wilmot, Ced Gyles, and Rube Ludwig at the 1948 victory parade.

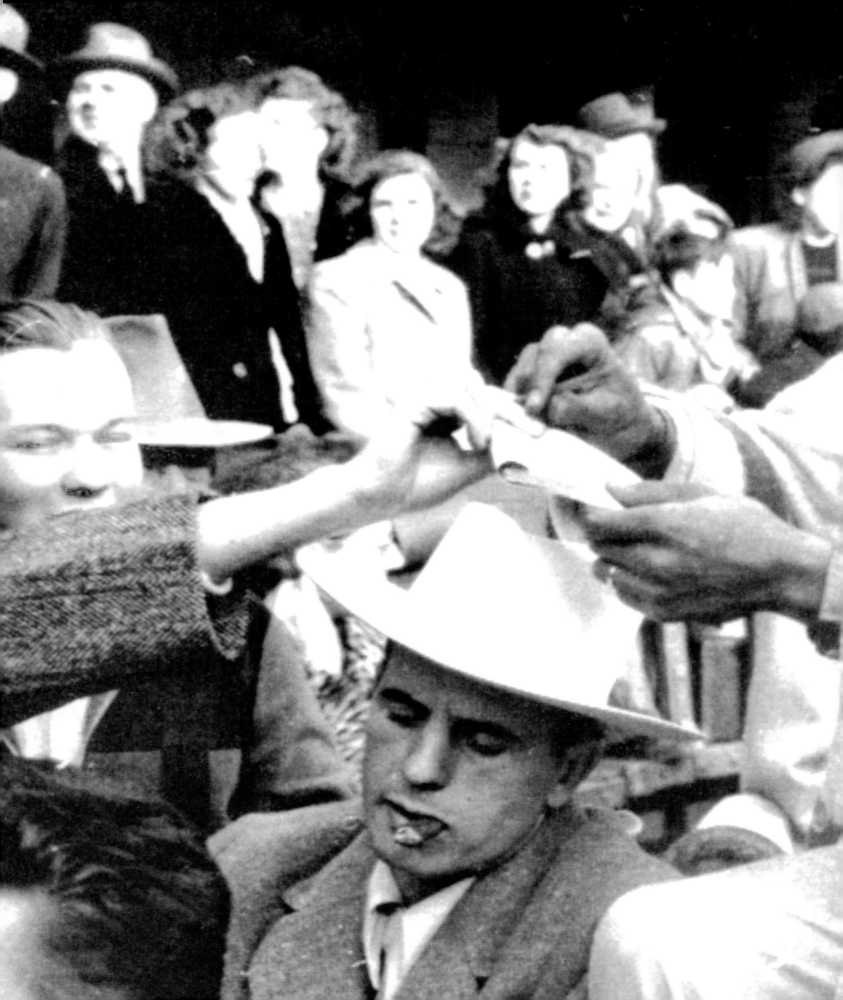

Woody Strode at the 1948
victory parade.

square dances, and general highjinks, the Stamps lived a Spartan existence and practised in secret, with Lear paranoid about someone discovering his pet strategies – to the extent that he worried about airplanes flying over the practice field and had the team do their film study in a locked basement.

One of the things he was trying to keep secret was a gimmick lifted straight from the playbook of the Rough Riders – who, for the familiar reasons of eastern media bias, entered the championship game as heavy favourites. Ottawa had enjoyed great success that season employing the "sleeper" play, in which a receiver found a way to camouflage himself against the crowd of players on the sideline before springing into action and catching the other team unawares. Lear added it to the Stamps' Grey Cup playbook – though he and his players later denied that it was planned. In fact, in a pre-game meeting with Canadian Rugby Union officials, Lear actually went so far as to ask that all players on the bench be pushed back so that Ottawa would be discouraged from employing this play, which he denigrated as bush-league tactics.

THE CULTURE OF CANADIAN FOOTBALL

IF EVER THERE WERE contrasting styles or cultures of the game, the 1948 Grey Cup brought them into sharp relief. The eastern game was much older, yet was still an exciting brand of football, as exemplified by the great Tony Golab, who led the Rough Riders into the 1948 contest. The Calgary Stampeders, however, were led not just by a group of players that was unbeaten in all fourteen games leading into the title affair, but by a loyal cowboy following that literally descended on Toronto.

In just their third full season, the Stamps posted a perfect 12–0 record in the regular season – a feat still unduplicated – under rookie head coach Les Lear. On the day, they were outgained 349 yards to 264, gave up 291 rushing yards to a virtual who's who of 1948 football, yet found ways to win with a mixture of five key elements:

offence, defence, special teams, "big plays," and fan support. Calgary forced six Ottawa fumbles, came from behind twice, and scored the game's first touchdown on the now-outlawed "sleeper" play, giving Calgary a 5–1 lead just before halftime.

The 1948 Grey Cup truly was a game that changed "the game" itself. Reinforcing its importance is the fact that the announced attendance of 20,013 – then a Grey Cup record – was many thousands less than it might have been had Toronto's Varsity Stadium been any bigger. Post-game accounts suggested that many more fans "had to be content with [a] radio description of the game . . . one cowboy watched from a telegraph pole on Bloor St." The real impact of the 1948 Grey Cup was best summed up by one Torontonian: "This thing has done more to bring the east and the west together than the building of the railway."

Les Lear won two Grey Cups with Calgary.

In the final moments of the second quarter, with the game still scoreless, the Stamps executed the sleeper play to perfection, pulling off a double surprise by concealing the receiver on the opposite side of the field from the two team benches. The Stampeders had the ball on the Ottawa 14-yard line. At the end of one play, Calgary end Norm Hill fell down near the sideline, and didn't get up. Many fans in the stands at Varsity Stadium noticed him, lying prone near the sidelines, but the Ottawa players and coaches didn't. (Legend has it that some of them were distracted, gazing into the stands, because of the arrival of figure skater and national sweetheart Barbara Ann Scott.) Another Stamp took his place in the formation. At the snap, Hill jumped up and headed for the end zone, while Ottawa defenders scrambled madly to catch up with him. Quarterback Keith Spaith faked a pass the other way, then lobbed the ball to Hill, who bobbled it momentarily. An Ottawa defender recovered in time to knock him to the ground, but the tipped ball landed back in his hands as he fell to the turf for the touchdown, giving Calgary a halftime lead. (It was the first and only time the sleeper play was employed in a Grey Cup game, though it wasn't officially banned under CFL rules until 1961.)

In the third quarter, the Rough Riders rallied to pull ahead 7–6, and, entering the final period, appeared to have control of the game. In those tense moments, Lear didn't just coach – he was in uniform as well, and came onto the field when he felt the need to get his players to settle down and focus.

One of the stranger plays in Grey Cup history finally, and definitively, turned the tide Calgary's way. Scrimmaging on his own 40-yard line, Ottawa quarterback Bob Paffrath threw a lateral pass to Pete Karpuk, who was unable to catch the ball. As was the custom at the time, the referee's horn sounded, signalling an infraction – the play was offside – but unlike the modern official's whistle, that didn't mean there was a stoppage in play. Apparently confused, no Ottawa player jumped on the ball. Instead, Woody Strode walked over, took a look, heard his teammate Chuck Anderson holler, "Pick it up and run like hell," and did just that, until he was finally tackled on the Ottawa 10-yard line.

On the next play, Calgary scored the winning touchdown in a game that finished 12–7, capping an undefeated season.

Afterwards, the party at the Royal York was, understandably, one for the ages. This account was written for *The Globe and Mail* by William French, who would go on to enjoy a long and distinguished career as the newspaper's literary editor. In 1948, he was a rookie reporter, fresh out of school, sent to describe the exotic events unfolding at the Royal York. And though it's hard to miss the big-city condescension, it also sounds like he might have enjoyed the fun, despite himself.

New Year's Eve came a little early this year.

It arrived Saturday night, when the hilarious followers of the victorious Calgary Stampeders staged a spontaneous celebration at the Royal York. They ushered in

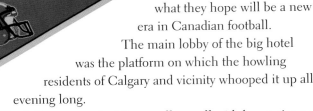

what they hope will be a new era in Canadian football.

The main lobby of the big hotel was the platform on which the howling residents of Calgary and vicinity whooped it up all evening long.

The lobby was packed from wall to wall with humanity, so much so that two singing cowpokes strumming on their guitars had to take refuge on a table-top for fear of strumming somebody's teeth.

Once on the table, the cowboys – whose names were Oogie and Bev, not Slim and Shorty as you'd expect – were joined by a perky cowgal who took charge of the sing-song.

The mob sang everything, lustily and slightly out of tune. First came all the songs about the West, including Texas. One of the most popular was a ditty call "Vive le Cal-garee," in which the choir gave vent to its bursting civic pride.

What was left of the goalposts arrived in the lobby shortly after the game and was put up for all to see. A foresighted bell-hop lashed them to the balcony railing.

People stood four deep around the mezzanine balcony. It was like watching a bull-fight in the arena below and space for looking was as scarce as it had been for the game in the afternoon. The spectators were a different breed than the merrymakers. They didn't join in the singing and cheering and seemed a little puzzled by it all.

A little old lady with grey hair wanted to know the name of one of the Calgary players – any one – so she could write to Calgary and get his autograph.

Several people in the throng wore black ribbons. They were Ottawa fans in mourning for their team.

When members of the team went through the lobby on their way to the civic reception, centre of attention was Woody Strode the towering all-star end and idol of the fans. Woody was besieged by autograph hounds.

Stampeder President Tom Brooks appeared, carrying the Grey Cup, and a great cheer went up. In acknowledgment, Tom took a drink out of the symbol of Canadian grid supremacy.

There was a great bustle and cheers when five cowpunchers, each carrying a case of refreshments, passed through the lobby in Indian style. They escaped into an elevator.

After Oogie and Bev stopped a-strummin' and plinkin' on their geetars – their fingers were sore – the party broke up into small eddies of interest, each group singing a different song. Throughout the din, a man wearing an ogre-like rubber mask ran around kissing all of the women in sight. He got away with it, too.

The exhibition was exuberant and uninhibited, staged by a thoroughly happy group of people. Last night the Calgarians boarded their special train and started the long journey back across the prairies to the city they love.

It's a long winter.

That "long journey back across the prairies" in fact turned out to be more of the same, another wild party train – except that, unlike on the ride to Toronto, the players were now unencumbered, free to connect with their wives or girlfriends and join in the celebrations. When the Stamps returned to Calgary, they were welcomed by a crowd of 30,000 people – that in a city with a population of just over 100,000.

A year later, the Stamps would be back in the big game, this time losing to the Montreal Alouettes. By then, a tradition had been established that continues un-changed more than half a century later. Anyone who travels to the Grey Cup game,

The 1948 Grey Cup team in their trademark Stetsons.

GREY CUP ECONOMICS

TICKETS FOR THE 2011 Grey Cup game in Vancouver had sold out by July 21 – more than four months (129 days) in advance of the game. The face value of tickets ranged from $125 to $375, and 54,313 fans watched the British Columbia Lions defeat the Winnipeg Blue Bombers in the refurbished B.C. Place Stadium. Of course, just because the tickets officially sold out doesn't mean there wasn't a booming secondary market, right up until game time.

Compare those prices to the first Grey Cup game, held at Rosedale Field in 1909. Bleacher seats were sold for 25 and 50 cents, and the best places in the house went for $1.25. In 1911, seated admission went for $1.50, while standing room in front of the main grandstand could be had for 75 cents. Fans flocked into Varsity Stadium at those prices as the national fi-nal's popularity boomed, particularly for games held in Toronto.

Tickets remained around the $1.50 level even until the great 1948 game that saw an influx of Calgary fans. That would soon change, as Grey Cup gate receipts grew from just $19,718 in 1946 to more than $115,000 in 1951, when tickets for the Ottawa–Saskatchewan classic sold for as much as $5.65. The price hit $10 in 1956, and escalated to $15 for best seats in 1967. Gate receipts by then had gone well beyond the $300,000 mark. In 1976, the Grey Cup finally sur-passed the $1,000,000 mark in gate receipts, and that figure has grown steadily ever since as fans continue to sell out the game in every CFL city. From little more than a local event in 1909 that brought in $2,616.40, the Grey Cup Festival is now a multimillion-dollar cultural event.

no matter what their allegiance, can count on running into kindred spirits, often in crazy get-ups, hailing from every corner of this vast country, gathered together to celebrate. And though it remains murky as to whether a horse was ridden into the lobby of the Royal York in 1948, many a horse has been into many a hotel lobby since.

Other large sporting events, other championship games, have become glossily corporate and impossibly expensive, separating the haves from the have-nots, with stadiums often filled by those with no real passionate rooting interest, there simply because of connections or because it's the place to be. The players themselves remain hidden away, and the best parties come with velvet ropes attached, with security guards at the door making sure that only the right people are granted entrance.

In a Grey Cup city, even in the security-conscious atmosphere of the twenty-first century, it is still very possible to run into one of the competing players on the street in the days before the game. It is possible – heck, likely – that a night on the town will involve running into some of the game's legends, there to join in the festivities. And the centre of the Grey Cup isn't a black-tie gala, isn't a VIP-only celebration. It is in the Spirit of Edmonton room, or Riderville, or Tiger Town, or one of the other pop-up parties – as simple as a hotel ballroom, with a band on the stage and drinks available and fans packed in like sardines – where even in tough times for Canadian football the game's beating heart resides. There is nothing else exactly like it in the great wide world of sport.

Thank Calgary for that. Thank the square dancers, the pancake flippers, the guys with the guitars, the man on the horse – if indeed there was a man on a horse – for teaching this country how to throw a party, and how to celebrate itself.

1957

TOUGH AS STEEL

Jim Trimble was a great big bear of a man: huge hands, huge head, huge body, and a huge, over-the-top personality. Even in a sport populated by giants, he was hard to miss, and long before superstar coaches with gargantuan egos and outsized personas became commonplace, long before trash-talking became part of the modern sports landscape, Big Jim made it his personal art form.

Perhaps his act wouldn't have played so well in other places in the relatively conservative, genteel times that were the late 1950s. Perhaps in other places they would have preferred a coach who didn't spout off quite so much about the short-comings of the opposition, who wasn't quite so willing to settle arguments with his fists, who never hesitated to let people know he wasn't just the best football coach in Canada but the best in all of North America.

But in Hamilton, the blustery former steelworker from McKeesport, Pennsylvania, was a perfect fit, and in 1957, the coach, his team, and his town would celebrate a famous victory, signalling the beginning of a decade of dominance – at least in the east. In one of Canada's great football cities, it was a perfect match of style, success, and personality.

For the rest of Canada, though, the 1957 Grey Cup game would be remembered not so much for the triumph of the Hamilton Tiger-Cats, but for one of the most

Angelo Mosca, in fourteen CFL seasons, earned an all-star spot five times.
Pictured here at Ivor Wynne Stadium after the Tiger-Cats 1972 victory.

TICATS

SCOREBOARD	QUARTERS				FINAL SCORE
	1st	2nd	3rd	4th	
WINNIPEG	0	0	0	7	7
HAMILTON	13	0	0	19	32

TORONTO DAILY STAR

66TH YEAR ★★★★ Authorized as second-class mail, the Postmaster, Ottawa. SATURDAY, NOVEMBER 30, 1957—60 PAGES 5c Per Copy. 35c PER WEEK HOME DELIVERED

Gilchrist Star As Cats Bring Grey Cup East

Varsity Stadium, Nov. 30—The dullest and most one-sided Grey Cup game in 10 years ended in a Hamilton victory and the return of the Grey Cup to the East, as the Tiger-Cats whipped Winnipeg Blue Bombers 32-7.

The Cats were just too powerful for the crippled Bombers, battered them for three quarters and then broke the game wide open with three touchdowns in the final 15 minutes.

It's the first time the East has won the Grey Cup since 1953, when Hamilton defeated the same Bombers, 12-6.

Not since the late 1940's, when Argos shut out the Bombers twice in succession, has there been a more one-sided game.

The Ticats took a 13-0 first quarter lead, and except for a couple of Winnipeg threats that fizzled out, their domination was never in question.

Hamilton fans rushed onto the field at the end of the game and mobbed their heroes.

FAN TRIPS BAWEL IN FLIGHT

The game was marred by a fan who tripped Hamilton's Ray Bawel near the Winnipeg bench at the Bomber 40-yard line as he raced toward a certain touchdown with an intercepted pass. As police took the fan away, the officials penalized Winnipeg half the distance to the goal line and Hamilton went on to score anyway.

Cookie Gilchrist, with two touchdowns, was the Cats' big man, with Gerry McDougall, Bernie Faloney and Bawel getting the other Hamilton majors. Steve Oneschuk hit on only two of five convert tries, mainly because of poor snaps.

Homebrew quarterback Barry Roseborough saved Winnipeg from a shut-out when he tossed a 15-yard touchdown pass to Dennis Mendyk late in the game. Kenny Ploen converted.

Ploen, the Bombers' first-string quarterback, was taken from the game late in the third quarter with an injured leg, and while he made a brief come-back in the last quarter, finally had to give up.

It was a typical Hamilton win. Their defensive team controlled the opposition, wore them down, and set the stage for the last quarter steamroller.

Winnipeg had their chances. Gerry James was stopped on the six-
(Continued on Page 2, Col. 1)

SUKARNO SAFE AS 4 GRENADES THROWN, 7 DIE

Jakarta, Nov. 30—(AP)—President Sukarno of Indonesia narrowly escaped death when unknown assassins threw four hand grenades at him, a government communique said today. Sukarno was unhurt.

The grenades were thrown at a school party attended by the Indonesian head of state and his children. First reports said seven persons were killed in the attack.

Scoring Plays

Dennis Mendyk fumbled on the Winnipeg 45 and Hamilton end Ray Bawel picked up the ball and raced for the touchdown. Steve Oneschuk converted. Hamilton 7, Winnipeg 0.

Bernie Faloney plunged from the five. Oneschuk failed to convert.

Gerry McDougall ran over two Winnipeg players for a 27-yard Hamilton touchdown on the first play of the quarter. A bad snap washed out the convert. Hamilton 19, Winnipeg 0.

Cookie Gilchrist bashed five yards for a touchdown. The convert was blocked. Hamilton 25, Winnipeg 0.

Gilchrist ran 17 yards for a touchdown and Oneschuk converted. Hamilton 32, Winnipeg 0.

Roseborough threw a 13-yard pass to Mendyk for a touchdown. Ploen converted. Hamilton 32, Winnipeg 7.

WINNIPEG, WHO CAME EAST with a reputation as a tough ball club playing in a tougher league than the Big Four, found today that Ticats defence set up all their touchdowns as the Tiger-Cats whipped Winnipeg, who had trouble moving the ball on the ground or in the air.

Mistakes Did It -- Grant

By GORD CAMPBELL

If you wanted to be so close to this you could cut it, all you had to do was be in the Winnipeg dressing room after their one-sided loss to Hamilton.

As a result of fast coach Bud Grant who emerged to go on a TV show replied when asked when the doors will be open, replied in "about five minutes" when they got over it.

Grant refused to make excuses for his team's defeat but did remark that he thought...

Hamilton was out as much of a precision team as Edmonton. However, he blamed the defeat on the fact the Bombers made too many mistakes and was the first to admit Hamilton deserved to win.

Gerry James, chewing the red standing homebrew footballer in Canada this year, not later about it all.

"I don't want this to sound like sour grapes," he said, "but we played out worst ball game of the season. Hamilton was better...

a tough and tough, like we figured, and deserved to win.

The turning point was when I fumbled on the Hamilton four yard line at the beginning of the second half. We were hot then and the score was still 13-0. After that fumble, the boys seemed to lose the hope," he continued.

"Just figure it this way, we carried the ball 260 times in Western conference and fumbled once. Here I carried it good times and fumbled four times," he said.

THE WEATHER—SNOWFLURRIES

SATURDAY-SUNDAY

The Toronto and vicinity forecast is: A few snowflurries today. A few rising periods and cold Sunday. Winds becoming westerly 20 into this afternoon.

Wind, yesterday, 5 a.m. W. 8; noon, NW 8, 8 p.m. NW 3.

Time	Temp.	Weather	Bar.
Low since 1841 (1880)	35		
Low since 1841 (1873)	-5		

A year ago, high 29, low 21.

INDEX

Amusements—27-28		Crossword—52		Radio, TV—23-24	
Births, Deaths—38		Health—49		Sports—31-34	
Books—39		Horoscope—55		Suburban—13	
Churches—14-15		Markets—16-17		Travel—16-17	
Comics—57		Racing—34		Want Ads—20-45	

TICATS CASHED OPPORTUNITIES BOMBERS DIDN'T

By MILT DUNNELL
Star Sports Editor

Varsity Stadium, Nov. 30—The Red River band wagon which had rolled triumphantly out of the West broke down completely and ended a total wreck, its load of platinumed highlighters who brought the Grey Cup back to the East for the first time since 1953.

The Cats were the last eastern club to hold this most coveted prize in Canadian sport and this same Winnipeg team was the victim that year as well. This was a contest between a Hamilton team that cashed in on every opportunity and a Winnipeg team that cashed in on practically none.

Especially in the second quarter

Especially in the second quarter the Bombers were like a dice shooter who builds up his loot until he goes for the big pass and then rolls snake-eyes.

Fumbles Costly

Three times in those 15 minutes, the Blue Bombers surrendered the ball inside the Hamilton 30-yard line, without getting a single point. Once they were on the seventh, and once on the 12th.

They still had a chance to get back into the ball-game starting the third quarter when they were 13 points behind. It looked as if they intended to get that far, but their hopes were crushed when Jerry James, Golden Boy of the West, recently voted the outstanding homebrew player in Canadian
(Continued on Page 2, Col. 1)

HAMILTON TO 'BUST OPEN' MAYOR VOWS

By JIM PROUDFOOT

Mayor Lloyd Jackson of Hamilton promised to "bust wide open tonight.

The Hamilton mayor told the successful players as they celebrated their easy Grey Cup victory, that the Ambitious City would stage a victory celebration to end all victory celebrations tonight.

The Tiger-Cats will arrive in Hamilton around 10 p.m. tonight.

His worship had to about to be heard over the din in the Cats' dressing-room, Ralph Toohy led the charge into the room and all players were shouting at the top of their voices. Ignored in the corner was a refrigerator filled with soft drinks, as the players opened magnums of champagne. The Grey Cup was carried in and the players quaffed champagne out of it.

Hamilton coach Jim Trimble paid tribute to the Winnipeg Blue Bombers in discussing his victory. He said "They gave us a real fight up until halftime but we began to wear them down. One team was in much better physical shape.

Additional stories and picture of today's Grey Cup game are on pages: 2, 3, 4, 5, 7, 9.

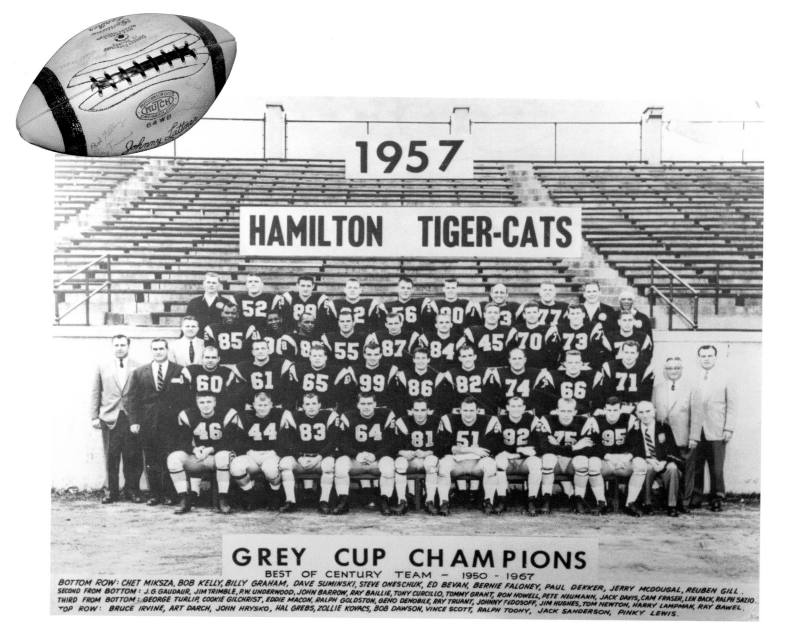

1957

HAMILTON TIGER-CATS

GREY CUP CHAMPIONS
BEST OF CENTURY TEAM — 1950 - 1967

BOTTOM ROW: CHET MIKSZA, BOB KELLY, BILLY GRAHAM, DAVE SUMINSKI, STEVE ONESCHUK, ED BEVAN, BERNIE FALONEY, PAUL DEKKER, JERRY McDOUGAL, REUBEN GILL.
SECOND FROM BOTTOM: J.G. GAUDAUR, JIM TRIMBLE, P.W. UNDERWOOD, JOHN BARROW, RAY BAILLIE, TONY CURCILLO, TOMMY GRANT, RON HOWELL, PETE NEUMANN, JACK DAVIS, CAM FRASER, LEN BACK, RALPH SAZIO.
THIRD FROM BOTTOM: GEORGE TURLIP, COOKIE GILCHRIST, EDDIE MACON, RALPH GOLDSTON, GENO DENOBILE, RAY TRUANT, JOHNNY FÉDOSOFF, JIM HUGHES, TOM NEWTON, HARRY LAMPMAN, RAY BAWEL.
TOP ROW: BRUCE IRVINE, ART DARCH, JOHN HRYSKO, HAL GREBS, ZOLLIE KOVACS, BOB DAWSON, VINCE SCOTT, RALPH TOOHY, JACK SANDERSON, PINKY LEWIS.

bizarre moments in the history of three-down football – and there have been more than a few – when the name Ray "Bibbles" Bawel entered into this country's sporting lore.

Identity is always part of the equation in sport. Rooting for a home team is, by extension, rooting for home, for friends and family and neighbourhood, for all of those things that define the place that you come from, projected onto your favourite team. In the modern world, with every game from everywhere available to just about everyone, it is certainly possible to adopt faraway teams and faraway uniforms, to pledge allegiance to players you will never see in person. But that is merely a technological extension of the pure and organic act that is heading for the

The 1957 Hamilton Tiger-Cats
and the ball used in the
Grey Cup game.

park, for the diamond, for the rink, to cheer on those you know, who are wearing the colours of home.

In its modern configuration, Canadian football has been played in nine different cities (not counting the brief American experiment). And in each one of those nine places, at one time or another in its history, its CFL team has been central to how it defined itself.

But when it comes to CFL football as a pillar of local identity, there are two towns that stand above all the rest.

One is Regina – really, the whole province of Saskatchewan, and its far-flung diaspora – where wearing the green has become an even more potent symbol of fidelity in the twenty-first century than it was when Ron Lancaster and George Reed were the gods of Taylor Field.

The other is Hamilton, albeit for very different reasons. Regina is an urban "island" surrounded by a sea of wheat fields; Hamilton is stuck squarely in the middle of the most populous region of Canada, the Golden Horseshoe of Southern Ontario. Before all of the communities between Oshawa and Grimsby converged into one great megaplex with Toronto as the dominant centre, Hamilton stood out from its neighbours because of its heavy industry, because of steel, because it was the smaller, unfashionable burg down the road from Canada's biggest and richest city.

Hamiltonians forged an identity that centred on pride in their working-class heritage and pride in the city's grit and toughness – plus just maybe a little chip on the shoulder. From the very earliest days of Canadian football, there was a perfect convergence between that civic self-image and the way the locals played the game. Hamilton players were the roughest in a rough sport, and their fans prided themselves on being just as tough. The Hamilton team might have not played the prettiest football, the flashiest football, but no team would be more ferocious. All the local heroes – from Brian Timmis, the "Old Man of the Mountain," who refused to wear a helmet long after other players had adopted them; to John Barrow, the great rock of the defensive line; to Angelo Mosca, almost a cartoon villain in the CFL, who used to name his own All-Meanie Team and who morphed easily into an off-season job as a professional wrestler; to Grover

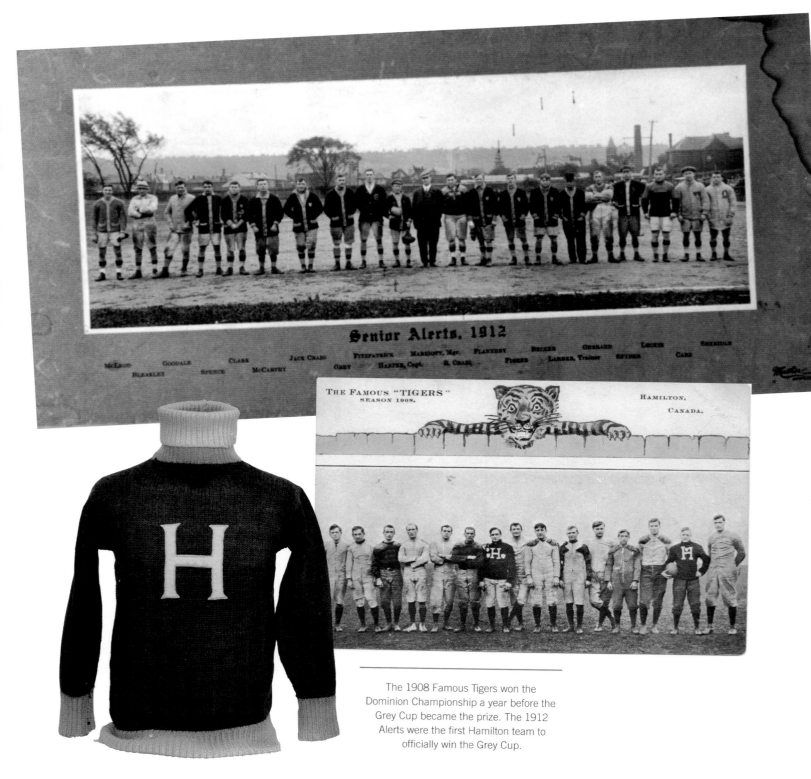

Senior Alerts, 1912

FITZPATRICK   MARRIOTT, Mgr.   FLANNERY   BECKER   GERRARD   LOCKIE   SHERIDAN

McLEOD   GOODALE   CLARK   JACK CRAIG   GREY   HARPER, Capt.   B. CRAIG   FISHER   LARMER, Trainer   SNIDER   CARR

BLEAKLEY   SPENCE   McCARTHY

THE FAMOUS "TIGERS"
SEASON 1908.

HAMILTON,
CANADA.

The 1908 Famous Tigers won the
Dominion Championship a year before the
Grey Cup became the prize. The 1912
Alerts were the first Hamilton team to
officially win the Grey Cup.

GARNEY HENLEY - Halfback
6'   180 lbs.
HAMILTON TIGER-CAT FOOTBALL CLUB

Garney Henley won four Grey Cups with the Tiger-Cats over his fifteen-year career.

Covington, and Joe Montford, and the rest – were cut from the same cloth.

Fifteen times teams from Hamilton have won the Grey Cup – and, if you include the pre–Grey Cup championship in 1908, the city enjoyed at least one victory in every decade of the twentieth century. The Hamilton Alerts took the Cup once, the Tigers five times, the wartime Flying Wildcats once, and the Tiger-Cats – born of a merger of the city's two franchises in 1950 – eight times. (Hamilton teams have also made fourteen losing appearances in the Grey Cup game.) Many of those sides featured great quarterbacks, great running backs, athletes who succeeded because of their speed and skill and finesse. Has there been, for instance, a more elegant and graceful figure in the history of Canadian football than Garney Henley? Henley came to Hamilton from South Dakota via the Green Bay Packers' camp and starred as both a defensive back and a receiver. He was part of the 1967 championship team that featured what many argue was the greatest defensive lineup in league history, and was a star still in 1972, when the Ticats won the Grey Cup at home on Ian Sunter's dramatic final-play field goal.

But utter the phrase "Hamilton football" and anyone who knows the game thinks immediately of something else entirely: grinding, borderline-dirty defence;

big, nasty guys patrolling the trenches; and fans who mirror their team in their passion and lack of pretence, and who for decades made Ivor Wynne Stadium (known prior to 1971 as Civic Stadium) the least friendly environment in the CFL for any visiting team.

The 1957 edition of the Tiger-Cats team was a perfect reflection of all that, beginning with Trimble. He had been recruited by Hamilton general manager (and future CFL commissioner) Jake Gaudaur from Philadelphia, where, during his brief tenure as head coach of the National Football League's Eagles, Trimble had earned a reputation for being hard on his own players almost to the point of cruelty. Trimble's confidence and bombast seemed undiminished by his failings with the Eagles, or by the fact that, during his first CFL campaign in 1956, his Ticats were humbled in the eastern final by the Montreal Alouettes. He remained fully secure in his own genius, determined to build a team designed not just to beat then-dominant Montreal in the east, but to conquer the flashy Edmonton Eskimos, who had topped the Als in each of the previous three Grey Cup games.

Entering the 1957 season, Hamilton made two blue-chip additions to its roster to go with Ralph Goldston and Cookie Gilchrist, who had arrived the year before. The first was Barrow, an All-American defensive tackle out of the University of Florida, who, like many players of the day, turned down the NFL in favour of a bigger paycheque in the CFL, and would become the anchor of arguably the greatest defensive front in Canadian football history. And the second, quarterback Bernie Faloney, who had starred on a national championship team at the University of Maryland in 1953 and helped the Eskimos win a Grey Cup in 1954, came to the Tiger-Cats following two years of military service.

The 'Cats only scored 250 points in fourteen games during the 1957 season, but they also surrendered precious few, and finished first in the east, ahead of a surprising Ottawa team and Montreal. The Alouettes knocked off the Rough Riders in the semifinal. In

66   STEPHEN BRUNT

the first game of the two-game, total-points final, they were competitive with the Ticats, losing 17–10, before being humbled 39–1 at Civic Stadium, a result that sent the Ticats to their first Grey Cup appearance since their championship season in 1953.

Meanwhile, out west, the Winnipeg Blue Bombers shocked the defending champion Eskimos, beating them in the best-of-three final (the third and deciding game went to two overtime periods). Their rookie head coach also had Philadelphia ties – Bud Grant had played with the Eagles under Trimble. Personality-wise, though, he was Trimble's polar opposite, quiet and self-effacing. Their great Grey Cup rivalry would go four more rounds after their first meeting, in 1958, 1959, 1961, and 1962, and Grant would win them all. But on November 30, 1957, in what was the first championship game to be televised from coast to coast, the team Grant fielded at Varsity Stadium was already seriously depleted by injury, and that situation would worsen as the game went on. Running back Gerry James broke a finger (he kept playing, but fumbled four times); quarterback Kenny Ploen hurt a knee; and the Bombers lost their punter, Charlie Shepard, in the first quarter, giving the Ticats a huge field-position advantage, because their punter, Cam Fraser, was the best in the game.

Hamilton scored their first touchdown when Gilchrist hammered Dennis Mendyk, and Ray Bawel ran the fumble back 54 yards for a touchdown 6:15 into the first quarter. Another fumble led to another touchdown three minutes later. There was no scoring in the second or third quarters, but the opportunistic Ticats effectively put the game away in the fourth, taking a 32–0 lead, even though the Bombers' offence would outgain Hamilton's by a considerable margin on the day.

As Gord Walker wrote in *The Globe and Mail*: "Jim Trimble's hardy warriors didn't rattle or shake with an adverse roll of the dice. They were shoved around considerably, but an interception here, a fumble recovery there, then a booming punt from the toe of Cam Fraser, and the Bombers were back on their haunches wondering where all of their offensive gains had gone."

Then came the great slapstick moment – though at the time, not everyone was laughing.

Bawel, a multi-sport star athlete at the University of Evansville in Indiana, had played for Trimble in Philadelphia. When he was released by the Eagles after the 1956 season, his old coach

Bernie Faloney joined the Tiger-Cats in 1957 and became a star in the league, winning two Grey Cups with the team.

persuaded him to come north and give the Canadian game a try. He was a skinny guy, but quick, a skilled defensive back, and in the '57 Grey Cup he was enjoying what had to be the game of his life. In addition to his fumble-return touchdown in the first quarter, Bawel had picked up another fumble by Gerry James inside the Hamilton 10-yard line with the Ticats up 12–0 in the third quarter – a moment most regarded as the real end of the Bombers' comeback hopes.

Then, with five minutes left in the game, and Hamilton in full control, the Bombers lined up in punt formation from their own 50-yard line. Gerry Vincent was doing the kicking because of the injury to Shepard. Instead of punting, the desperate Bombers attempted a fake, with Vincent throwing a pass, but Bawel wasn't fooled. He stepped in front of Winnipeg receiver Ernie Pitts, intercepted the ball, and immediately set off towards the Blue Bombers' end zone.

Whether Bawel would have made it will remain a matter of conjecture. But as he was sprinting past the Bombers' bench, before any Winnipeg player could get near him, Bawel tripped, fell forward, and then was tackled at the Winnipeg 42-yard line.

He immediately jumped to his feet, ran back down the sideline, and angrily confronted a man wearing a black cap and overcoat standing among the Winnipeg players on the sideline. The mystery man held up his hands in front of him, as if expecting Bawel to throw a punch. Then, as Walker described it in *The Globe and Mail*: "The spectator, threatened at first by some players, faded into the crowded background, actually walked down and in front of the Hamilton bench where incensed players were looking downfield to see if they could spot him, stepped over the players' bench, then disappeared into an exit immediately behind the bench."

There was understandable confusion on the field. Referee Paul Dojack, knowing that there was nothing in the rule book to deal with that kind of fan interference, was forced to improvise. The Ticats argued that he ought to simply award them a touchdown. Instead, he ruled that the ball be placed half the distance to the goal line, since he believed that there was a chance Bawel would have been tackled. Trimble and his players weren't happy with the call, but they were comfortably ahead in any case, and when Cookie Gilchrist ran the ball over from 16 yards out two plays later, the weirdest play in Canadian football history became a moot point.

The mystery lingered, though. In the winners' dressing room afterwards, Bawel

THE "LONGEST" GAME

IN 2010, THE CANADIAN Football League conducted an in-depth video-based review of each Grey Cup game to ensure that the record book was accurate and more comprehensive than ever. Right away, one game stood out particularly as what may be termed the longest game: the 1962 Grey Cup, which was held on December 1 *and* December 2. Heavy fog rolled in from Lake Ontario, making it impossible to see well, if at all – especially for fans watching on TV. The game was suspended with 9:29 to play in the fourth quarter and the score 28–27 in favour of the Winnipeg Blue Bombers. Hostilities were resumed the next day, which turned out to be clear, but not another point was scored. Winnipeg won the Grey Cup, and the "Fog Bowl" gained legendary status in Grey Cup annals.

The 2005 game went to overtime, but the extra period took the form of a "shootout," in which Edmonton and Montreal took turns on offence, with the Eskimos scoring ten points to the Alouettes' seven to prevail, 38–35. But it was these same two teams that staged another form of "longest game" in 1956, and we have the Varsity Stadium clock operator to thank for that.

On November 24, 1956, the Eskimos and Alouettes found time to reel off a stunning 235 plays, including a total of 191 rushing or passing attempts! The game saw a play run every fifteen seconds. So, how did that offensive explosion happen? The only explanation is that the game timekeeper did not start the clock on the referee's whistle, but on the ball being snapped.

In another bizarre twist, there would have been even more plays in the 1956 game, but they ran out of footballs! When Edmonton's Jackie "Spaghetti Legs" Parker scored from seven yards out with a few seconds to play into a crowded end zone, one enthusiastic fan stole the last remaining ball and ran off into the night. Referee Harry Bowden had no choice but to declare the game over, as the field was completely overrun with happy fans.

displayed a smear of shoe polish on his ankle – proof positive that he had been tripped. But who had done the deed? The next day, the Toronto *Telegram* offered a cash reward to anyone who could identify the perpetrator. No one came forward – though Bawel did later receive an anonymous gift: a $150 watch bearing the inscription "1957 Grey Cup Game – The Tripper."

It would be two decades later before David Humphrey was comfortable telling his story in public – though by then, his moment of infamy had become a bit of a running joke. Who would have suspected that the Tripper would turn out to be a highly respected justice of the Superior Court of Ontario?

In 1957, Humphrey was already a prominent Toronto defence attorney, and an Argonauts fan, with no clear rooting interest on Grey Cup day. He slipped into Varsity Stadium thanks to being recognized by a few buddies from the Toronto police force, who were also happy to let him stand along the sideline. And, yes, alcohol was involved: Humphrey was one of many fans at the game that day armed against the cold with a discreet flask of whiskey.

As he would explain many years later, he had become upset after seeing a man in the crowd who had been a jury foreman in a case that Humphrey had argued. His client, accused of murdering a thirteen-year-old girl, had been sent to the gallows, which the lawyer believed deeply was a miscarriage of justice. The jury foreman saw Humphrey and extended his hand, but Humphrey refused to shake it. And then, upset, he took a couple of deep swigs from the flask – and then, perhaps, a couple more.

But beyond that, how to explain a moment of temporary insanity? Humphrey never really could, though he came to enjoy his own notoriety, and his name would forever be paired with Bibbles Bawel.

Bawel never played another game of professional football. He went back to Indiana and back to school, earned a graduate degree, did a bit of coaching, and helped to build a successful business. He would be inducted into the Indiana Sports Hall of Fame.

On his plaque, there's no mention of the moment that made him instantly famous in Canada, or of the play that made him forever part of Grey Cup lore.

1964

WEST COAST RISING

I t is not often that a Grey Cup is a true grudge match.

Over the course of a year, from November to November, so much changes. Players come and go, fortunes rise and fall. Even when the same two teams happen to come together in consecutive championship games, as has happened more than occasionally, usually so much water has passed under the bridge that it is as though they are meeting for the first time.

But not always. Sometimes it's chapter two. That was the story in 1964, when the defending champion Hamilton Tiger-Cats met the British Columbia Lions for the second year in a row. The 'Cats were the dominant eastern team of the late 1950s and early 1960s, when they appeared in nine Grey Cup games in eleven years. The Lions, born in 1954, had never won the Grey Cup, had made their first appearance only the year before. And hanging in the air from the 1963 game was the memory of one notorious play, which in Vancouver and environs they still haven't forgotten almost a half-century later.

Just ask Joe Kapp and Angelo Mosca.

One thing must be said about British Columbia football fans: they are patient.

Canadian football was a late arrival in Vancouver, a city in which rugby retained its popularity much longer than it did in Eastern Canada (rugby remains very much a part of the B.C. sports landscape to this day). The first football clubs were formed

The B.C. Lions celebrating their winning of the 99th Grey Cup game, 2011.

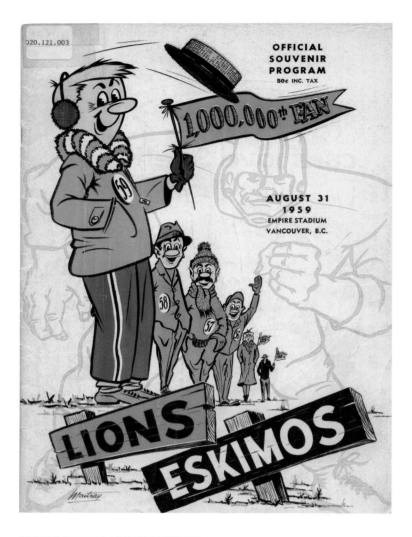

OFFICIAL
SOUVENIR
PROGRAM
50¢ INC. TAX

1,000,000ᵗʰ FAN

AUGUST 31
1959
EMPIRE STADIUM
VANCOUVER, B.C.

LIONS
ESKIMOS

in the 1930s, but Canada's west coast wasn't part of the Grey Cup competition until well into Canadian football's modern era.

In 1951, a group of Vancouver businessmen, inspired by *Vancouver Sun* columnist Andy Lytle, approached the Western Interprovincial Football Union about adding a team to the existing four franchises. They were encouraged, and a year later returned with a $25,000 goodwill bond in hand, only to be rejected, with Winnipeg and Saskatchewan voting against expansion. But the Vancouverites were undeterred. In 1953 they tried once more, and this time they were told to come back once they had a 15,000-seat stadium, and 6,500 season's ticket holders. These requirements were fulfilled when Vancouver hosted the 1954 British Empire Games, which led to the construction of Empire Stadium. The stadium became the home of the newly formed British Columbia Lions and a regular host of the Grey Cup game, beginning in 1955 – the first year the game was staged outside the east. (Still, even after Vancouver had met all of the original conditions, the Lions had to agree to cover the travel expenses of visiting teams before they were finally granted entry to the league.)

The task of building the Lions was handed to Annis Stukus, whose remarkable career in Canadian sport included stints as a football player and coach, sportswriter and broadcaster, consultant to the Toronto Huskies in the inaugural season of the National Basketball Association, and general manager of the Winnipeg Jets of the World Hockey Association, where he signed Bobby Hull to a landmark contract. The job wouldn't be easy. There was no expansion draft to seed the franchise, and with only nine Americans allowed, Stukus would somehow have to find enough Canadian players to fill out a competitive roster.

Stukus was starting from scratch – and it showed. In the first game of that

Left: Annis Stukus was a CFL player in the thirties and would go on to spearhead CFL expansion to the West, first with the Edmonton Eskimos, then the B.C. Lions.

first season, on August 28, 1954, the Lions shocked just about everyone by leading the Winnipeg Blue Bombers 6–1 at halftime. But they lost that one, and then every other game that season too, except for one at-home win September 18, when they topped the Calgary Stampeders 9–4.

The Lions improved from 1–15 to 5–11 in 1955, and then to 6–10 in 1956, though they still finished out of the playoffs, and Stukus was fired. Then things got worse: 4–11–1 in 1957; 3–13 in 1958.

Finally, in 1959, a glimmer of hope: the Lions finished 9–7 and made the playoffs for the first time, thanks in large part to the heroics of a running back from the University of Iowa who was part of a Rose Bowl–winning team the previous January: Willie Fleming. British Columbia was clobbered in the western semifinal by Edmonton by a combined score of 61–15, but, for the first time, the long-suffering Vancouver fans felt their pain might be rewarded.

Still, it would take a little while. In 1960, they were back in fourth place, and back out of the playoffs. On the field, the 1961 season was an out-and-out disaster: the Lions finished 1–13–2. But that year, they added two key building blocks: Tom Brown, an All-American linebacker and offensive lineman from the University of Minnesota, and quarterback Joe Kapp, who came over from Calgary in midseason in a trade for four B.C. players.

Joe Kapp, quarterback of the B.C. Lions first Grey Cup victory in 1964, also played in the Rose Bowl and the Super Bowl, the only player to appear in all three events.

Kapp wasn't exactly a sure thing, because he was coming off a knee injury that had severely diminished his exceptional running abilities. But his pedigree was impeccable. An All-American at the University of California, where in 1959 he led the Bears to the Rose Bowl (losing to Willie Fleming's Hawkeyes), Kapp had finished fifth in voting for the Heisman Trophy and had been drafted by the Washington Redskins of the National Football League. The Redskins didn't sign him, and he was lured north by Jim Finks, then the Stamps' general manager. After beating out future Buffalo Bill (and United States senator) Jack Kemp for the starting job, Kapp took the Stampeders to the playoffs in 1960. But after the knee surgery, Finks had his doubts that Kapp would ever fully recover, and one game into the 1961 season he made the deal to send him to the Lions.

"I came to Vancouver in the trade and the city came alive," Kapp remembers. "The people got behind us. And we weren't the Vancouver Lions – we were the British Columbia Lions. Players made their lives here."

Well, perhaps it wasn't quite so instantaneous, but soon enough things started to gel. In 1962, coach Dave Skrien arrived, and Kapp threw for 3,279 yards and 28 touchdowns as the Lions finished fourth with a 7–9 record. Finally, the franchise had reached a tipping point, and Kapp, with his big personality, became a celebrity – arguably Vancouver's first true modern sports hero. His fame even earned him a number of commercial endorsement deals, including one with Squirrel brand peanut butter, for which Kapp visited communities all over the province, driving a peanut butter–coloured convertible.

"That's why they called me Nutty Joe," he says.

The 1963 season was a magical one in Vancouver, thanks in large part to Fleming. Already established as a 1,000-yard rusher, he enjoyed a season for the ages, rushing for 1,234 yards on 127 carries – an astounding 9.7 yard average. The Lions finished at 12–4, on top of the Western Division, then beat the Saskatchewan Roughriders two games to one in the best-of-three western final – winning the final game emphatically, 36–1, at Empire Stadium. As a bonus, they would play in their first-ever Grey Cup game right there, at home, while the eastern champion Hamilton Tiger-Cats would have to make the long journey west into unfriendly territory.

One moment from that game has remained burned in the memories of B.C. Lions fans ever since. With Hamilton leading 7–0 late in the first half, Fleming took a pitch from Kapp, ran wide, and was tackled by Gene Ceppetelli almost at the side-line following a short gain. A beat – maybe two – later, Mosca came flying in, after running across much of the width of the field to get there. He launched himself at the prone running back and actually sailed right on over him. Technically, he didn't pile on, and he certainly didn't spear Fleming with his helmet. No penalty was called on the play. But on the way by, Mosca's knee smacked Fleming in the head. Fleming suffered a concussion and was lost for the rest of the afternoon.

Hamilton never looked back, and won the game 21–10.

Was the Mosca hit really dirty? Was it really the difference? By and large, the answer to those questions depended on where in Canada you lived. In Vancouver and environs, you'd get an emphatic yes to both. In Hamilton, they'd agree with Ticats coach Ralph Sazio, who said after the game, "We're from Steeltown and we understand that football isn't football until you hear the leather pop."

But, for the record, Kapp says that losing Fleming wasn't the whole story of the Lions' loss. "Good football teams can overcome that kind of thing if your balance is there. They took our ace away, and we had to drop down to a king. There are no excuses, though. Hamilton was probably the best defensive team in the league at that point." (But Kapp was not always so sanguine on the subject. Just a couple of hours after he uttered those words, in the days leading up to the 2011 Grey Cup game, Kapp and Mosca, by then both in their seventies, got into a brawl at a CFL

Willie Fleming scored the game-breaking touchdown of the 1964 Grey Cup, getting revenge for the Mosca hit of the year before.

Action from the 1964 Grey Cup game, B.C.'s first trophy-winning season.

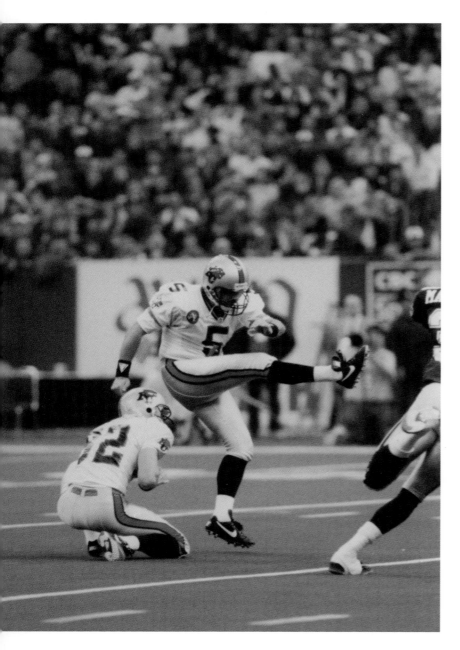

Lui Passaglia won three Grey Cups with the Lions before moving to the front office. Seen here playing in the 1994 Grey Cup game.

Alumni Association luncheon that became a world-wide media sensation.)

At the time he was injured, twenty-four minutes into the game, Fleming had gained only twelve yards on five carries. The Ticats controlled him, and the Lions offence in general.

"The Lions seemed to be college boys playing a game, but the Ticats are pros who practice a high and violent art," Dick Beddoes wrote – but that was the eastern perspective. The headline over Jim Taylor's story in the Vancouver *Province* the next morning reflected the view from the west coast: "Dirtiest Player Sidelines Star: Mosca Puts Fleming In Hospital."

In fact, Fleming never did go to the hospital. After being checked out by team doctors, he spent the rest of the game watching from the sidelines in street clothes. But as to Mosca's "dirtiness," even he probably wouldn't argue. In addition to his football exploits, he enjoyed a successful parallel career as a professional wrestler, was always willing to wear the black hat, embellished his reputation as a tough, mean player, and certainly didn't shy away from the infamy, from the notoriety – or from being the most hated man in British Columbia. All of that was good for the Mosca business.

It's telling that, after the '63 game, Skrien seems to have been nearly as interested in talking about a Mosca hit on Kapp as Mosca's hit on Fleming.

"I never saw a more deliberate attempt to injure a player than once when Mosca hit Kapp, knocked him down, fell over him, and then hit him an elbow in the face," Skrien said. "What upset me was that Mosca laughed like the whole thing was hilarious."

Which perhaps explains why Kapp – along with several of his teammates – refused to shake Mosca's hand after the game. And it may also explain their dust-up, nearly fifty years later.

(Following the Grey Cup defeat, angry, drunken Vancouverites took to the streets, congregating at the corner of Georgia and Granville. It didn't quite qualify as a riot, like the one after the 2011 Stanley Cup finals, but still, 319 people were arrested by the Vancouver police.)

THE FIRST GREAT GREY CUP TEAMS: COLLEGIATE CHAMPIONS

IN 2011, THE GREY Cup and Vanier Cup games were held jointly in Vancouver as part of a football festival weekend. The link between the two games is undeniable, as Canadian Inter-university Sport (CIS) football graduates are at the heart of most CFL clubs. The annual Canadian Evaluation Camp and draft have become essential events on the CFL schedule. The gap between the collegiate and pro levels is wide today, but this has not always been the case. In fact, collegiate teams won seven of the first twelve Grey Cup games.

The University of Toronto Blues won the Grey Cup from 1909 to 1911, becoming Canada's senior football champions three times running. The last collegiate team to win the Cup, Queen's University, strung together three championships from 1922 through 1924 and were the predominant football power of their day. Over those three games, Queen's outscored opponents 78–4, disposing of "professional" teams from Edmonton, Regina, and Toronto's Balmy Beach with ease. The 54 points and nine touchdowns they scored against Regina in 1923 remain Grey Cup records, unmatched by any club – professional or otherwise – since then.

This scoring record needs just a bit of qualification, however, as under the rules of the day, the team scored upon was forced to kick off. Simply put, Queen's marched down the field and scored, then gratefully received the kickoff and did it all over again. The unfortunate Rough-riders barely touched the ball that day, by most accounts.

During its run of championships, Queen's won twenty-six consecutive games over all forms of opposition. The key players in that era were two charter members of the Canadian Football Hall of Fame, Harry "Red" Batstone and Frank "Pep" Leadlay. They combined for 19 points in 1923 and were unquestionably the dominant players of their time. Their backfield kicking and running skills were unparalleled and given that players played both offence and defence in that era, they were on the field continuously. To provide a modern perspective of the challenge facing Queen's opponents, the magnitude would be akin to playing a hockey game against a team with both Wayne Gretzky and Mario Lemieux on the ice for the full sixty minutes. The Queen's roster included many others stars, such as John "Red" McKelvey, Liz Walker, and Bud Thomas.

Returning to the link between Canadian college and professional football, Batstone and Leadlay actually conducted their careers in reverse. First they played for the IRFU (semi-pro) teams in Toronto and Hamilton, and then went on to star for the collegiate powerhouse at Queen's. Batstone left the game in 1928 to become a very successful doctor, but remained to help many CRU committees administer the game. Leadlay returned to the Hamilton Tigers after Queen's, retiring in 1930. Between them they won nine Grey Cup games. Both are now enshrined in the Canadian Sports Hall of Fame.

Above: An early Varsity football game.

Whatever the truth, whatever the interpretation, the Mosca hit on Fleming set the stage beautifully for the 52nd Grey Cup game one year later, on November 28, 1964, when the two teams met again at Toronto's Exhibition Stadium. Hamilton and British Columbia both topped their divisions, the Lions finishing with an 11–2–3 record and beating the Calgary Stampeders in the western final.

It would be a very different game, played on a very different kind of day, than it had been the year before. The teams met in what could best be described as Vancouver weather – cold rain, which resulted in a slippery field – and afterwards some of the Lions players suggested that their familiarity with those conditions had been an advantage, especially considering that the Ticats seemed to struggle with their footing, and with holding on to the football, all day long.

But this was also a different, more confident Lions team. "Well, we got Willie for a full game," Kapp says, when he was asked what had changed between 1963 and 1964. "And we were one year better, and believed in ourselves."

A 35-yard Kapp-to-Fleming pass set up B.C.'s first score, with fullback Bob Swift piling over for the touchdown. (Swift would leave the game injured shortly thereafter, and his emergency replacement, Bill Munsey – normally a defensive back – would come on to play a key role in the Lions' victory, scoring two second-half touchdowns, one on an 18-yard run, one on a fumble recovery.) British Columbia stretched their lead to two touchdowns on a broken play, when holder Pete Ohler was unable to control the snap on Peter Kempf's short field goal attempt. The Lions' Jim Carphin alertly figured out that something had gone wrong, and did as he had been instructed to do – run into the end zone. Ohler picked up the ball and hit him with a pass for the score, the decisive play of the game.

Fleming broke free for a 46-yard touchdown run to make it 20–1 B.C. at the half – it was widely noted that the hole in the Hamilton line that he ran through corresponded exactly to Mosca's position – and though the Ticats threatened in the third quarter, and mounted a late, furious charge in the fourth, the Lions' first-ever Grey Cup victory was secure: final score 34–24.

This would be no dynasty. In 1965, with both Kapp and Fleming hobbled by injuries, the Lions were back in fourth place in the west, and by the end of the 1966 season, Kapp was off to the Minnesota Vikings of the National Football League, where he would start in a Super Bowl game (he is the only quarterback to date to have played in a Rose Bowl, a Grey Cup, and a Super Bowl). The great patience of those loyal B.C. fans would be tested through the rest of the decade and all of the next. It wouldn't be until 1983 that the Lions again qualified for the Grey Cup, losing a heartbreaker at home in the brand new B.C. Place, 18–17, to the Toronto Argonauts.

Two years later, a Lions side led by a brilliant young coach named Don
Matthews would not be denied. They were dominant all year long, and hammered
the Tiger-Cats 37–24 in the Grey Cup game at Montreal's Olympic Stadium.

In 1988, the Lions were back in the big game and suffered another gutting one-
point loss, 22–21, to the Winnipeg Blue Bombers at Lansdowne Park in Ottawa.

Back home in 1994, in an unprecedented cross-border Grey Cup matchup
against what was then known simply as the Baltimore Football Club, hometown
boy Lui Passaglia's last-play field goal not only won a championship, it sealed a
26–23 victory for Canada over the United States in a game that seemed to have
much more at stake than simple silverware.

The Lions won their fourth Grey Cup in 2000, beating Montreal 28–26 in the
final after finishing the regular season only 8–10, and then accomplishing the near-
impossible feat of winning two playoff games on the road.

Wally Buono arrived from Calgary in 2003 as coach and general manager, signalling a new era of stability and excellence in Vancouver. The Lions lost to the

Argos in the 2004 Grey Cup game, but were back two years later, when they again beat the Als, 25–14.

And then, in 2011, in what turned out to be Buono's last game as head coach, his Lions became the first team to recover from an 0–5 start to the season and win the Grey Cup. They defeated the Winnipeg Blue Bombers 34–23 at the refurbished B.C. Place – making it the first time a team had won the Grey Cup at home since the '94 Lions' victory.

It can be argued that the 1964 Grey Cup victory was different than any that had come before, because of the nature of the place, because of its sports history, because of its geography. Thousands of miles from central Canada, where so many of the country's economic and cultural and sporting conversations had originated, magnificently bracketed by the mountains and the ocean, Vancouver existed apart from the rest of Canada, especially in the era before easy commercial air travel.

The Vancouver Millionaires had won the Stanley Cup way back in 1915, but Vancouver didn't became part of the modern National Hockey League till 1970. Before the 1963 and 1964 Grey Cup games, the biggest local sporting event in the second half of the century had been the famous Miracle Mile in 1954 – just a few weeks before the Lions' first game – when Roger Bannister famously duelled with John Landy in the Empire Games.

Winnipeg, Saskatchewan, Calgary, and Edmonton had all become part of the Grey Cup tradition decades earlier, and by the time the Lions came into being, all had been participants in the big game, and all but Saskatchewan had celebrated championships.

The West Coast, though, hadn't been invited to the party.

When the Lions landed at the Vancouver airport, returning from their triumph in 1964, they were greeted by thousands of fans who had braved the pouring rain – the tarmac was a sea of umbrellas. They watched linebacker By Bailey, who had been part of that first Lions team in 1954, emerge from the plane holding the Grey Cup high.

And, as Kapp remembers it, the celebration that began that day went on and on and on.

"I don't think any of us recovered for several weeks," he says.

1969

O, CANADA!

This was a perfectly, particularly Canadian moment, capping off a decade when the country came of age, when its citizens felt a new sense of confidence about their place in the rapidly changing world of the 1960s. The nation was still basking in the glow of Expo 67, the world fair it hosted as part of its centennial celebrations, an announcement of Canada's arrival on the global stage. Montreal was a hip, stylish, cosmopolitan city. The prime minister, Pierre Elliott Trudeau, was young, dashing, and glamorous – and, as it turned out, even knew how to kick a football.

On the field, Russ Jackson, arguably the greatest Canadian-born player of all time, was about to enjoy a brilliant finale to a career. Meanwhile, lurking in the background, as yet out of sight and certainly out of mind as the country partied on, were harbingers of a national crisis that would erupt a year later, with kidnapping and murder and tanks rolling through Canadian streets.

On November 30, 1969, at the Autostade, the Rough Riders were playing the Roughriders in the 57th Grey Cup, and all of that was part of the mix.

This was just the second Grey Cup game to be played in Montreal (back in 1931, the Montreal AAA Winged Wheelers had beaten the Regina Roughriders 22–0 at Percival Molson Stadium), and the only one ever to be played at the Autostade – or

Mark Kosmos and Art Green celebrate the last Ottawa Grey Cup win, 1976.

the Automotive Stadium, as it was formally known, because it had been paid for by the major Canadian-based automakers – a much-unloved, cold, concrete monstrosity that had been built in Montreal's Victoriatown neighbourhood to host concerts and a rodeo display during Expo 67.

The Alouettes moved to the Autostade in 1968 from their traditional home on the campus of McGill University, and would remain there until the Olympic

Russ Jackson, widely considered the greatest Canadian-born quarterback, seen here in the 1969 Grey Cup game.

STEPHEN BRUNT

Stadium opened in 1976. The Autostade was regarded as a state-of-the-art building, at least in terms of its construction – rather than being a single entity, it had 19 separate, interlocking sections, which in theory could be picked up and reassembled elsewhere. For a brief moment, the Montreal Expos considered beginning their existence there in 1969, before making the wise decision to set up shop instead at tiny, intimate Jarry Park.

(At the end of the 1966 season, the Ottawa Rough Riders also played a single "home" game at the Autostade, the second game of their two-game, total-point eastern final against the Hamilton Tiger-Cats. They were forced to make the move because their actual home stadium, Lansdowne Park, was already in the process of being partially demolished and rebuilt as a Canadian Centennial project.

"It was terrible," Russ Jackson remembers. "The field [at the Autostade] was just awful. It was muddy in some places and frozen in others.")

The 57th Grey Cup was also, as far as anyone can tell, the only one to be featured in a soft porn film, an entirely forgettable Quebec-made movie called *Deux femmes en or* (Two Women in Gold). The plot synopsis (perhaps a bit awkwardly translated): "Two women living in the suburban of Montreal find difficult time waiting for their frequently absent husbands. They decide for fun to call as many delivery men as possible to have sex with them." All that as the football game played in real time in the background on the women's TV set.

But the live action at the stadium itself took place in a far more serious political and cultural context: the Riders and 'Riders played under the suspected threat of a terrorist attack from a separatist organization that would become familiar to all Canadians ten months later, during what became known as the October Crisis: the

Ottawa had previously won two Grey Cups as the Senators (1925 and 1926), but the 1940 team, pictured here, was the first to win as the Rough Riders.

Front de libération du Québec. Three hundred police officers were deployed around the stadium, just in case something happened, as were hidden sharpshooters. Montreal mayor Jean Drapeau promised CFL commissioner Jake Gaudaur that the game would be played without incident, and he wasn't taking any chances.

Jackson says that the players were unaware of the additional security though he learned later that a plainclothes RCMP officer had been ordered to follow him whenever he came to Montreal.

Ottawa's first football club was formed in 1876, and organized football has been played in the nation's capital ever since. The club was called the Ottawa Senators when they won championships in 1925 and 1926, and the Rough Riders when they won in 1940, beating Toronto Balmy Beach in the only two-game, total-points Grey Cup final in history.

The first Ottawa triumph of the modern era came in 1951, when they beat the Saskatchewan Roughriders 21–14. A long drought followed, with the Ottawa teams finishing behind their eastern rivals in Toronto, Montreal, and Hamilton. But the city's football fortunes began to change for the better with the arrival of coach Frank Clair and, the ascendance of the great Bobby Simpson in 1956 and the signing of Jackson and Ron Stewart in 1958. Clair, nicknamed The Professor, was one of the CFL's true characters, an absent-minded football genius who often forgot the names of his own players and who had already won Grey Cups with the Toronto Argonauts in 1950 and 1952.

In 1960, Clair coached Ottawa to a surprising Grey Cup win, employing a two-quarterback system, alternating Jackson with a young American from Pennsylvania named Ron Lancaster. They split time during games, and neither knew who would be starting until Clair gave the word during the pre-game warm-ups.

Long time Rough Rider Bob Simpson won two cups with Ottawa during his career (1950–62).

A ROUGH RIDE

IN THE UNLIKELY SETTING of the Autostade in Montreal, it was certain – matters of spelling notwithstanding – that a group of "rough riders" would win the 1969 Grey Cup game.

Ottawa's Rough Riders had adopted the nickname in 1898, but then dropped it in favour of Senators for the 1925 and 1926 seasons before switching back. They might have been better advised to stick with the Senators; after winning back-to-back titles as the Senators, they proceeded to go five years (1928–32) with only one regular-season victory! The Regina Rugby Club, meanwhile, had begun calling itself the Roughriders in 1924. It is a historical oddity that, during the years when Ottawa couldn't even win a game, Regina made five consecutive trips east to play for the Grey Cup.

In 1951, the western 'Riders returned to the Grey Cup after a seventeen-year absence, and Canadian football had its first Roughriders–Rough Riders matchup, with Ottawa claiming victory by a 21–14 margin. Both clubs went on to suffer through lengthy dry spells – by the time they met again in 1966, they had combined for exactly one Grey Cup appearance (Ottawa, in 1960). The eastern Riders, behind star quarterback Russ Jackson, rolled to an 11–3 regular-season record and made short work of Hamilton in the eastern final, winning by a combined score of 72–17. But in the championship game, Jackson's former teammate Ron Lancaster led Saskatchewan to the first title in team history, by a score of 29–14.

The 1969 game was a story of a great start and a rough ride to the finish for the Roughriders of Saskatchewan. They led 9–0 after limiting Ottawa to 26 yards of offence and one first down in their first six possessions. But it is often the big play that turns a game around, and Ottawa found its man in Canadian Ron Stewart. He touched the ball just seven times in the game but gained 153 yards and scored touchdowns on the only two passes he caught all day. Of his 112 yards receiving, 111 came after the catch, as he turned a pair of short swing passes into scores from 80 and then 32 yards out.

The two sets of "rough riders" met a fourth time, in 1976, and Tony Gabriel's game-winning catch brought the Grey Cup to the nation's capital for the ninth time in team history. The eastern Riders would make only one more trip to the Grey Cup, in 1981, and folded in 1996. The CFL returned to Ottawa in 2002, but the team, now called the Renegades, bowed out after four losing seasons. The Green 'Riders, however, have made frequent appearances at the Grey Cup in recent years, beating Winnipeg in 2007 and dropping a pair of close decisions to Montreal in 2009 and 2010. Ottawa is preparing to return to the CFL in the next few years, and will have its sights set on a tenth national championship.

Above: 1951 Grey Cup 'Riders vs. Riders game.

That rotation lasted only until 1963, when Lancaster was traded to Saskatchewan, where his Hall of Fame career played out. In 1966, he led the Green 'Riders to their first Grey Cup victory, beating Jackson and the Rough Riders in the championship game. But that loss turned out to be only a temporary setback for what would later be acknowledged as the greatest Ottawa team of them all. In 1968, the Rough Riders defeated Calgary 24–21 in Toronto to win the Grey Cup, setting the stage for the 1969 season, and Jackson's triumphant swan song.

In the post-Jackson years, there would be a few other great football days for Ottawa: the 1973 Grey Cup, a 22–18 win over Edmonton keyed by a great defence dubbed the Capital Punishment Gang. And in 1976, three players who had arrived the year before – quarterback Tom Clements from Notre Dame University, quarterback Condredge Holloway from the University of Tennessee, and receiver Tony Gabriel, traded to the Riders by the Hamilton Tiger-Cats – were the stars. Clements's winning throw to Gabriel in the 1976 Grey Cup game, in which Ottawa again defeated Saskatchewan, is immortalized in CFL lore as simply "The Catch."

That was the end of the line. There would be only one more Grey Cup appearance by an Ottawa team, and a highly unlikely one at that: in 1981, after finishing the season with a 5–11 record, the Rough Riders upset the heavily favoured Hamilton Tiger-Cats in the eastern final – a game remembered best for Pat Stoqua's 102-yard catch-and-run touchdown.

Ottawa entered the Grey Cup game against the powerful Edmonton Eskimos as huge underdogs. But led by Gabriel and quarterback Julius Caesar Watts, they shocked the Esks – and just about everyone else, perhaps including themselves – rolling to a 20–1 halftime lead. After the break, though, Warren Moon led a furious Esks comeback, capped by Dave Cutler's winning field goal with three seconds left on the clock.

"We shouldn't have showed up for the second half," Gabriel joked later.

What followed that last flicker of glory were fifteen seasons of bad ownership, bad management, bad coaching, and bad, losing football. At the end of the 1996 season, the Ottawa Rough Riders ceased operations, leaving the loyal football fans of the city high and dry.

There was briefly new hope with the unveiling of the expansion Ottawa Renegades franchise in 2002. But the team folded before the 2006 season without ever having qualified for the playoffs.

As early as 2014, football is scheduled to rise again in Ottawa, in a rebuilt stadium on the site of Lansdowne Park.

Russ Jackson and Ron Stewart, 1969 Grey Cup.

Before the 1969 season, Russ Jackson told Frank Clair that it would be his final year playing football. A Hamilton boy, a graduate of Westdale High School and McMaster University, he had originally come to the Riders expecting to play defensive back. But a series of injuries gave him a shot at playing the position at which he had starred in college – quarterback – and Jackson never looked back. He was the first Canadian-born QB since Joe Krol to be recognized as the league's best,

and the last Canadian to be named the CFL's most outstanding player. Jackson was an elegant athlete who could run nearly as well as he could throw. And he was cerebral, able to run Clair's complicated offence and to read the situation and change plays at the line of scrimmage – a skill that would come in handy during his last championship game.

At age thirty-one, his retirement announcement seemed premature, even during an era when fewer athletes played late into their thirties. Jackson was at the top of his game, and Clair figured he had at least four or five more seasons in him. But Jackson wanted to take his life in a different direction, to pursue a career in education that would eventually lead to a job as a high school principal, and not even a season that was arguably the finest of his professional career would prove enough to change his mind. "I told Clair this was going to be it," Jackson remembers. "Twelve years is longer than I ever thought I would play. There was no reason other than my personal reasons to get out. We [Jackson and his wife, Lois] had three young kids. And I wanted to get on with my education." (Jackson had been commuting between Ottawa and Toronto two or three times a week during the football season while completing his teaching degree.)

The Ottawa Rough Riders and the Saskatchewan Roughriders were the CFL's dominant teams in 1969. Each lost only three games during the regular season – and Saskatchewan defeated Ottawa the only time the two met, 38–21. "Saskatchewan knocked the crap out of us in Regina," Jackson remembers. "We got the hell beat out of us. But that gave us some ideas of what they were going to try to do in the Grey Cup."

Entering the playoffs, the Ottawa Rough Riders were the clear favourites, matched up against Toronto in the two-game, total-points eastern final. But they made things interesting, travelling to Exhibition Stadium for the first leg and losing to the Argos 22–14.

In the days between the first and second games, Leo Cahill, Toronto's outspoken coach, stood up at a meeting of the Argos' Playback Club, and declared, "It will take an act of God to beat us."

That statement still stands, right up there with Jim Trimble's "We'll waffle 'em," as the greatest example of hubris in CFL history.

Of course, what followed was precisely that "act of God" – Ottawa won the second game at home, 32–3, to comfortably qualify for the Grey Cup.

Game day at the Autostade dawned cold and blustery. The field was frozen and slick, forcing the players to don broomball shoes in the hopes of gaining a bit of traction. For the first time, the Grey Cup was being played on Sunday rather than Saturday (other than the famous Fog Bowl of 1962, when the game was suspended and completed the following day), which would become the new norm.

Prime Minister Pierre Trudeau kicking off the 1969 Grey Cup game.

Ron Stewart playing in the 1966 Riders Grey Cup loss.

Prime Minister Trudeau walked onto the field for the ceremonial kickoff, wearing a white knit peaked cap in a style then highly fashionable, with a red carnation stuck in the crown. He added a long, matching white scarf. (He wasn't the only prime minister in attendance: Saskatchewan's favourite son, John Diefenbaker, was also there, though his hat was made of fur.)

When it came time to kick, Trudeau removed his matching white mittens. And he wore a pair of football cleats.

Saskatchewan's coach, Eagle Keys, understood exactly the challenge his team was facing, and having beaten Ottawa in the 1966 Grey Cup game and in the teams' lone meeting in 1969, he must have felt confident that he had the formula for success. On offence, his Roughriders would ride the arm of Lancaster and the powerful running game of George Reed, who had been the dominant figure in winning the 1966 championship. On defence, they would unleash a fierce pass rush featuring two of the greatest linemen in CFL history, Bill Baker and Ed McQuarters, to try and disrupt Jackson's rhythm, and especially his propensity for throwing the long bomb – a play the Riders liked to call "the Arrow" – to wide receivers Whit Tucker and Margene Adkins. With Ottawa's star running back and receiver Vic Washington sidelined by injury, it stood to reason that if the Saskatchewan rush could get to Jackson, the Ottawa attack would grind to a halt.

All of that was sound, in theory, but if the excellent Ottawa defence could shut Reed down, Saskatchewan's attacking options would be severely limited. And the westerners' game plan failed to account fully for Jackson's superb improvisational abilities, not to mention the still-potent talents of a diminutive running back from

Queen's University named Ron Stewart, who was also approaching the end of his career. ("With Washington out, Stewy became more a part of our offensive thinking," Jackson says.)

The Rough Riders knew what was coming, and they were ready, but it was Saskatchewan that grabbed the early advantage. In the first quarter, Ottawa punter Bill Van Burkleo slipped on icy turf, turning the ball over and setting up a Lancaster touchdown pass to Al Ford. The lead grew to 9–0 before the end of the first quarter when Ottawa coach Frank Clair opted to concede to a safety rather than punt the ball out of his own end zone.

Frank Clair led the Rough Riders to three Grey Cups in his thirteen years with the team. Pictured here at the Autostade in Montreal.

Though no one knew it that day, Clair was coaching his last CFL game (he would continue as Ottawa's general manager through 1978, winning two more Grey Cups). He wore his trademark black horn-rimmed glasses and chain-smoked continuously on the sidelines, from the opening kickoff all the way to the final gun.

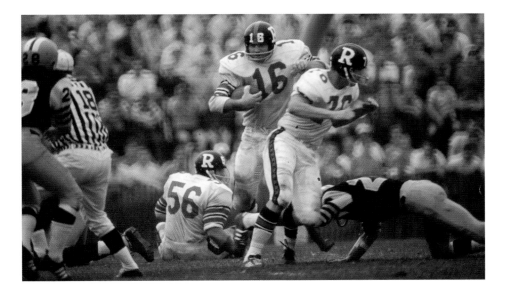

Jim Mankins (16) played three seasons in Ottawa, winning Grey Cups in two of those.

THE CFL RECORD BOOK

MANY OF THE GREAT players in Canadian football history, and many honoured members of the Canadian Football Hall of Fame, did not necessarily shine in Grey Cup competition. Examples include the great Dick Shatto, who retired in 1965 as the game's leader in receiving and overall yardage but never played in a Grey Cup game. The same goes for the B.C. Lions' Jim Young, who had a wonderful thirteen-year CFL career but did not see Grey Cup action, either. George Reed, the number-two rusher in league history, did get into four games, but was on just one winning team, as was seventeen-year veteran and teammate Roger Aldag, who won in his only appearance in 1989. Hal Patterson and Ronnie Stewart played in a combined eleven Grey Cups and yet were limited at times, due to the extraordinary attention paid to them by the opposition. They each posted some good games and some others where they had only a minor impact.

Patterson turned in one of the most significant regular-season performances in history on September 29, 1956, when he caught eleven Sam Etcheverry passes for an incredible 338 yards and two touchdowns – the convert on the second of those TDs provided Montreal with the margin of victory in a 44–43 win over Hamilton. (On the day, Etcheverry passed for 561 yards.) Since then, only two CFL receivers have gone over the 300-yard mark in a game, but no one has topped Patterson's mark.

Notwithstanding his great 1969 Grey Cup performance, Ronnie Stewart proved to be one of the most outstanding Canadian football players throughout his regular-season career from 1958 to 1970. His finest moment came on October 10, 1960, with only 16 touches of the ball all day and not a single reception. In 15 carries, Stewart set the single-game rushing record with 287 yards in a 51–21 win at Montreal. The next nearest mark by any CFL player (and the next eight best totals were produced by imports, in what has long been a position dominated by Americans) was by George Reed, on twice as many carries (30 for 268 yards). Stewart's mark remains among the finest efforts in any game by a Canadian-born CFL player.

Above: Legendary Rough Rider Ron Stewart.

The Ottawa offence finally came to life in the second quarter. Just as planned, Saskatchewan's rush had pretty much eliminated the eastern Riders' trademark long passing game to Tucker and Adkins. So Jackson, turned to the run, handing the ball to Stewart and fullback Jim Mankins, and to quick, short passes. He hit tight end Jay Roberts for Ottawa's first touchdown, closing the gap to 9–7.

Ford ran the ensuing kickoff back 77 yards, but the Roughriders blew that opportunity when Reed fumbled at the Ottawa 19-yard line. Soon after came the signature play of the game. Anticipating a Saskatchewan blitz, Jackson called a screen pass to Stewart. Just before the rush swallowed him up, he flipped Stewart the ball in the flat, with two huge offensive linemen already roaring down the field in front of him, ready to clear the path. Eighty yards later, Stewart crossed the Roughrider goal line, essentially untouched, giving Ottawa a lead they would never relinquish.

Saskatchewan had their chances to get back into the game. In the third quarter, they were first and goal on the Ottawa 7-yard line, but stalled there, and Jack Abendschan's short field goal attempt went wide for a single, narrowing the score to 14–10. Later in the quarter, Ford slipped behind defensive back Don Sutherin, but he dropped a perfectly thrown pass from Lancaster.

Then, a fumbled punt set Ottawa up for what would be the clinching score: scrambling away from the Saskatchewan pass rush, at one point completely reversing field to escape McQuarters in a way that would remind younger CFL fans of Doug Flutie, Jackson bought time, and then hit Mankins with a touchdown pass, making the score 21–11 Ottawa after three quarters.

Jack Gotta had a 30–26 record in his four seasons as Ottawa's head coach.

In the fourth quarter, Jackson stepped under centre, anticipated the blitz coming again, and changed the play, signalling to Stewart that he ought to run a quick route over the middle. "He was watching for it," Jackson remembers. "He knew they were coming. I almost got tackled before I delivered it." Stewart caught the ball and ran 32 yards for a touchdown, making the score 28–11.

"I think we got 'er," Clair said to assistant Jack Gotta, secure now that the win was assured.

A single point off a missed field goal by Sutherin created the final margin of victory: Ottawa 29, Saskatchewan 11.

Trudeau presented Jackson with the Grey Cup. As Jackson remembers it, he jokingly opted to swap his football helmet for the prime minister's cap.

"I can't," Trudeau said. "Margaret knit it for me."

Then Jackson sprinted off the field, holding the trophy high. It wouldn't quite be the final glimpse Canadian fans would have of the great number 12. The following spring, he made a cameo appearance in the CFL all-star game as the defending Grey Cup champions took on the best from the rest of the league (and there, with Prince Charles looking on from the stands, Jackson's last pass as a professional football player was intercepted). Everyone agreed that he could have played on, and played well, and at least one other team, the B.C. Lions, attempted to lure him out of retirement, but Jackson stuck to his guns and went on to a career as a high school principal. With his departure, the 1960s Ottawa Rough Rider dynasty came to an end.

But that wasn't quite the end of the Grey Cup story in 1969. Three weeks after Ottawa's victory, the Cup itself was stolen from Lansdowne Park. It wouldn't be recovered until the following February, when a tip led police to a locker at Toronto's Royal York Hotel. There, the old mug, which had survived so much over the previous sixty years, was discovered, safe and sound.

Commissioner Gaudaur decided then and there that there would be no more risks taken with the great historic relic. A replica Cup was commissioned by the CFL, one that could be used as a stand-in in certain circumstances – just in case.

Trudeau awarding the Cup to the Grey Cup champion Rough Riders, 1969.

100 GREY CUPS 103

1978

COMMITMENT TO EXCELLENCE

The name certainly has a nice ring to it: City of Champions. Edmonton is many things, including the capital of the province of Alberta, but that title has stuck now for nearly four decades, and it's not hard to understand why. The most northerly outpost of big-time professional sport on the continent is famous for the way the community rallies both around events and behind the iconic, title-winning teams that helped put it on the map. If Edmontonians have an extra bit of swagger – especially when they look down the road towards their great provincial rivals in Calgary – it is because of that legacy of sporting success.

Hockey is obviously a major part of that, in the form of the Edmonton Oilers who, during the heydays of Wayne Gretzky and Mark Messier, won five Stanley Cups in seven years and played fast and beautifully. But long before then, football was Edmonton's game, especially during two landmark dynasties when the Eskimos dominated the Canadian Football League. Since the Second World War, no franchise has won more Grey Cups than the Esks (all time, they trail only the Toronto Argonauts, 15 Cups to 13, but the Argos enjoyed a head start of almost half a century), and no organization has enjoyed such a consistent reputation for doing things the right way, for being one step ahead of the competition.

That winning image was forged during the most dominant championship run in CFL history, beginning with the 1978 Grey Cup game, the first of five consecutive

Tom Wilkinson and Danny Kepley after defeating the Alouettes at the Olympic Stadium in Montreal, 1979.

EDMONTON ESKIMOS
1893

Back---- G.Williams,H.Blair,L.Forbes,Dick Hardisty,(captain)N.Kelly,referee,
Cresswell,Macdonald,Edmonston,L.Adamson,Braine,A.Adamson,H.Hope,N.Jackson,
G.Armsted,F.Corris,J.Forbes,(touch judge.)

victories, a string that no other team has come close to matching. It's fitting that the opponents were the Montreal Alouettes. No two cities, never mind two cities so geographically and culturally distinct, have so rich a shared Grey Cup history, having met a remarkable eleven times in the championship game.

Edmonton's victory in 1978 came in their fifth Grey Cup appearance in six years, with the foundation for future triumphs fully in place. The roster already contained the beginnings of what would become a long and unbroken succession of brilliant quarterbacks – extending all the way to Ricky Ray thirty years later. Tom Wilkinson, the wily old vet from Wyoming, was under centre that day. Backing him up on the sidelines in the absence of the injured

Bruce Lemmerman was a rookie fresh from the University of Washington named Warren Moon. Moon was the latest in a long line of African-American quarterbacks who came north for the chance to play a position that in the National Football League had been all but reserved for whites, an informal prejudicial policy that, as an unintended consequence, enriched the CFL enormously.

By the time the dynasty had played out, Wilkinson would be retired and Moon would be established as the starter – and as one of the greatest players in CFL history. The line of quarterbacks – and regular Grey Cup appearances – would continue through Matt Dunigan, Tracy Ham and Damon Allen. That's five Hall of Famers in a row, a feat no other franchise has come close to accomplishing.

The first Edmonton football team was established in 1893, early days for the Canadian game, and nicknamed the Esquimaux. But in the decades that followed, as western leagues came and went, there would be long stretches in the 1920s and 1940s when there was no Edmonton club at all.

Two Edmonton teams were the first western clubs to venture east and challenge

The Edmonton Eskimos won three consecutive Grey Cups between 1954–56. Seen here in the 1954 Grey Cup game.

Left: The 1893 Edmonton Eskimos.

for the Grey Cup. In 1921, an early version of the Eskimos made the trip to Toronto, where they were beaten 23–0 by the Argonauts in the championship game. Canada's athlete of the half century, Lionel Conacher, played in his first and only Grey Cup game that day, scoring 15 points for Toronto. He gave the home team an edge, plus it didn't hurt that several American college players recruited by Edmonton were not entirely familiar with the Canadian rules. A year later, the Edmonton team, renamed the Elks, arrived in Kingston, Ontario, at midnight on Grey Cup day – following a four-day train trip – to challenge the powerful side from Queen's University. The Elks actually led 1–0 at the half, but the heavily favoured home team woke up after the break and cruised to a 13–1 win. Afterwards, unhappy both with the officiating and with what they interpreted as tepid hospitality, the Elks turned down an invitation to attend a post-game dance with the Queen's student body.

In 1923, that Edmonton team went out of business. The modern Eskimos were formed in 1949, the product of local enthusiasm (and perhaps just a little bit of local envy) whipped up when the Calgary Stampeders became the first western team to win the Grey Cup in 1948. Twenty thousand Edmontonians paid a dollar each for a share in the club, which remains to this day one of the CFL's publicly owned franchises. The task of building the new team, which adopted the colours of green and gold, was handed over to a very familiar face in Canadian football circles: Annis Stukus, who a few years later would take on the same task with the expansion B.C. Lions. Stukus got things started, selling tickets, pumping up local enthusiasm, and recruiting talent wherever he could find it. From the foundation he constructed emerged a team that, in only the fourth season of its modern incarnation, made it all the way to the Grey Cup game, where the Eskimos were beaten by the Toronto Argonauts.

Two years later, the Esks were back representing the west at Varsity Stadium as prohibitive underdogs against the powerful Montreal Alouettes, a team that featured the all-world quarterback/receiver tandem of Sam Etcheverry and Hal Patterson, along with a host of other stars. No one gave Edmonton much of a chance, but they hadn't fully factored in the genius of one of the greatest players ever to grace the three-down game.

Jackie "Spaghetti Legs" Parker came to Canada from Mississippi State, taking the advice of one of his college coaches, Darrell Royal, who had spent the 1953 season in Edmonton before going on to a long and storied career at the University of Texas.

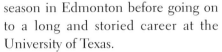

Parker could do just about everything that could be done on a football field – he played running back and defensive back and quarterback, he kicked, and he ran back kicks, all with remarkable athleticism. In the 1954 Grey Cup game, the entire country discovered his talents, most famously when he ran Chuck Hunsinger's fumble back 90 yards for a touchdown in the final minutes, just as Montreal was driving to put the game away. Instead, with the convert, Edmonton won 26–25, and then beat the Als for the Grey Cup the next two years in succession, 34–19 in the 1955 game and by a lopsided 50–27 margin in 1956.

That would be Edmonton's last Grey Cup win for nearly twenty years. In 1960, the Esks again made it as far as the championship game, temporarily interrupting the run of Grey Cup appearances by Bud Grant's Winnipeg Blue Bombers, before losing to the upstart Ottawa Rough Riders. It would be another thirteen years before they got that far again, a rise in fortunes directly tied to the arrival of Wilkinson in 1972. He had originally come north to play for the Toronto Rifles of the Continental Football League (a team coached by the flamboyant Leo Cahill), where he spent two seasons before being signed by the Argonauts as a backup in 1967. Wilkinson became the team's starter, with moderate success, but was never really allowed to settle into that role, as the Argos seemed determined to find somebody to replace him. Wilkinson was traded to British Columbia in advance of the 1971 season. He played there for a year, and then was cut during training camp before the 1972 season began.

It's easy to understand why coaches had their doubts about Wilkinson. He didn't have much of an arm, wasn't much of a runner, wasn't an imposing physical speci-

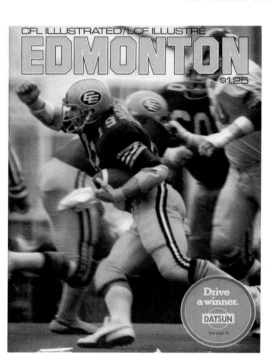

men by any means – in fact, he tended to look a little soft around the middle. And while most quarterbacks seem to have been born with a kind of Big Man on Campus swagger, Wilkinson was modest and self-effacing and certainly not straight out of Central Casting.

Edmonton, with the very capable Bruce Lemmerman established as its starter, decided to give Wilkinson a look as a possible backup. Wilkinson said later that if he'd been cut again, he might have stopped by the Calgary Stampeders' camp on the way home to Wyoming to see if they were interested, but otherwise would have been finished with football forever. Instead, he stuck with the Esks in '72, and by 1973 he was the starter as they advanced to their first Grey Cup since 1960, losing to the Ottawa Rough Riders, 22–18. They were back again a year later, with Wilkinson again under centre, and again they lost, this time 20–7 to the Alouettes.

Finally, in 1975, on a frigid day at Calgary's McMahon Stadium – the first Grey Cup ever played on the prairies – the Eskimos defeated the Als 9–8, when Montreal kicker Don Sweet missed a final-play field goal that could have won the game. For Edmonton, this victory was but a taste of greater things to come.

In 1977, the Eskimos organization took a huge leap of faith. When head coach Ray Jauch decided to leave the sideline for a job in the front office, the Esks hired as his replacement thirty-six-year-old Hugh Campbell, who during his playing career as a wide receiver had been Ron Lancaster's favourite target with the Saskatchewan Roughriders. Campbell had no professional coaching experience and was barely older than some of his players, though he had successfully rejuvenated the football program at tiny Whitworth College in Spokane, Washington, after retiring from the 'Riders.

There were plenty of experienced alternatives at the time who had paid their coaching dues and would have seemed a far surer bet. But Campbell turned out to be something special, one of the finest football minds of his generation. For the next three decades – interrupted only by a short foray into the United States Football League and National Football League in the 1980s – he was the central figure in Edmonton football, and one of the most influential in the entire CFL.

Hugh Campbell won ten Grey Cups, the first coming as a player in 1966, then five as a coach for the Eskimos dynasty, and the final four as GM or President of the Eskimos.

Campbell led the Esks to the Grey Cup in his rookie season, where they once again faced the Alouettes, this time at the brand new Olympic Stadium in Montreal. Because of the scramble to get the building ready in time for the 1976 Games, a few of its frills had fallen by the wayside – including the innovative, retractable canopy-style roof that was supposed to be suspended from a monumental (though also unfinished) tower. As a result, the Big O remained open to the elements, and in the late autumn of 1977, those elements included a heavy snowfall the night before the big game. The grounds crew took care of that, clearing the field; but then, in order to prevent the still-wet field from freezing solid, they decided to seed the artificial turf with salt pellets. The result by kickoff time was a slick, icy mess that no variety of athletic footwear, no matter how state-of-the-art, could get an adequate grip on.

It was Tony Proudfoot, the Als' defensive back, who improvised a solution that proved key to the Als' eventual victory. As legend has it, during the pre-game warm-up, with the terrible field conditions already obvious, Proudfoot spotted an electrician working on the sideline set-up, employing a heavy-duty staple gun. He borrowed it, fired a few staples into the end of his cleats, and found that it gave him better traction. Soon enough, nearly all of his teammates followed suit. Montreal beat Edmonton 41–6 in what would become known as the Staples Game.

Tom Wilkinson and Danny Kepley with the Grey Cup after the Eskimos' 1979 win.

LAST-MINUTE GREY CUP HEROES

OF THE FIRST 99 Grey Cup games, twelve have been won by a team scoring the deciding points in the final minute of play or in overtime. The most recent of those finishes came in 2009, when Montreal kicker Damon Duval made a 33-yard field goal on the final play to overcome a 27–25 deficit and win the game. The Alouettes' comeback was aided by Saskatchewan's now famous "too many men" penalty, which negated Duval's miss from 43 yards out on the previous play.

The first of these late-game heroics came in 1939, when Winnipeg's Art Stevenson punted the ball out of the end zone with the score tied at 7. Joe Krol turned the very same trick in 1947, for Toronto. Since then, there have been two overtime games, the first of which was won on an 18-yard end run by Winnipeg quarterback Ken Ploen in 1961. The most recent overtime decision came in 2005, under the new shootout format in which teams alternate possessions. Edmonton took the lead at 38–35 with a field goal by Sean Fleming and then stopped Anthony Calvillo and the Alouettes to secure the win. Another seven contests have been decided in regulation time by field goal kickers, the first of them by Hamilton's Ian Sunter in 1972. Lui Passaglia did the same thing in 1994, but this time in front of a home crowd at B.C. Place Stadium.

The play that stands out the most, perhaps, is the only final-minute, game-winning touchdown in Grey Cup history. It was scored by Tony Gabriel on a 24-yard pass from Tom Clements with just twenty seconds left to play in 1976. The win was the last in Ottawa's long history in Canadian football.

GREY CUPS WON IN THE LAST MINUTE

YEAR	WON	LOST	TIME	SCORE	GAME-ENDING PLAY
2009	MTL	SSK	0:00	28–27	Duval 33-yard field goal on the final play
2005	EDM	MTL	O/T	38–35	Overtime shootout: after Fleming's 36-yard field goal, Edmonton prevented Montreal from scoring
1998	CGY	HAM	0:00	26–23	McLoughlin 35-yard field goal on the final play
1994	BC	BAL	0:00	26–23	Passaglia 38-yard field goal on the final play
1989	SSK	HAM	0:02	43–40	Ridgway 35-yard field goal
1987	EDM	TOR	0:45	38–36	Kauric 49-yard field goal
1981	EDM	OTT	0:03	26–23	Cutler 27-yard field goal
1976	OTT	SSK	0:20	23–20	Clements 24-yard pass to Gabriel
1972	HAM	SSK	0:00	13–10	Sunter 37-yard field goal on the final play
1961	WPG	HAM	O/T	21–14	Ploen touchdown run 3:02 into the second 10-minute overtime period
1947	TOR	WPG	0:00	10–9	Krol punt to the deadline from 25-yard line on the final play
1939	WPG	OTT	0:45	8–7	Stevenson punt to the deadline from 8-yard line on the final play

Other Late Game-Winning Scores:

2002	MTL	EDM	0:19	25–16	Montreal stopped a game-tying Edmonton 2-point convert attempt (Montreal then returned the subsequent short onside kickoff for a touchdown)
2000	BC	MTL	0:44	28–26	B.C. stopped a game-tying Montreal 2-point convert attempt
1988	WPG	BC	2:55	22–21	Kennerd 30-yard field goal
1983	TOR	BC	2:44	18–17	Barnes 1-yard pass to Minter
1954	EDM	MTL	2:30	26–25	Parker 90-yard fumble return and convert by Dean
1944	MSH*	HAM	3:00	7–6	Davey punt to the deadline from 10-yard line

*Montreal St. Hyacinthe/Donnacona Navy Combines

In Edmonton, the media and fans weren't willing to believe that it was all about the shoes – they thought that was merely an excuse for a terrible performance. The criticism left the Eskimos' players and coaches with chips on their shoulders, with a feeling that they had something to prove as they entered the 1978 CFL season.

It was a landmark year in Edmonton. The city hosted the enormously successful Commonwealth Games in early August, the first of what would turn out to be a long line of international sporting events. As a happy by-product, the Eskimos gained a new home. Following a final game at Clarke Stadium on August 23, they moved next door to Commonwealth Stadium, a beautiful outdoor facility that was the second-largest in the league – and which would be packed with Eskimos' fans more often than not.

During the regular season, the Eskimos established their clear superiority in the west. Wilkinson had found a new commitment to physical fitness, losing twenty pounds, and the rookie Moon showed flashes of brilliance as his backup. In the western final, the Esks knocked off the Stampeders, advancing to the Grey Cup game in Toronto.

Meanwhile, in the east, the Alouettes had struggled a bit in adjusting to their new coach Joe Scannella, who had taken over when Marv Levy moved to the NFL. They finished second behind Ottawa, beat the Tiger-Cats in the semifinal, and then travelled to Lansdowne Field, where they knocked off the first-place Rough Riders in the eastern final.

Thus the scene was set for a rematch between the great historic rivals at sunny and frigid Exhibition Stadium.

It's the truth in any brand of North American football that quarterbacks get too much of the credit in the good times and too much of the blame in the bad. They're the ones in the spotlight, the ones who handle the ball on nearly every play. They're the stars, they get paid the most money, and everyone knows their names and numbers. But it's also true that, just as the cliché suggests, most football games are won or lost in the trenches, by the dominance of one set of linemen over another, which either allows the quarterbacks and running backs and receivers to make those flashy plays or prevents them from doing so.

If Wilkinson and Moon and Campbell were the brains of the Eskimo dynasty, its beating heart was found among the ranks of defensive linemen and linebackers, especially two of the CFL's all-time greats: Dave "Dr. Death" Fennell and Dan Kepley. In the 1978 Grey Cup game, it was they and their defensive teammates who made life very difficult for quarterbacks Joe Barnes and Sonny Wade and Montreal's exciting young running back David Green. Never would the Als' offence really get on track, and only an offensive miscue by the Eskimos really kept it close. In the tense final moments, with the game on the line, it was the Edmonton defence that saved the day.

Warren Moon led the Eskimos to five consecutive Grey Cups.

That said, the play for which the game is best remembered involved neither the Edmonton offence nor the defence, but its special teams. With the Eskimos leading 3–0 in the first quarter, and facing third and two on the Montreal 15-yard line, Campbell sent in the ever-reliable Dave Cutler and the rest of the field goal team. A routine three points seemed in order.

But early in the week leading to the Grey Cup, Campbell had added a trick play to the Esks' repertoire, though the players had only had the chance to practise it once. At a time when absolutely no one suspected it, he made the risky call.

As always, wide receiver Tom Scott initially lined up behind Wilkinson, the holder, and Cutler, the kicker, waiting for Wilkinson to look over the defence and then direct him to whichever side of the line needed shoring up. Thus instructed, Scott moved up to take his position on the left end, where he faced Montreal linebacker Carl Crennell.

But then Scott went in motion, moving laterally behind the line and in front of

Wilkinson, who called for the snap. Cutler offered up a reasonable pantomime of the kick he knew he wasn't actually going to make, then moved to the position vacated by Scott, where his job was to try and block Crennell. Meanwhile, from his knees, Wilkinson flipped Scott a shovel pass, and the receiver slipped through a small crack on the right side of the line, gaining eight yards and a first down.

Two plays later, Jim Germany ran over from the two, and the Eskimos' lead was 10–0.

Until the final play of the third quarter, that margin seemed comfortable enough. The Esks led 14–4 at the half, and stretched it to 17–3 not long after the break. Their defence looked impenetrable.

Then, scrimmaging on his own 10-yard line, Wilkinson attempted a routine hand-off to running back Jim Germany. They never connected, the ball hit the turf, was recovered by the Als, and in the opening moments of the final quarter, Joe Barnes scrambled for the touchdown, narrowing the Edmonton lead to 17–10.

Things got wild after that. The Alouettes' own superb defence rose to the occasion, stopping the Eskimos' offence cold. A late hit by Edmonton's David Boone knocked Barnes out of the game, forcing Scannella to hand the reins to Sonny Wade. Don Sweet's field goal narrowed the score to 17–13, but Cutler replied after a botched Montreal fake punt resulted in Wade being tackled at his own 21-yard line.

LEAD CHANGES AND THE GREATEST COMEBACK EVER

THROUGHOUT GREY CUP HISTORY, the results of games have often been in doubt up until the last minute, and lead changes are known to be frequent. The three contests that stand out were played in 1987, 1998, and 2005. On six occasions in each of these games, the lead team changed on the scoreboard, and all of these contests saw the winning points scored in the final minute or in overtime. In 1987, the lead changed hands five times in the fourth quarter alone, and Jerry Kauric's 49-yard field goal, the longest winning kick in Grey Cup history, sealed the game for Edmonton. Calgary's 1998 win over Hamilton and Edmonton's triumph in overtime in 2005 also saw the lead swapped back and forth six times.

The largest-overall winning comeback ever recorded was by the Edmonton Eskimos in 1981. With their run of three consecutive championships on the line and a fourth in real danger, they fell behind 20–0 just 3:14 into the second quarter to the Ottawa Rough Riders (a team that posted a regular-season record of 5–11). The Riders were widely considered to be double-digit underdogs that day, with rookie quarterback J. C. Watts leading their offence. Ottawa scored four times in their first six possessions and held Warren Moon to just nine passing yards and two interceptions in the early going. The Esks' two-quarterback system paid off yet again, however, as veteran Tom Wilkinson came in to lead the final four series of the first half to settle things down. Moon and the Esks' defence came out of the locker room after the halftime break and simply blew the Rough Riders away. Moon scored twice himself, led four scoring drives, and completed a game-tying two-point conversion to Marco Cyncar with 4:05 to play. After yet another defensive stop, Moon moved the Eskimo offence on the ground to set up Dave Cutler's game-winning field goal from 27 yards out with three seconds on the clock, in one of the most exciting Grey Cup games of all time.

With the score 20–13, the Als had one last gasp. Wade drove them as far as the Edmonton 27-yard line in the game's dying moments, but the Eskimo defence held firm once more.

And so the Edmonton dynasty began – but not without a touch of slapstick. As the captains, Wilkinson and Kepley, were carrying the ancient trophy off the field between them, a drunken fan ran into them, knocking the Cup to the ground and breaking it in half.

Of course, by that point in its history, the old mug had survived far worse.

Wilkinson was named the game's most valuable player, though he completed only 15 of 25 passes for an unremarkable 111 yards. True to his character, he acknowledged afterwards that he didn't really deserve it.

"I don't think I should have been named the game's most outstanding player," he said. "But I'll take the car that goes with it."

Tracy Ham joined the Eskimos in 1987, after the dynasty years, but managed to lead them to another Grey Cup in his first season with the team.

Over the next four seasons, the Eskimos would roll on, dominating Canadian football as no team had before, or has since, adding one Grey Cup victory after another: a 17–9 win over the Als in 1979; a 48–10 win over Hamilton in 1980; a 26–23 thriller over longshot Ottawa in 1981, with Wilkinson coming off the bench to ride to the rescue; and finally, a 32–16 demolition of the Argonauts back at Exhibition Stadium in 1982.

It would never again be quite so good again for Edmonton fans – or for any other fans in professional football – but it was a rare season thereafter when the Esks weren't at least in contention. (It wasn't until 2006 that their thirty-five-year streak of qualifying for the Western Conference or Division playoffs was finally broken.) Dunigan arrived in 1983, just as Moon was departing, and in 1985, the year Allen was signed to back him up, the Eskimos were back in the Grey Cup game, losing to the Hamilton Tiger-Cats. A year later, it was Allen, subbing for an injured Dunigan, who led Edmonton to a thrilling 38–36 victory over the Argos in the 75th Grey Cup.

In 1990, with Tracy Ham now their starting quarterback, the Eskimos lost the final to Winnipeg. The following season, Ron Lancaster was hired as the Eskimos' head coach, the beginning of yet another golden era for Edmonton football. Winning their final eight games of the season, the Esks captured the Grey Cup in 1993, their eleventh championship in franchise history, with Allen named for the second time the game's most outstanding player. With Danny McManus at quarterback, they lost to Doug Flutie and the Toronto Argonauts on a memorably snowy Grey Cup day in Hamilton in 1996.

The new century brought more good tidings. After losing the 90th Grey Cup game at home in 2002 to the Montreal Alouettes, the Esks came back the next year to beat them for the championship, the first for Ricky Ray. And then, in 2005, in one of the most remarkable Grey Cup games ever played, they outduelled the Als one more time, 38–35 in overtime.

Fans of every other team in Canada would have loved to have had it so good for so long.

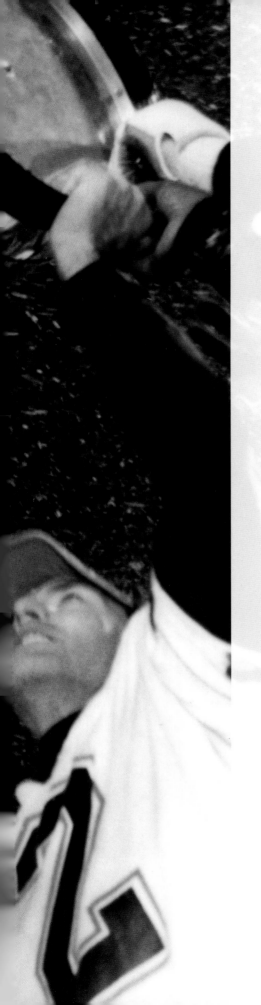

1983

THE ARGOS BOUNCE BACK

It was all a little bit ho-hum. On November 29, 1952, the Toronto Argonauts won the 40th Grey Cup game, defeating the Edmonton Eskimos 21–11 at Varsity Stadium. The western champions struck early with a Normie Kwong touchdown to lead 5–0. But the hometown Argos scored fifteen points in the second quarter, and really, that was all she wrote.

The victors were hardly a novelty act. The Argos had won the Grey Cup in 1945, 1946, 1947, and 1950 (their great star Joe Krol was part of all of those, plus a wartime win with the Hamilton Flying Wildcats, so the 1952 championship would give him six in his illustrious career). And going back in history, it was the tenth Grey Cup for an Argonauts team, and the twenty-fourth time in the history of the game that at least one of the participants had had "Toronto" in its name.

No wonder, then, that the post-game scene described by *The Globe and Mail's* Gord Walker seemed unusually muted.

"It was difficult to judge from the first trickle of Argonaut players into their dressing room whether they had won or lost. Billy Bass was first in, tossed off a matter of fact, 'that's it' and went to his locker. Joe Krol followed, wore a slight smile, but didn't express his thoughts vocally. Then came Doug Smylie, who whipped off his helmet and hurled it savagely at his locker. Al Bruno was

Doug Flutie, one of the CFL's greatest players, won three Grey Cups through his career and was named the MVP of the game each time.

Lionel Conacher was a star in the NHL as well as CFL. Seen here practising football in his Chicago Black Hawks jersey.

the first victory indicator. You couldn't mistake what his wide grin meant."

Sure, they would remember the '52 Grey Cup game. It was the first one ever televised – though only locally, in Toronto and environs (Annis Stukus started the telecast with a chalkboard talk about strategy, and the picture disappeared for a full twenty-nine minutes in the third quarter before reappearing for the end of the game).

But another Toronto Grey Cup? Didn't they all start to blur together? Soon enough, surely, there would be another to add to the long list.

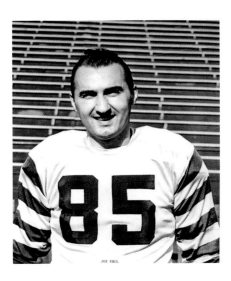

It is unique in Grey Cup history, the long walk in the desert of one of the oldest and most storied franchises in the Canadian game. The Toronto Argonauts were, in most years, the wealthiest team in the CFL. In the modern era, they would regularly import big-name players and big-name coaches, luxuries unavailable to clubs operating on tight budgets. Each acquisition would, in turn, be greeted as a saviour, as the one to take the Argos back to the same Promised Land where Krol and company had led them in 1952.

But somewhere along that road to glory, something always went wrong.

There would be no more Grey Cup appearances in the 1950s.

There would be not a one in the 1960s.

In 1971, a glamorous, star-studded team coached by Leo Cahill and quarterbacked by former Notre Dame star Joe Theismann finally managed to avoid all of the land mines that sidelined all of those other Argonaut teams on the way to the championship game. They arrived at the 59th Grey Cup in Vancouver's rain-soaked Empire Stadium as favourites over the Calgary Stampeders. The Argos fell behind early, but in the fourth quarter they were poised to finally break the curse. With the score 14–11 for Calgary, Dick Thornton intercepted a Jerry Keeling pass and returned it to the Stampeders' 11-yard line, which seemed to guarantee at least a tying field goal. What followed instead was arguably

Joe Krol was an integral part of the Argo teams that won five Grey Cups in his seven years with them, (1945–53).

GREY CUP HIGHLIGHTS

ASK TWO OR MORE fans to name the greatest play or individual performance in Grey Cup history, and you're sure to provoke a debate. What follows, however, is a list of plays that went a long way toward influencing or changing the outcome of a Grey Cup game. Most fans should be able to find a play or a game-long effort that they remember having watched live, seen on a highlight reel, or witnessed in person.

YEAR	PLAYER	TEAM	THE PLAY
1921	Lionel Conacher	TOR	Scored 15 of Toronto's 23 points — in five different ways — before leaving after the third quarter to play all 60 minutes in a hockey game that evening.
1931	Warren Stevens	MTL	Threw the first Grey Cup touchdown pass to Kenny Grant (37 yards).
1935	Fritz Hanson	WPG	Returned a punt 70 yards for a touchdown without the aid of blocking to give a western club the Grey Cup title for the first time ever.
1938	Red Storey	TOR	Scored three fourth-quarter touchdowns to lead Toronto to a 30–7 comeback win.
1947	Joe Krol	TOR	Accounted for all 10 Toronto points, including a 35-yard TD pass to Royal Copeland and the game-winning punt single on the final play.
1948	Norm Hill	CGY	Scored a touchdown on the famous "sleeper play" from Keith Spaith, helping Calgary complete an unbeaten season and win their first Grey Cup.
1953	Vito Ragazzo	HAM	Hooked up with Ed Songin on a 55-yard pass and run to provide the game-winning points for Hamilton's first Grey Cup win as the Tiger-Cats.
1954	Jackie Parker	EDM	Returned Chuck Hunsinger's "fumble" 90 yards for a touchdown to set up Edmonton's 26–25 win.
1955	Sam Etcheverry	MTL	Passed for 508 yards and two touchdowns in Als' 34–19 loss to Edmonton.
1957	Ray Bawel	HAM	Scored in the first five minutes on a 50-yard fumble return and was later tripped by a fan while returning his second interception of the day for an apparent touchdown.
1958	Norm Rauhaus	WPG	Blocked Cam Fraser's punt into the end zone and recovered on the final play of the first half.
1961	Kenny Ploen	WPG	His 18-yard run settled the first Grey Cup overtime win in favour of Winnipeg.
1964	Bill Munsey	BC	Scored a touchdown on both offence and defence, including a 65-yard fumble return, giving the B.C. Lions their first Grey Cup win.
1966	Ron Lancaster	SSK	Threw for three touchdowns to lead Saskatchewan to their long-awaited first Grey Cup win.
1969	Russ Jackson	OTT	Led Ottawa to a 29–11 win in his final game, throwing a Grey Cup–record four touchdown passes.
1969	Ron Stewart	OTT	Touched the ball just seven times but gained 153 yards with two touchdowns.
1971	Reggie Holmes	CGY	Recovered Leon McQuay's fumble late in the game at the Calgary 12-yard line to help preserve the Stampeders' first win since 1948.
1972	Ian Sunter	HAM	Last-play field goal from 34 yards won the Grey Cup at home for Hamilton. The winning drive was aided by four great catches by Tony Gabriel and Garney Henley.
1976	Tony Gabriel	OTT	Scored the only last-minute Cup-winning touchdown in history on a 24-yard pass from Tom Clements.
1977	Vernon Perry	MTL	Returned an interception 77 yards in Montreal's 41–6 win over Edmonton.
1981	Dave Cutler	EDM	Completed the greatest Grey Cup comeback (after trailing 20–0) with a 27-yard winning field goal.
1982	Warren Moon	EDM	In his final CFL season, he passed for 319 yards and ran for 91 more to complete Edmonton's run of five straight Grey Cup wins.
1986	Grover Covington	HAM	Recorded five of Hamilton's record 13 sacks in a 39–15 upset win over Edmonton.
1989	Dave Ridgway	SSK	Ended what has been termed "the greatest Grey Cup ever" with a 35-yard field goal with two seconds left to play, breaking a 40-all tie.
1991	Raghib Ismail	TOR	His 253 kick-return yards included a touchdown on a kickoff in the fourth quarter.
1994	Lui Passaglia	BC	Made last-play field goal at home, redeeming himself after a miss a minute earlier.
1996	Eddie Brown	EDM	His amazing touchdown catch in the snow came after kicking the ball up into his arms.
1998	Mark McLoughlin	CGY	Made last-play 35-yard field goal to win — one of three in the final quarter.
2000	Chuck Levy	BC	Denied Montreal's final effort to tie the game by defending a two-point convert.
2007	James Johnson	SSK	Made a Grey Cup–record three interceptions, including a second-half touchdown.
2009	Damon Duval	MTL	Given a second chance after Saskatchewan's "too many men" penalty, Duval hit a 33-yard field goal on the final play to give Montreal their first Grey Cup since 2002.

STEPHEN BRUNT

the most famous fumble in Canadian football history. The Argos' elusive and enigmatic running back Leon McQuay took a hand-off from Theismann, slipped to the turf, and dropped the ball. Calgary's Reggie Holmes recovered. Opportunity lost.

But that wouldn't end the torture for Toronto fans. The Argo defence held, and the Stamps were forced to punt from deep in their own end with 1:53 left in the game. Trying to corral a bouncing ball near the sideline, Argos returner Harry Abofs kicked it into touch – and in the process educated almost every fan watching about one of the more obscure rules of the Canadian game. If he had knocked the ball out of bounds with his hands, the Argos would have retained possession and would have had one more chance to tie or win the game. But because he kicked it, Calgary was given possession, and they then ran out the clock to seal the victory – breaking their own long drought, with the first Grey Cup win for the Stamps since 1948.

Back in ancient times – after the 1937 Grey Cup game, in which Toronto squeaked by the Winnipeg Blue Bombers 4–3 – fans first talked about the "Argo Bounce," a lucky break that seemed to come Toronto's way exactly when required.

By 1971, though, the phrase was laden with irony. The following season, the Argos went 3–11, Cahill was fired, and after the next season Theismann headed for the National Football League. The franchise's championship hopes would be mired in futility for the rest of that decade and into the next.

What changed the Argonauts' fortunes, finally, and brought their Grey Cup drought to an end, were a new coach and a temporary abandonment of the endless quest for big name stars.

After finishing a franchise-worst 2–14 in 1981, the Argos handed the reins to Bob O'Billovich, a Montana native who had been a defensive back and backup quarterback with the Ottawa Rough Riders before becoming an assistant coach with the team. O'Billovich understood the idiosyncrasies of the league and knew the nuances of Canadian football in a way that many of his Argo predecessors did not. He hired as his offensive coordinator one of the most innovative thinkers in the sport, Darrell "Mouse" Davis, who had popularized a scheme known as the run-and-shoot, which used motion and multiple wide receiver sets and turned out to be a perfect fit with the three-down, big-field game.

Davis only stayed in Toronto for one season, but it was a memorable one. Employing the starting quarterback

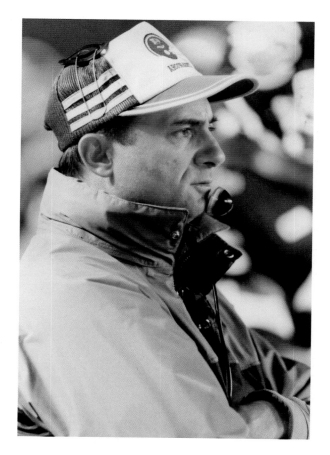

Bob O'Billovich broke the Argos' thirty-one year Grey Cup drought in 1983.

Joe Theismann led the Argos to the Grey Cup final in 1971, but couldn't end their long Cup drought, losing to the Stampeders, 14–11.

Condredge Holloway led the Argos to their first Grey Cup win in 31 years.

tandem of Condredge Holloway and Joe Barnes (who had won championships in Ottawa and Montreal, respectively), he helped the Argos go from worst to first in the CFL East in 1982. "A lot of the things we brought in on offence were pretty new and creative," O'Billovich says. "We applied a lot of the run-and-shoot concepts to our game. With the unlimited motion, we were able to do some things that no one had seen before." The Argos' run wasn't halted until the Grey Cup game, where they were hammered 32–16 by the powerhouse Edmonton Eskimos, who won their fifth consecutive championship. (That game is best remembered for the cold, torrential rain that fell at Exhibition Stadium, which convinced local politicians that the city needed a domed stadium. The SkyDome – later renamed Rogers Centre – which included the world's first fully retractable roof, opened to great fanfare in 1989, and hosted the Grey Cup game that year.) "It was a close game going into the half, and then the second half the rain came down hard," O'Billovich remembers. "It affected us more than it did Edmonton because we relied on the pass so much. That was the first time that Toronto had been in a Grey Cup in thirty years. They had a parade – and we didn't even win. I think there were about 20,000 people downtown the day after the game. I said to the players, 'Imagine the kind of turnout they're going to have if we actually win it.'"

They would soon find out. The Argonauts were the best team in the east in 1983 and, after a tough win over the Hamilton Tiger-Cats in the eastern final, advanced to the Grey Cup game, which was played in the brand new B.C. Place Stadium – the first Grey Cup in history to be played indoors. Nearly 60,000 fans packed the place, and almost all of them were there to root for the hometown B.C. Lions, who had finally broken Edmonton's stranglehold on the west. Much of the credit for that went to their bright, young rookie head coach Don Matthews, who had been an assistant on the Eskimos' staff during the Edmonton dynasty.

Those Lions, led by the great wide receiver "Swervin' Mervyn" Fernandez, who caught a long touchdown pass from Roy Dewalt to open the scoring, were the better team in the first half. The Argos tied the game 7–7 on a touchdown pass from Holloway to Jan Carinci, but their offence struggled as B.C. employed an overloaded defensive front designed specifically to nullify the run-and-shoot. Holloway, who had come down with the flu in the days before the game, was largely ineffective. Just before halftime, when Lui Passaglia's field goal put B.C. up 17–7, Joe Barnes – who was the only player on the Argo roster old enough to have been born when they last won the Grey Cup – started warming up on the Toronto sideline.

The game turned in the second half. With Barnes under centre, the Toronto offence adjusted and began to move the ball. But three drives stalled short of the goal line, and three times the Argos' field goal kicker, Hank Ilesic, missed – so that instead of a potential nine points, they picked up only two, to narrow the score to 17–9. Ilesic, who had signed with the Edmonton Eskimos out of high school as a punter (he was nicknamed "Thunderfoot" because of his booming kicks) had placekicking added to his duties for the first time after moving to the Argos for the 1983 season.

O'Billovich remembers the conversation he had with Ilesic on the sidelines after he missed the third field goal attempt.

Canadian-born punter Hank Ilesic won seven Grey Cups over his 19-year career.

"I said, 'Hank, we're going to need those points. This is a close game.'"

"Don't worry, coach," Ilesic said. "I'll make it when it counts."

To his credit, he did. After switching the shoe on his plant foot to provide a better grip on the artificial turf, Ilesic was good on a 43-yard field goal in the fourth quarter, which narrowed the score to 17–12. Meanwhile, the Toronto defence completely stymied Dewalt and the B.C. offence in the second half.

With the clock ticking down, the Argos regained the ball at their own 49-yard line and began one of the most memorable drives in the team's long and glorious history. Most CFL fans remember how it ended; what they may have forgotten is how it almost came apart: Barnes connected with Paul Pearson on a pass over the middle, and when he was hit, Pearson fumbled the ball, which popped straight up in the air. Had the Lions recovered, the Grey Cup would almost surely have been theirs. Instead, Pearson's teammate Emanuel Tolbert plucked the ball out of mid-air and saved the day.

That set up a play that would become iconic for Toronto football fans. With 2:55 left on the clock, the Argos scrimmaged on the Lions' two-yard line. Barnes took the snap and rolled left, instantly under pressure. He then flipped a short pass to running back Cedric Minter, who cruised across the goal line – and finally, it seemed, deliverance was at hand.

Still, there were tense moments yet to come for the long-suffering Toronto fans. The Argos failed on a two-point convert attempt that would have given them a three-point lead. Instead, down by just one, with lots of time on the clock to move into position for a winning field goal, the Lions got as far as their own 46-yard line before a holding penalty set them back. A long bomb from Dewalt to Jacques Chapdelaine that would surely have won the game glanced off the receiver's finger-tips. The Argos would get the ball back, and then be forced to punt, setting up one final, failed Lions Hail Mary. Only then did the celebration begin, as O'Billovich was carried off the field on his players' shoulders.

"Absolute elation," he says, when asked how it felt.

Afterwards, all of the Toronto players told the same story. The difference this time, they said, was the Argos were truly a team.

"That wasn't the Toronto way for so long," Holloway said. "They used to go out and buy one guy, an Anthony Davis or a Terry Metcalf. They'd tell him to go and win it. They told me that two years ago. But Coach O'Billovich changed that way of thinking. He turned the Argos into a team."

"What you're seeing is the beginning of a dynasty," said hometown boy Carinci, who remembered crying when Leon McQuay fumbled in 1971. "I grew up in Toronto, and I know very well about the 31 years. I've suffered a lot, too. I think of all the high-priced players and coaches who have come in here over the years, but couldn't do it. . . . It turns out all we needed was a team, which is what Obie built."

"We brought a winning attitude," O'Billovich says. "We changed the culture of Toronto pro sports franchises at that time. It was just a tremendous experience. It had taken so long for that to happen and to be a part of history – that something nobody can ever take away from you. It's a memory firmly etched in every mind of every player that represented the Toronto Argonauts in that Grey Cup game, and [of] every coach. It was pretty special."

O'Billovich was right about the victory parade. It took over much of downtown Toronto as the Argos celebrated their first Grey Cup since 1952. But Carinci wasn't quite right about the dynasty – the remainder of the 1980s would be pretty much a

washout for the Argonauts. Barnes was traded to Calgary in 1985, and after the Argos lost the 1987 Grey Cup game to the Eskimos, 38–36, O'Billovich was fired in 1989, though his stellar CFL career continues today, with Hamilton his latest (and perhaps final) stop.

The Argos' fortunes wouldn't change for the better until 1991, and then in dramatic fashion, when the team was purchased by California-based wheeler-dealer Bruce McNall, who also owned the Los Angeles Kings of the National Hockey League. His partners in the enterprise were the actor John Candy, a lifelong passionate Argos fan, and Wayne Gretzky, then the greatest hockey player on earth. McNall had acquired Gretzky from the Edmonton Oilers in 1988 in the most famous trade in hockey history.

McNall arrived intent on making a splash, and there's no question he succeeded. The Argos in the past had generated plenty of publicity for bringing in big talent, but never anything like this: in advance of the National Football League draft, Toronto signed the player projected to go first overall, Notre Dame's sensational receiver and kick returner Raghib "Rocket" Ismail. It was an enormous risk, at an enormous cost, but in the short term, at least, it paid off. A huge crowd packed the SkyDome for the season's opener with the Blues Brothers providing halftime entertainment. Beyond the sizzle, the Argos delivered on the field, finishing first and winning the eastern final 42–3 over the Blue Bombers in front of 50,000 fans. They advanced to the first-ever Grey Cup game played in Winnipeg, where their opponents would be the Calgary Stampeders.

The game's signature moment on that frigid day was Ismail's 87-yard kickoff return for a touchdown in the fourth quarter – both the moment and Ismail untouched by a frozen can of beer that was hurled from the stands and just missed him as he cruised into the end zone. Final score: Toronto 36, Calgary 21.

By the time the Argonauts next appeared in the Grey Cup, McNall was in jail, Candy was dead, Gretzky had long since surrendered his ownership stake, and Ismail was playing in the NFL. But Toronto had acquired another superstar – arguably the greatest player in the history of the Canadian game – Doug Flutie, who arrived from Calgary before the 1996 season. That sensational Toronto squad, coached by Don Matthews, won two consecutive Grey Cups.

The first, played in Hamilton's Ivor Wynne Stadium, transformed into a winter wonderland by an unexpected blizzard, was a riveting game of give and take between the Argos and the Edmonton Eskimos. The teams traded kick-return touchdowns – Jimmy "the Jet" Cunningham brought a punt back 80 yards, but

SOMETIMES, IT TAKES TWO

BY 1982, AS THE Argos faced the Esks in the last of Edmonton's five straight Grey Cup victories, they had a pair of QBs that could well have been the regular starter anywhere. And the following season, Condredge Holloway and Joe Barnes each attempted more than 250 passes, the first time in CFL history that had ever occurred. Neither missed much time to injury, and Holloway started a little more than Barnes, but each was effective in leading the club to a 12–4 mark and first place in the east for the second consecutive season.

The true test of their interchangeability came in the 71st Grey Cup, against the British Columbia Lions. For the first time ever, the game was being played indoors – at the brand-new B.C. Place Stadium, before 59,345 fans, most of whom were backing the Leos. Holloway played most of the first half and engineered only one score before he was pulled late in the half. At halftime, the Argos faced a tough 17–7 deficit, but Barnes, who would be named the game's offensive MVP, was the spark Toronto needed as he came off the bench to pro-

duce 203 second-half yards and five drives that led either to field goal attempts (Hank Ilesic had a tough day, going 1-for-4) or the game-winning touchdown. Barnes moved the Argos consistently throughout his turn, passing for 175 yards and picking up another 36 on three scrambles out of the pocket.

The other side of the story was the outstanding second-half defence put up by Toronto. The Argos shut down the Lions completely, forcing six two-and-outs and a pair of turn-overs. Defensive MVP Carl Brazley was a key player for the Argo "D," as he made six tackles, forced a fumble, and made two B.C. turnovers on his own with a fumble recovery and an interception.

The 1983 Argonauts are only one of two only teams since 1950 (a span of sixty-two Grey Cup games) to have shut out an opponent in the second half of a Grey Cup, and their come-back from a 10-point deficit at the half was just the fourth of that magnitude in Grey Cup history.

Above: Condredge Holloway combined with Joe Barnes to give the Argos a 12–4 record in the 1982 season.

134   STEPHEN BRUNT

WARRIOR

THERE ARE CFL QUARTERBACKS who have started more Grey Cup games than Hall of Famer Matt Dunigan, and some who have won more games as well. But none can match him for the sheer number of teams that he led into the CFL's championship game. The talented import from Louisiana Tech started three straight Grey Cup games, from 1986 to 1988, as well as the 1991 and 1992 contests – a total of five in a span of just seven seasons, and, most remarkably, for four different clubs. Everywhere Dunigan went, except for expansion Birmingham (whom he led into the playoffs, at least) and a brief stint in his final year in Hamilton, he guided his teams into the Grey Cup. A remarkable achievement, but one that came with a price by every season's end.

Dunigan's efforts to get his teams to the championship did not come without personal sacrifice, often in the form of the hellacious hits he absorbed in 194 career CFL games. In fact, he missed fifty-two games for a variety of injuries across fourteen seasons. His statistics show just how worn down he would become by the post-season: his passer rating in Grey Cup games was 55.3, compared to a regular-season mark of 84.5. In several of his Grey Cup appearances, notably with the Argonauts in 1991 against Calgary, injuries limited his ability to move and throw at all. A look at the 1991 game stats, however, sum up his influence: Toronto – Dunigan: 12 of 29 for 142 yards; Calgary – Barrett: 34 of 56 for 372 yards. Final score: Toronto 36, Calgary 21. Dunigan made his 12 completions count for two touchdown passes and did not throw an interception, while Barrett was picked off three times and Calgary's turnovers led to half of the Argos' 36 points that day. That is Grey Cup guts and leadership writ large.

In his final Grey Cup appearance in 1992, Matt Dunigan faced incredible pressure from the Calgary defence (Wally Buono's first championship team) and stayed standing for three quarters. He finally gave way to Danny McManus after two sacks and dozens of hits. By the end of his career, Dunigan had played on two championship teams and was inducted into the Canadian Football Hall of Fame in 2006 after passing for 43,857 yards – he remains fifth in all-time yardage – and launching 306 passes for touchdowns. For Dunigan, the game was as much a matter of will as of skill, and he epitomized what it must have taken for a player of modest physical stature (5'11", 180 pounds) to impact the CFL game.

Henry "Gizmo" Williams topped that, taking back a kickoff 91 yards for the Eskimos – and both quarterbacks, Flutie and the Esks' Danny McManus, put on a show. The two teams combined for 41 points in the second quarter alone, with the Argos finally prevailing 43–37 (though Edmonton Eskimos fans will forever point to a Flutie quarterback sneak on a third-down gamble, and a fumble that wasn't called a fumble . . .).

A year later, following a second consecutive 15–3 regular season, the Argos returned to the Grey Cup, this time at Edmonton's Commonwealth Stadium, where, until the western final, all signs pointed to a rematch against the hometown Eskimos. But the Saskatchewan Roughriders, who finished third in the west with an 8–10 record, upset Calgary in the semifinal and then beat the Eskimos at home, 31–30, to become one of the true Cinderella teams in Grey Cup history. It appeared that most of the province of Saskatchewan had emptied, as fans of the Green 'Riders poured into Edmonton for the big game. But against Flutie and company, the magic wore off. Adrion Smith's 95-yard kickoff return for a touchdown to open the second half was the decisive blow in what finished as a comfortable 47–23 Toronto victory. For the second year in a row, Flutie was named the Grey Cup's most valuable player.

Michael "Pinball" Clemons joined the Argos organization in 1989 and has been there ever since, winning three Grey Cups as a player in the 1990s and one as head coach in 2004.

Flutie departed in 1998, and tough times followed. In 2003, Toronto actually fell briefly into bankruptcy before new owners took charge in time for the 2004 season. What followed was a real feel-good story: coached by Michael "Pinball" Clemons, as popular an athlete as Toronto has ever known, the Argos rose from the ashes to finish second, and then upset the Montreal Alouettes in the eastern final at Olympic Stadium to advance to the Grey Cup. The game was held that year in Ottawa, and the opponents would be the B.C. Lions.

That Grey Cup will be remembered for Clemons's emotional call-and-response speech to his players, captured by television cameras, just before they stepped onto the field.

"A guy who understands perspective about life and what's important," he said. "Part of it is, this is when you truly care about somebody and you're willing to work together with them and you're really, truly willing to do it, not just for your own good but for their good first. When you're willing to think about somebody else first, they truly become family.

"Who are we?"

"FAMILY!"

"Who are we?"

"FAMILY!"

"Who are we?"

"FAMILY!"

"Now, when we go out there today, we've been talking about playing at another level. We've been talking about being dominant. And you know the reason why we've been dominant the last few weeks.

"What's the word?"

"PAIN!"

"What's the word?"

"PAIN!"

"Because you've got to hit somebody in this game. That's why we've been dominant. When we go out there today, there's going to be a bigger audience than has ever seen a football game in this country in history. It's the biggest crowd ever. Now we've got a chance to do what we've been talking about. We're talking about playing this game at a level that nobody, nobody, nobody, in any league anywhere has ever played this game . . . Guys, let's go out there today as a family and get it done from the first whistle to the last . . .

"Win on three: one, two. . ."

"WIN!"

Win they did, 27–19, the fifteenth championship in the history of the Argonaut football club, the most by any team. And no Argo bounce was required.

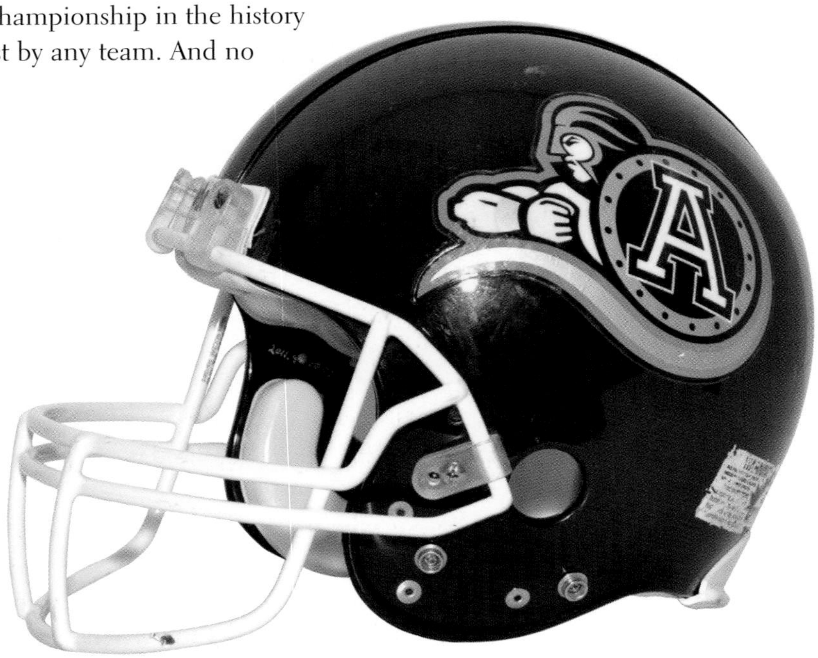

1995

BALTIMORE, CANADA

The 83rd Grey Cup Game was a first, and a first . . . and a last.

The early 1990s had been a time of turmoil for the Canadian Football League. Shifting cultural currents and unsteady ownership had put the very future of the ancient game in jeopardy. Yes, there had been challenging times before, but never had the CFL been so close to extinction.

And so, in desperate times, one takes desperate measures. At a moment when the Canadian-ness of the Canadian game seemed to be of diminishing importance for Canadians, and when the Internet revolution seemed to have rendered lines between countries and cultures arbitrary and unnecessary, CFL governors began to think the previously unthinkable. Faced with an apparently unsolvable dilemma, they decided that the only path to survival was through growth – not within Canada, but into the United States, putting teams in markets that were unserved by the National Football League. That bold, risky strategy required the CFL make several significant compromises. For instance, in some places, it was nearly impossible to squeeze a full Canadian field into stadiums built for the American game. And it hardly made sense for American-based teams to be forced to employ Canadian players, so for them and them only, out went the non-import quota that had been a fundamental of the CFL for decades.

Even with the grand plan still a work in progress, and with some of the U.S.

Mike Pringle helped bring the Grey Cup south of the border for the first – and only – time.

BALTIMORE'S GREATEST LEGACY

ONE OF THE POSITIVE aspects of the CFL's short-lived incursion into U.S. markets was the introduction of a player who would become one of its brightest stars.

Mike Pringle was selected 139th in the 1990 National Football League draft by the Atlanta Falcons, but made it into just three games, carrying the ball twice for a total gain of nine yards. Released in training camp in 1991, Pringle spent the following spring with the Sacramento Surge of the World League before playing three games with the Edmonton Eskimos.

Between 1992 and '93, the World League shut down, while the CFL expanded. Surge owner Fred Anderson was granted the CFL's first U.S. franchise, the Sacramento Gold Miners, and Pringle appeared in all eighteen games, gaining more yardage as a receiver than a running back. An off-season trade sent him to Baltimore, and at age twenty-seven he enjoyed the greatest of breakout seasons, setting a CFL record with 1,972 rushing yards. The team, coached by Grey Cup fixture Don Matthews and quarterbacked by CFL veteran Tracy Ham, finished second in the East Division and made it all the way to the championship game, where they lost to the B.C. Lions on Lui Passaglia's field goal with 0:00 showing on the clock.

Pringle was named the CFL's Most Outstanding Player in 1995, after again leading the league with 1,791 rushing yards. With a 15–3 record, the Stallions led the CFL South Division and defeated Winnipeg and San Antonio en route to the 83rd Grey Cup game, played for the first time ever at Regina's Taylor Field. Baltimore's defence (which forced six turnovers) and special teams were the story of the game, but Pringle gained 137 yards, helping put the Stallions in position for five Carlos Huerta field goals. Baltimore defeated the Calgary Stampeders, 37–20, and for the first and only time, the Grey Cup was captured by a non-Canadian team . . . but not for long.

Even as the Grey Cup was being presented, it was known that the NFL's Cleveland Browns had designs on playing in Baltimore in 1996. As the other four U.S.–based franchises folded, Stallions owner Jim Speros considered other American sites before electing to move to Montreal and revive the Alouettes name. The Denver Broncos signed Pringle to an NFL contract, but when he was cut late in training camp, he rejoined his former team north of the border.

In 1998, Pringle broke his own record for rushing yardage, with 2,065, while establishing league highs for carries (347)

and 100-yard games in a season (14) and winning his second Most Outstanding Player award.

Though the Als won the Grey Cup in 2002, Pringle saw action in only six regular-season games. A year later, he signed with Edmonton, rushing for 1,376 yards and contributing to the Eskimos' Grey Cup win. The seven-time CFL all-star retired after the 2004 season, having broken George Reed's career records for rushing yards and yards from scrimmage, and tying Reed's mark for touchdowns (since broken by Milt Stegall). He was inducted into the Canadian Football Hall of Fame in 2008.

Above: Mike Pringle returned to Canada after the U.S. expansion
to win two more Grey Cups as an Eskimo and an Alouette.

ownership not entirely stable, off the CFL went
into unknown territory – first Sacramento, California, followed in short order by San Antonio,
Texas; Baltimore, Maryland; Shreveport,
Louisiana; Birmingham, Alabama; and
Las Vegas, Nevada. The traditional east–
west split would be thrown out the window; now
the Grey Cup would be a battle of North versus South,
and in all likelihood, of Canada versus the United States.

The first international Grey Cup game
took place in 1994, as what was then known
as the Baltimore Football Club (the NFL had prevented them from using the Colts name) lost to the
British Columbia Lions on a last-play Lui Passaglia field
goal at B.C. Place, a matchup that began to stir some of
the same overtly patriotic feelings that would be on full
display in Vancouver sixteen years later when it hosted the
2010 Winter Olympic Games.

By 1995, though few outside the CFL's inner circle
knew it, the great American experiment was actually on its
last legs. Teetering ownership in several U.S. cities, tepid
fan support, and the imminent move of the NFL's
Cleveland Browns to Baltimore conspired to knock down
the house of cards. But there would be one last spectacular
gasp, as a powerful Baltimore team coached by Don
Matthews – and now called the Stallions – rolled through
the playoffs, setting up a Grey Cup match against the
Calgary Stampeders, quarterbacked by the great Doug Flutie.

That was rich subtext indeed. And then there was the setting.

Regina had always held a special place in the hearts of those who love Canadian
football. The smallest city to have a team, the focus of a vast, though sparsely populated, province, it has always seemed the pure and perfect embodiment of the connections between identity, place, and rooting interest. There was a romance to the
idea of Saskatchewan football that reached all the way down to the seven- and
nine-man teams playing in high schools where the student population was too
small to permit fielding a full 12-man squad. For those who knew their history, there
were the tales of those quixotic teams that came east in the 1920s and 1930s and had
their heads handed to them by the eastern powers when they challenged for the
Grey Cup. All of that passion wasn't fully rewarded until 1966, the first time the

Green 'Riders won the Cup, and the championships since were few and far between. Some years, the 'Riders seemed a hopeless cause. But the beating heart never stilled.

It had long been conventional wisdom that a city as small as Regina could never play host to the Grey Cup. This was a big-time, big-city event. For much of its history, the game had been played only in Toronto, and then – with the construction of Empire Stadium – it made regular stops in Vancouver. The opening of Olympic Stadium in Montreal created another, spectacular venue. And other cities occasionally had their turn – Ottawa and Hamilton, Calgary and Edmonton, and in 1991, for the first time, Regina's prairie rival, Winnipeg.

Bringing the Grey Cup to Regina, though, was something else again, and in an era when it seemed that being bigger, splashier, and more expensive was all that mattered, a small-town championship game didn't exactly seem to line up with the CFL's larger objectives. What would those people in San Antonio and Baltimore and Las Vegas think when they saw "Regina" on the marquee?

Still, the decision had been made, and strangely enough, it was Larry Ryckman, the owner of the Stampeders and one of the more gung-ho proponents of U.S. expansion, who came up with the perfect analogy. The Grey Cup in Regina, he said, would be just like the 1994 Winter Olympics in Lillehammer, Norway. At a time when the Olympic spectacle was becoming ever more grandiose, those Games had been staged in a sleepy rural town where people skied and sledded to work and to buy their groceries, where speedskaters were superstars, where the connection between the sports and the culture and the environment and the history was organic and obvious every moment of every winter day. It was a journey back to the sports' roots, to the origins, and Ryckman rightly figured that Regina would be the same – or at least it would be, if you substituted people wearing watermelons as hats for picturesque Norwegians.

In a strange and unsettling moment in Grey Cup history, Regina turned out to be the perfect tonic. The Roughriders didn't come close to qualifying – they finished 6–12 that season, in sixth place in the new CFL North Division and out of the playoffs. But still, the people of Saskatchewan responded as though it were Ron Lancaster and George Reed taking the field for the home team. The week leading up to the game was like none in the history of Grey Cup, a celebration of the province and its football heritage – stories of whole houses painted green, of fan loyalty that stretched through generations, of impossibly long journeys made just for the chance to watch a ballgame. Every Grey Cup event, no matter how modest, the kind of stuff at which jaded, big-city fans might have turned up their noses, was packed to the rafters and beyond. For the Canadians from outside the province who were in attendance – and for the handful of puzzled and amazed Americans,

Don Matthews is the second winningest CFL coach of all time, and the only coach to win a Grey Cup in the U.S.

including a smattering of reporters, who followed the Stallions north to this strange and exotic land – it was tough to resist the appeal of something so honest and genuine, in a culture increasingly driven by artifice and superficiality and baseless hype. What happened in Regina in 1995 was 100 per cent real, 100 per cent genuine – and more than a little bit magical.

As for the game itself, well, there the storybook narrative ended. A prairie zephyr swept through Taylor Field and was so strong at one point, before kickoff, that the crowd had to be evacuated from a section of temporary stands that had been constructed in one end zone to increase capacity to Grey Cup standards. The gusts were enough to earn the Wind Bowl a place alongside the Fog Bowl and Mud Bowl, storied Grey Cups played under crazy climatic conditions.

The bottom line was there would be no stopping Baltimore, not even by Flutie and a Calgary team that, for all of its dominance during the era, won only a single

Grey Cup, in 1992. The Stallions were just too good. Operating without any kind of roster restrictions based on nationality, Matthews stacked his team with superb players at all positions – including on special teams, which to a large degree was where the game was decided. Chris Wright scored on an 82-yard punt return to give Baltimore an early 7–0 lead. Calgary fought back with two field goals, and then a Flutie touchdown pass early in the second quarter put them ahead 13–7.

But then the Stallions took over, with three field goals and a touchdown off a blocked punt – more of that special-team dominance. They were up 23–13 at the

ALL KINDS OF WEATHER

IN RECENT YEARS, GREY Cup weather has frequently been a non-issue, as the game has been held indoors thirteen times since the opening of B.C. Place Stadium in Vancouver in 1983. Rogers Centre in Toronto (known formerly as the SkyDome) and a covered Olympic Stadium in Montreal have hosted five of those warm and dry contests since 1989. However, the other eighty-six Grey Cup games have been played in a wide variety of weather conditions, ranging from a sunny but frosty –17°C day in Winnipeg in 1991 to the 90 k.p.h. wind conditions in the 1995 Wind Bowl in Regina. Snow-covered, frozen fields seemed to be the norm in the 1920s and 1930s, followed by years of muddy fields with the game at the mercy of early Canadian winters. The most recent of the "coldest" games came at Edmonton's Commonwealth Stadium in 2009, under –5°C conditions, and these types of games have usually led to a few more fumbles or dropped passes than usual.

Two other games stand out particularly among those most affected by the conditions on the day: the 1962 Fog Bowl and the 1950 Mud Bowl, both held in Toronto. In 1950, the field was described as at best "muddy," but a look at the existing film reels of the game offers a better description – a quagmire. The footballs were so heavy and waterlogged that Toronto tried just three passes all day, completing one for seven yards. Winnipeg managed to complete just three passes themselves and had a total of three first downs in the entire game. The oddest image of the day came when a dazed Winnipeg star

Buddy Tinsley fell face down into the mud. Legend has it that the officials saved him from drowning, but the Winnipeg star claimed otherwise. The other lasting memory is of backup Winnipeg quarterback Pete Petrow and his dazzlingly clean jersey after he came off the bench late in the game to join a sea of mud-blackened uniforms.

The strangest Grey Cup, and one seen only in part, even by the 32,655 fans in attendance, was the 1962 Fog Bowl between Winnipeg and Hamilton at Exhibition Stadium. Unseasonably warm 47°F weather brought in fog off Lake Ontario that persisted throughout the day. Eventually, the fog became so thick that the final 9:29 of the game had to be postponed until the next day, with Winnipeg leading 28–27.

An interview with Kenny Ploen of the Blue Bombers revealed the real issue that arose with the continuing the next day – the players had less than twenty-four hours to get into game shape after stiffening up. In today's game, players generally have a week in between games, so the turnaround was a tough one for the sixty players dressed that day. There were no points scored after the action resumed under clear conditions; only four first downs were made, and neither team was able to move the ball much past the midfield stripe. Hamilton completed a 38-yard pass in the final minute, but a Joe Zuger punt on the final play was covered by Ploen at the two-yard line and ended the longest game seen, more or less, in Grey Cup history.

Opposite: The infamous Mud Bowl of 1950.

half, and after the two sides traded touchdowns in the third quarter, Baltimore closed the show, with Carlos Huerta (who seemed untroubled by the howling gale) kicking two more field goals in the fourth, and running back Mike Pringle taking control, running behind the superb Stallions' offensive line, eating up yards and eating up the clock.

The final score was 37–20. Baltimore quarterback Tracy Ham was named the game's most valuable player, but in truth the win was in every way that mattered a total team victory by one of the best in CFL history. Counting the regular season

and playoffs, the Grey Cup victory was the Stallions' eighteenth of the season. No CFL team had done that before, and none has since.

In the dressing room after the game, the Stampeders players couldn't help but feel that they had disappointed more than just their hometown fans. In each of the previous two seasons, they had entered the playoffs as Grey Cup favourites, and both times, they had floundered before even reaching the big game.

But this loss felt worse.

"We let the country down," linebacker Matt Finlay said. "It's a sad day for Canada. I've loved the CFL my whole life. Everyone wanted to keep the Cup in Canada."

Only receiver Dave Sapunjis tried to take the long view.

"It's sad for us," he said. "But maybe this will be good for CFL football in the United States. Maybe this will spark a little more interest in our game down there."

As he prepared to transport the Grey Cup outside of Canada for the first time, the champions' owner, Jim Speros, seemed wildly confident about the future. He knew that the Browns – renamed the Ravens – were coming to Baltimore for the 1996 season, which probably meant that the Stallions, who been drawing close to 30,000 fans a game at the old Memorial Stadium, would have to pack up and move elsewhere.

But they'd find a new home, he assured everyone. He was talking to all kinds of different people. The NFL's Houston Oilers were leaving for Tennessee. Maybe Houston was where the CFL would land next.

"It's back to business for us," Speros said. "But I've got a heckuva lot more leverage whatever I do. I'm carrying a proud chip on my shoulder tonight."

Who could have imagined in that moment that, by the time the next season began, the Grey Cup champions would not only be all that remained of the American expansion? Just as had been the case in Baltimore, they would find themselves in a city a beloved football team with a glorious past had fled years before.

Where the death of the American experiment led, indirectly, to the return of the CFL to Montreal – not by grand plan, not by design, but because there was no alternative.

In 1996, the Baltimore Stallions became the new Montreal Alouettes, and there, their story would play out like a fairy tale.

Tracy Ham moved from Toronto to Baltimore with the U.S. expansion. Both years there he made it to the Grey Cup final, winning the second year.

2001

THE MONTREAL RENAISSANCE

Never mind in the Canadian Football League – in any sport, in any era, this is one of the best, least likely, most poetic pulled-straight-from-a-movie-that-you-wouldn't-believe-for-a-second storylines – and one complete with a happy ending. How football was reborn in its birthplace, Montreal, is a tale that never gets old with the telling.

In 1987, after a long and painful decline, the Montreal Alouettes folded. It happened fast, on the brink of a new season. Suddenly, a franchise established in 1946, the team of Sam Etcheverry and Hal Patterson, of Sonny Wade and Don Sweet and Johnny Rodgers, with roots stretching back to the nineteenth century, was consigned to history, and too few tears were shed. Montreal had lost interest. The Olympic Stadium, once packed with more than 50,000 fans a game, was all but empty. Big-name player signings made no difference. A long love affair had simply burned out.

Nine years later, the CFL found itself in the midst of an identity crisis. Its attempt to expand to the United States had crumbled all at once. Only the most successful of the American teams, the Grey Cup champion Baltimore Stallions, had any interest in staying in business, and because the NFL was about to push them aside at venerable Memorial Stadium, the Stallions had become a team in search of a home. Other cities – other *American* cities – were floated as possible

The Alouettes after winning the 2010 Grey Cup in Edmonton.

destinations, before it became clear that the U.S. was no longer a viable option for the league. That left only one place in Canada with a suitable stadium: Montreal. The Stallions were rechristened the Alouettes and set up shop at the Big O, and in the beginning, it seemed that almost no one cared. The tiny crowds that turned up looked lost in the huge stadium. Few betting people would have laid a nickel on the new Als' chances for long-term survival.

But unbeknownst to just about everyone outside of the province of Quebec, something was happening there. Even in professional football's absence, the game at the grassroots level had been experiencing tremendous growth. In the CEGEPs, in the universities, young Quebeckers were playing and loving the sport that took hold when McGill University met Harvard way back in 1874.

So football was alive and well. All that was required to turn Quebeckers into fans again was a catalyst, something to make the old seem new – and the old seem new.

It is no small irony that the forced move of the Alouettes to another, much smaller, much funkier home, a place literally falling down around them, created the necessary spark. Forced out of Olympic Stadium for a playoff game by a previously scheduled U2 concert, the Als had nowhere to go but a crumbling old park on the downtown campus of McGill. It was no one's bright idea. It was the product of no genius marketing strategy. It was in every way a desperation move. And at kickoff time between the Alouettes and the B.C. Lions, it seemed as though nothing had changed in terms of the city's indifference: the stands looked pretty much empty.

But then, as the traffic congestion that had been holding them back began to ease, the fans started to arrive, to fill the place. A crowd that was young and fun-loving and drawn by the novelty of a game played right in the heart of a great, vibrant city, in cozy, atmospheric confines, by a team they were suddenly ready to embrace. The party that began that day continues unabated.

Of course, it didn't hurt that the team Montreal inherited from Baltimore was a powerhouse, a winner right off the bat.

On November 24, 2002, the circle was completed, when the new Alouettes arrived at Commonwealth Stadium and won the first Grey Cup for the city since 1977, defeating their historic *nemeses*, the hometown Eskimos, 25–16.

A heck of a lot had happened in the interim – there'd been ups and downs, death and resurrection – but by the time the trophy was raised, there was no argument that a new golden era of Montreal football was underway.

The long shared history of the sport of football and the city of Montreal divides neatly into five distinct chapters, one of which is the dark period when there was no team at all.

It begins, of course, at the very beginning, with the founding of the Montreal Football Club in 1868, and with the match between McGill University and Harvard University in 1874, which is generally regarded as the birth of the North American game. What the teams played that day would look a whole lot like rugby to a contemporary fan, and afterwards the Canadian and American games went their separate ways, occasionally cross-pollinating but evolving with several key distinctions in their rules, most notably the number of downs, the number of players, and the size of the field (the latter codified in the U.S. because they needed to fit the game into already-constructed stadiums that couldn't accommodate anything larger).

In 1907, the Interprovincial Rugby Football Union – the precursor of the CFL's Eastern Division – was formed, a body that would forevermore be known as the Big Four, with Montreal a charter member along with Toronto, Hamilton, and Ottawa.

Montreal's only pre-Alouette Grey Cup victory came in 1931, when the team was named the Winged Wheelers. (Finding the right moniker for the local club was an ongoing process: they were also at times known as the Hornets, the Indians, the Cubs, the Royales, and, much later, the Concordes.) The opponents that year were the Regina Roughriders, who came east with the usual high hopes. They thought they had seized an advantage when, the night before the game at Molson Stadium, they hired a local cobbler to add cleats to their boots, at a cost of $67. But the big day dawned, the weather was wintry and the field (a recurring Grey Cup theme) was frozen solid. Wearing cleats, the Regina players might as well have been wearing skates, while the home team got lots of grip by wearing running shoes. The game is remembered for the first touchdown pass in Grey Cup history, a 24-yard strike from Montreal's quarterback Kenny Grant in the third quarter. Beyond that, the home team was in control from start to finish, winning 22–0. The only thing marring the victory celebration was an unfortunate incident immediately after the game, when Montreal's Red Tellier levelled Regina's George Gilhooley with a punch. Tellier was banned for life by the Canadian Rugby Union – the only suspension in Grey Cup history – though

three years later, in a forgiving mood, the organization reinstated him.

Montreal football fell into decline thereafter. In 1936, the Montreal Amateur Athletic Association abandoned the sport, and teams that came after sputtered and nearly died. Following the Second World War, as football across Canada was returning to normal and the foundation of what would become the CFL was being put in place, three investors – Lew Hayman, Léo Dandurand, and Eric Cradock – bought the Montreal Big Four franchise, and after some consultation with the public, rechristened the team the Alouettes after the traditional song – a savvy and appropriate acknowledgement of the French-speaking majority in Quebec.

The Als were a hit right from the start. With the masterful Hayman in charge of building and coaching the team, they finished their inaugural season tied with the Toronto Argonauts for first place, and fans packed Delorimier Stadium – even though the home of the Montreal Royals baseball team wasn't exactly perfect for football, with the pitcher's mound right in the middle of the field. They lost to the Argos in the Big Four playoff (Toronto would go on to win the 1946 Grey Cup). Three years later, the Als finished second in the east, beat Ottawa in a two-game playoff, knocked off the Hamilton Tigers (back-to-back champions during a two-year stint in the ORFU) 40–0, and advanced to the Grey Cup game in Toronto against the defending champion Calgary Stampeders.

Once more, the conditions of the field were a problem – at least for the Stamps, who were outraged that no one had covered it with a tarpaulin during the snowy week before the big game. "We've just witnessed some bare-faced larceny," Stamps president Tom Brooks said afterwards, a reaction some might have construed as sour grapes. "Fans don't want to see a bunch of guys sliding around on their bellies or their backsides in a national final. The fans were robbed." The slippery pitch didn't seem to faze quarterback Frank Filchock, lineman Herb Trawick, or any of

The 1874 McGill–Harvard football game pictured here is regarded as the birth of North American football.

the other Alouettes stalwarts, as they comfortably won the new team's first Grey Cup, 28–15.

It would be twenty-one long years before Montreal's next championship, which suggests that there was a long, bleak era in the city's football history. But in fact it was during that drought that the sport enjoyed its first golden age in Montreal, with Sam "the Rifle" Etcheverry, a strong-armed quarterback from the University of Denver, and "Prince" Hal Patterson, a wonderfully gifted and elegant receiver from

ON THE DAY

IN 2001, A YEAR in which the CFL was dominated by its eastern teams, the western representative in the 89th Grey Cup had a losing regular-season record for the first time in league history. Edmonton captured first place in the West Division with an abnormally weak 9–9 record, while Calgary and B.C. earned playoff spots with marks of just 8–10. The East Division champion Winnipeg Blue Bombers finished up at 14–4 and made it past Hamilton easily to reach their twenty-second Canadian football championship game. Their lineup featured three Most Outstanding Player award-winners, led by quarterback Khari Jones, top Canadian Doug Brown, and offensive lineman Dave Mudge, plus Charles Roberts in his rookie season. On paper this game looked to be a blowout, but as it turned out on the day, the regular season often doesn't count for much.

The game's final stats package suggests an even match. Turnovers were equal; first downs, net yards, and sacks almost the same; passing little different; and each team had a 100-yard receiver – Marc Boerigter for Calgary and Milt Stegall for Winnipeg. If there was a statistical advantage at all, it was Calgary's ability to hang on to the ball – they had the ball for 33:02 and made a few more second-down conversions.

The 2001 contest was decided by yet another unlikely hero on special teams, long considered a vital part of the CFL game.

Heading into the game, Winnipeg boasted the league's top punt returner in Charles Roberts, while Calgary countered with the league's top kickoff-return specialist and overall yardage leader in Antonio Warren. The two kickers, Mark McLoughlin of Calgary and Troy Westwood of the Blue Bombers, had had off years and weren't much better in the Grey Cup, making only 3-of-7 on the day. So the game came down to a Grey Cup rarity: a blocked punt.

With Winnipeg stopped at their own 35-yard line late in the third quarter, the hero for Calgary became Willie Fells, who ran in a punt blocked by Aldi Henry from the 11-yard line to turn the game around and provide Calgary with a 24–12 lead. The Stamps withstood a late rally, and after McLoughlin's successful field goal, with 48 seconds left, Calgary had its fifth Grey Cup title in hand. The closeness of the statistics, and of the game itself, underlines the essential parity to be found in a league that has had, for the most part, only eight or nine teams since 1945. What it also shows is that "on the day," past performance may not mean much, and that Grey Cups are won in a variety of ways.

Kansas, who could play nearly every position on both sides of the ball, rivalling Maurice Richard of the Montreal Canadiens as the city's biggest sporting stars.

Three years in a row, the Alouettes went to the Grey Cup, in 1954, 1955, and 1956, and three years in a row they lost to the Edmonton Eskimos, by ever-increasing margins. The first one hurt the worst. Up by five late in the game and driving for another score, Chuck Hunsinger fumbled after taking a hand-off from Etcheverry, and Jackie Parker scooped up the ball and ran it back 90 yards for the deciding touchdown. Montreal fans and players would argue endlessly that it wasn't a fumble at all, but rather an incomplete illegal forward pass directed at lineman Ray Cicia, which should have resulted in a penalty, but not a turnover. Referee Hap Shouldice disagreed, and the Eskimos triumphed 26–25. Edmonton won again, 34–19, in the 1955 championship game, despite the fact that Etcheverry threw for over 500 yards, and then crushed the Als 50–27 in the 1956 Grey Cup.

Etcheverry and Patterson played on, but the Als no longer ruled the east. In 1960, Alouettes owner Ted Workman and general manger Perry Moss decided it was time for a change, seeing signs that Etcheverry was reaching the end of the

Opposite: Sam Etcheverry set a record for most passing yards in a Grey Cup game (508) in the 1955 Grey Cup game, a loss to the Edmonton Eskimos. His record stands to this day.

road. They engineered what is remembered in Montreal as one of the worst trades in sports history, sending Etcheverry and Patterson to the Hamilton Tiger-Cats in return for the Ticats' own star quarterback, Bernie Faloney, and defensive lineman Don Paquette.

Montreal fans reacted angrily, seeing the two greats shipped out of town. They became even angrier when they learned that Etcheverry had a no-trade clause in his contract, one that management clearly violated. Etcheverry then declared himself a free agent and signed with the St. Louis Cardinals of the National Football League. So Faloney stayed in Hamilton, where the Ticats dominated the east through much of the following decade. With his new team, Patterson would be catching passes from Faloney, and from succeeding Ticat quarterbacks, until an injury forced Patterson into retirement in 1967. And Don Paquette, a very good player but no superstar, became the answer to a trivia question.

The Alouettes all but disappeared from the radar in the 1960s. It was a desperate period, with only the genius of running back George Dixon providing any relief from nine consecutive losing seasons.

It's no small irony that an Als revival coincided with the return of Etcheverry, this time as head coach. He had come back to Montreal after his NFL playing

GREY CUP RIVALRIES

OF THE NINETY-ONE GAMES played since Edmonton was the first western team to go east and contest the Cup, twenty have matched the Eskimos against Montreal or pitted Winnipeg against Hamilton. The latter rivalry was played out mainly from 1953 to 1965, but the former – Edmonton and Montreal contests – seem to crop up repeatedly across Canadian football history. No other head-to-head matchups come close to these two great rivalries with the exception, perhaps, of the six Argonaut–Winnipeg games up to 1945.

Edmonton and Montreal's three consecutive meetings between 1954 and 1956 produced some of the greatest games and individual feats in Grey Cup history: Jackie Parker's 90-yard game-winning fumble return; Red O'Quinn's record 290 receiving yards; and the three highest total offensive outputs of all time. The Canadian Football Hall of Fame has inducted a whopping fourteen players from these two teams. The clubs met again five times in a six-year span in the 1970s, with Montreal finally winning in 1974 and 1977. All told, of Edmonton's twenty-four Grey Cup appearances, eleven have been against Montreal. The Als have played other clubs just seven times.

Winnipeg and Hamilton grabbed the stage in 1957 and dominated the game for almost a decade. They first met in 1935 and 1953, and would lock horns six more times by 1965. The Blue Bombers won four of the teams' six meetings between 1957 and '65, including the first Grey Cup to go into overtime, in 1961, and the Fog Bowl, played over two days in 1962. In the latter game alone, there were fourteen eventual Hall of Famers in the two lineups, along with many builders of the game among the two clubs' management groups.

The Tiger-Cats were the premier club of this era, reaching the Grey Cup nine times in eleven years before fading out of the picture after their 1972 last-play, 13–10 win over Saskatchewan on Ian Sunter's 37-yard field goal. They have been back to the Grey Cup just six times since then, and Winnipeg has not won since 1990.

Marv Levy led the Alouettes to two Grey Cups in the 1970s.

career ended to coach the Quebec Rifles of the United Football League for a single season in 1964, and then helped out as an assistant at Loyola College. In 1970, Etcheverry was hired as head coach for the Alouettes in the hope that he might bring back some of the old magic. Working alongside another great Alouette of the past, the team's new general manager, Red O'Quinn, Etcheverry almost completely turned over the team's roster with 24 new players, including an All-American quarterback and punter named Sonny Wade.

After finishing third during the regular season with an unremarkable 7–6–1 record, the Als embarked on an unlikely playoff run, going on the road to beat the Toronto Argonauts in the eastern semifinal, and then upsetting the first-place Tiger-Cats in the two-game, total-points final to reach their first Grey Cup game since 1956. Their opponents were another third-place team, the Calgary Stampeders, and the site was Toronto's Exhibition Stadium, where two teams walked out to find one of the worst fields in Grey Cup history (which was saying something). The natural turf came up in pieces – at one point, Wade picked up a clod and flung it away before taking a snap – turning the game into a bit of a fiasco. But in the end, Montreal fans weren't complaining, as the Als won 23–10, giving Montreal its first championship in twenty-one years.

That second Etcheverry Era didn't last very long. Following two more losing seasons, he was forced out as coach (though he would return briefly a decade later as general manager of the Montreal Concordes). Hired as his replacement was a diminutive gridiron intellectual named Marv Levy. Before taking his talents to the National Football League, Levy would be the architect of the greatest era in Alouettes history, as the team played in five Grey Cup games in six years and won two, in 1974 and 1977 (Levy's successor, Joe Scannella, was actually in charge for the last one).

In the 1974 Grey Cup, the Als beat the Eskimos 20–7 at Empire Stadium in Vancouver. On a windy day, which made things difficult for both offences, Levy made a key decision, replacing his ineffective starting quarterback, Jimmy Jones, with the veteran Wade. Wade didn't throw for a lot of yards, but he managed the game beautifully, and placekicker Don Sweet provided all of the necessary scoring, with 14 of the Als' 20 points, including four field goals – a Grey Cup record (at the time). On the other side of the ball, following an early first-quarter touchdown that would be the western champs' only score of the game, the Montreal defence completely shut down the Edmonton attack.

By rights, the Als should have won a second consecutive championship a year later, but the normally reliable Sweet was the goat this time (along with his holder, Gerry Dattilio, who bobbled the snap), missing a chip-shot field goal in the final minute that could have been the margin of victory. Instead, the Eskimos escaped with a 9–8 win.

The 1977 Grey Cup, played at the then brand-new Olympic Stadium in Montreal, will always be remembered as the Staples Game, after defensive back Tony Proudfoot had the bright idea of firing staples into the soles of his shoes to help gain a bit of traction on the icy field, and all of his teammates followed suit. The Als won, going away 41–6.

Barry Randall with the Grey Cup after the Alouettes' 1977 win.

Montreal lost two more Grey Cup games to the Eskimos, in 1978 and 1979 – the first of five straight championships for the great Edmonton dynasty – and then, entering the 1980s, football began its rapid decline in the city, sped along by bad ownership, unwise attempts to stir the market with the signing of big-money marquee American players, and by briefly rechristening the team as the Concordes, a name that proved to be meaningless in both official languages.

The fans – especially francophone fans – turned off.

When finally in 1987 the sad day came and they turned out the lights, it seemed as though hardly anyone cared enough to mourn. There wasn't even a conversation about the CFL someday returning to Montreal.

And then, fast forward fifteen years, when it all came together.

Anthony Calvillo holds the record for most CFL passing yards (over 70,000), most of those coming in his fourteen seasons with Montreal.

By 2002, the new Alouettes in their new/old home were firmly re-established in the hearts of Montrealers, and Percival Molson Stadium had become the fashionable place to be.

Though the team was stacked with talent from the day it unpacked, the Als in the early years of their revival failed to deliver a championship – and in fact earned a reputation for not being able to win the big one. They did reach the Grey Cup game in 2000 against the B.C. Lions, but fell agonizingly short, as a two-point convert attempt in the dying seconds, which could have sent the game into overtime, fell incomplete.

Two years later, the Als dominated the east during the regular season, rolling up a 13–5 record, and then dispatched the Argonauts in the division final to secure a berth in the 90th Grey Cup. There they faced the best team in the west, the Edmonton Eskimos, who enjoyed the advantage of playing at home in Commonwealth Stadium.

The Als' leader and star, as he had been since succeeding Tracy Ham as the starting quarterback, was Anthony Calvillo, whose tumultuous CFL career in many ways mirrored the challenging times the league had endured – and overcome. Calvillo arrived from Utah State, signing on with a brand-new team called the Las Vegas Posse, which held its training camp in the parking lot of a casino/hotel. There were nine other guys vying for the same job in what were obviously circumstances unlike any in the history of professional football. The then twenty-two-year-old Calvillo came out on top, and was the Posse's starter through the franchise's lone wild-and-wacky season of existence.

After the Posse folded, Calvillo was claimed by the Hamilton Tiger-Cats in a dispersal draft. But his confidence went south, as did the team, and after three seasons, many were ready to write him off. Calvillo signed as a free agent with the Alouettes as a back-up, where he was patiently groomed to take over when Ham retired.

He would mature into one of the greatest quarterbacks in Canadian football history, an accurate passer, a runner when necessary, but most of all a thinker, someone who fully understood the nuances of the game. That said, respect and recognition didn't come right away, and entering the 2002 Grey Cup, his doubters were still legion.

Calvillo's head coach, Don Matthews, was not among them. A man with a strong and sometimes polarizing personality, arrogant, condescending, and brilliant, Matthews had bounced from city to city, team to team, winning wherever he landed. He had coached Baltimore to the 1995 Grey Cup, but didn't follow the team to Montreal, instead signing on with the Toronto Argonauts, where he won consecutive championships with Doug Flutie as his quarterback. In 2001, he was out of football for the first time in his adult life when he received a call from the Als, who had just endured a disastrous backward step of a season.

Matthews now had a chance to win his fifth Grey Cup – a feat only Lew Hayman and Frank Clair had managed before him.

The 2002 game itself will not be remembered as a classic. Somehow, despite relatively mild temperatures and little precipitation, the grass at Commonwealth Stadium – the only stadium in the league to still have the real stuff (artificial turf wasn't installed till 2010) – was slippery enough to badly affect the play. The Alouettes handled the conditions better, and took control early, when Calvillo hit wide receiver Pat Woodcock for what turned into a 99-yard catch-and-run touchdown, the longest in Grey Cup history.

Edmonton made it close in the second half, and only a failed two-point convert attempt – shades of Montreal two years earlier – kept them from tying the game late in the fourth quarter. Jeremaine Copeland fielded the ensuing onside kickoff and ran it all the way back for the clinching touchdown in what finished as a 25–16 Montreal victory.

Though his statistics on the day were unspectacular, Calvillo was named the game's most outstanding player and understood that he had proved a point. "The critics can say what they want to say," he said. "But as long as I had the confidence of the guys in that locker room, that's all that mattered." If there remained any doubts, they were fully erased over the next eight years, as the Als appeared in six Grey Cups, and won back to back in 2009 and 2010. Meanwhile Calvillo surpassed the all-time career record for passing yards, not just for the CFL, but for all of professional football.

But leave it to a Canadian kid to sum up how it felt to have your name engraved on Earl Grey's famous mug.

"I've watched this game so many times growing up," Woodcock said amid the celebrations in the Alouettes dressing room. "It's the biggest day of the year for a football fan in Canada. You get together with family and friends, to make a big pot of chili and you watch the Grey Cup. To be able to score a touchdown in a game that I've watched so many times and dreamed of being in is the most exciting thing I can think of."

2007

RIDER PRIDE

Sometimes, the Grey Cup is more than just a football game. Sometimes, it can signal something larger, like the emergence of a whole new identity.

Eighty-four years before, a team representing Regina first made the trip east to challenge for the trophy, just the third western club to do so, facing an opponent it knew only by reputation. It might as well have been a trip to the moon.

Regina lost 54–0 to Queen's University that day in Toronto, which still stands as the worst beating in the history of the championship game. When they boarded the train for home, humiliated and ridiculed for their trouble, the Regina players must have wondered if it had really been worth the effort. Over the ensuing decades, other Saskatchewan sides probably felt the same way, suffering a series of gutting Grey Cup defeats while winning the big game only twice.

But early in the twenty-first century, change was afoot. As other parts of Canada fell into decline, Saskatchewan was in economic ascendance. After decades of out-migration, young people were sticking around to forge their future, and some of the province's vast diaspora were happily heading home.

A rising football team that twenty years before had teetered on the brink of extinction seemed to embody the province's new swagger, and its fortunes became even more of a focal point of local identity. Rider Pride had always been there, in good times and bad, but now it was even bigger and bolder than ever.

When the Saskatchewan Roughriders took the field at Toronto's Rogers Centre on November 25, 2007, to meet their regional rivals the Winnipeg Blue Bombers

The Roughriders ended a twenty-three year drought by winning the Grey Cup in 1989.

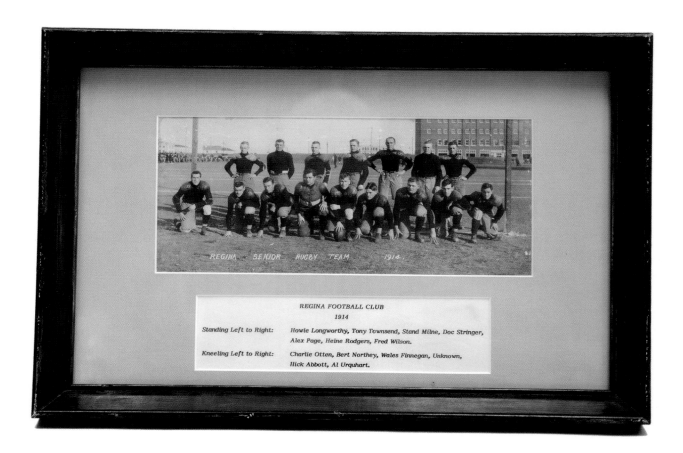

REGINA FOOTBALL CLUB
1914

Standing Left to Right: Howie Longworthy, Tony Townsend, Stand Milne, Doc Stringer, Alex Page, Heine Rodgers, Fred Wilson.

Kneeling Left to Right: Charlie Otten, Bert Northey, Wales Finnegan, Unknown, Hick Abbott, Al Urquhart.

in the 95th Grey Cup game, they were well on their way to becoming the wealthiest club in Canadian football. Saskatchewan games drew sky-high television ratings. 'Rider merchandise sold in astounding quantities. Game tickets were scarce and coveted. When the home team played, it seemed that nearly everyone in the province, male and female, young and old, was tuned in.

All they needed now was for the Roughriders to reward their passion by living up to growing expectations.

Enter a hero from another time. In 1989, in one of the most memorable Grey Cup games ever played, Kent Austin was Saskatchewan's quarterback, engineering the drive in the dying seconds against the Hamilton Tiger-Cats that led to Dave Ridgway's game-winning field goal, arguably the single greatest moment in Saskatchewan sports history.

Austin, long retired as a player, had no head coaching experience prior to the 2007 season, and had actually been fired from his job as the Toronto Argonauts' offensive coordinator the year before, allegedly because he failed to build a winning game plan around superstar running back Ricky Williams. Handed the reins to the Roughriders by general manager Eric Tillman, he quickly established himself as one of the brightest minds in the Canadian game. The 'Riders finished second in the west with a 12–6 record, edged the Calgary Stampeders at home in the semifinal, then upset the B.C. Lions in Vancouver in the western final, to earn their first Grey Cup trip since a longshot bid against Doug Flutie's Argonauts in 1997.

In 2007, for a rare instance in Saskatchewan football history, they arrived at Toronto's Rogers Centre – the site of that glorious 1989 triumph – as clear-cut favourites over the Bombers. That was in large part due to the fact that Winnipeg's starting quarterback Kevin Glenn, coming off a stellar season, had broken his arm in the fourth quarter of the eastern final victory over the Argos. Glenn's back up, Ryan Dinwiddie, was thrust into starting his first game, ever, and in the most difficult circumstances imaginable.

QUARTERBACKS

THE MAJOR THEMES OF the 2007 Grey Cup were the state of each club's quarterbacking heading into the contest, and the long Grey Cup droughts of each club. The Roughriders had had just two wins, and none since 1989, while the Blue Bombers, who had ten wins to their credit, hadn't won since 1990. So, relief was on the way for one team, but which would it be? Winnipeg, on the hunt for its eleventh title overall, and aiming to enrich its long history of success, seemed like the better bet.

Both teams revolved around the fortunes of their quarterbacks, with Saskatchewan led by the CFL's Most Outstanding Player that season, Kerry Joseph. A career-best 5,117 passing yards were enough for Winnipeg's Kevin Glenn to be named as the Most Outstanding Player in the east. The two would not meet in the Grey Cup, however; late in the East Division final, Glenn suffered a broken arm that put him out and thrust the starter's job on CFL rookie Ryan Dinwiddie, who had thrown just 24 passes during the regular season, largely in a mop-up role. In all of Grey Cup history, no quarterback had ever started a game with so little experience.

Dinwiddie did a creditable job in the first half, completing 8 of his first 13 passes, and Saskatchewan was only able to lead 10–7 on the strength of two late scores, one of which came off the first of three interceptions of Dinwiddie passes. The Bomber pivot bounced back, however, and his 50-yard touchdown strike to Derick Armstrong delivered the game's longest offensive gain and evened the score at 13.

Kerry Joseph overcame a slow start to engineer two second-half scoring drives as Saskatchewan gradually took control in Glenn's absence, which the Bombers keenly felt. That 13 of the 'Riders' 23 points came after Winnipeg turnovers highlights how much the Bombers missed Glenn. James Johnson's third and final interception of a Dinwiddie pass attempt was a Grey Cup record, and it allowed the 'Riders to run out the clock and achieve their third Cup victory – after a wait of almost two decades.

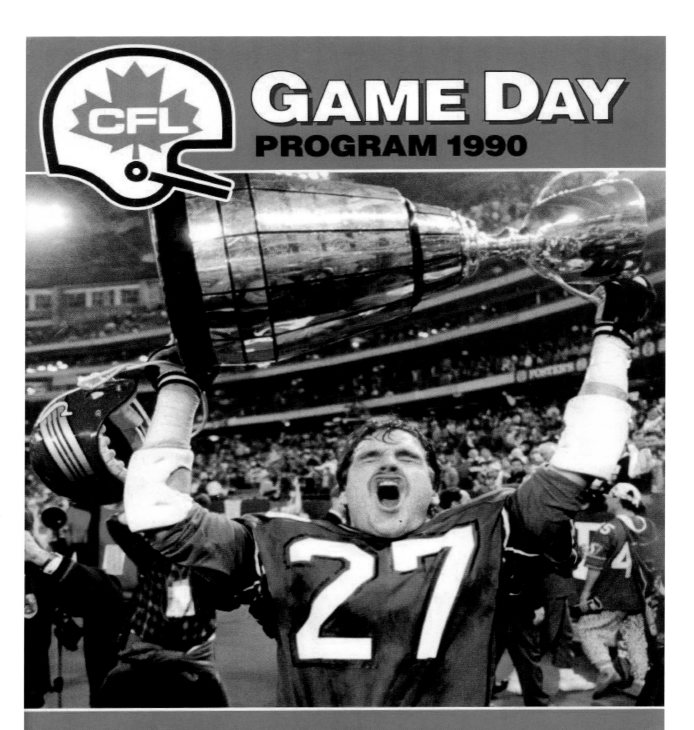

GAME DAY
PROGRAM 1990

SASKATCHEWAN vs. EDMONTON

The 'Riders' Jermese Jones celebrates their 2007 win.

Dinwiddie turned out to be part of the story – he had his moments, but the three interceptions he threw, one of which was returned for a touchdown by the game's MVP, defensive back James Johnson, were crucial to the outcome. Still, it was Saskatchewan's tough and aggressive defence and wide-open offence that ruled the day.

Fittingly, the clinching touchdown in a 23–19 victory came on a pass from quarterback Kerry Joseph to receiver Andy Fantuz, a graduate of the University of Western Ontario who, like Reed and Lancaster and Austin before him, would be adopted by the Green 'Rider faithful as one of their own. (Fantuz's popularity in the province would soar so much that they'd start selling a breakfast cereal with his picture on the box – Fantuz Flakes – as a way to raise money for charity. It flew off the shelves.)

The celebration of Saskatchewan's third Grey Cup victory, within the province and among those inside and outside of Canada who had a soft spot in their hearts for the place and the team, was one for the ages.

Austin departed after that single season of coaching, leaving for a job at his alma mater, the University of Mississippi, but this Grey Cup wasn't a one-off. It wasn't a fluke. More like a declaration.

FORWARD THINKING

THE BRAND OF FOOTBALL played in Canada up to 1928 was largely an offshoot of the game of rugby brought over from Great Britain. It evolved quickly from pure rugby into "rugby football," as evidenced by the original name of today's CFL East Division: the Interprovincial Rugby Football Union, or IRFU. Of course, the very innovation that makes football exciting, the forward pass, has always been a game-stopper in rugby, where it is illegal.

Most accounts of how the pass entered Grey Cup history point to 1931 and the Montreal AAA Winged Wheelers. Warren Stevens tossed a pass to Kenny Grant, and they combined for a 37-yard scoring play in the third quarter on the way to a 22–0 win over the Regina Roughriders. It is notable that Stevens was not the Wheelers' quarterback but a "flying wing," a player who could switch, or "fly," between what we would now call the forward line and the backfield and who was often the better passer in those days. (Similarly, Joe "King" Krol, primarily a halfback, did much of the passing for Hamilton and Toronto teams in the 1940s.)

The first actual use of the forward pass in Grey Cup play had come two years earlier, in 1929, by Regina and the Tigers at the old Hamilton AAA Grounds. The first attempt was thrown by Regina's Jersey Jack Campbell to Jerry Erskine. Reports of the day indicated that the Roughriders' 11 passes gained them around 100 yards and that Hamilton, a very conservative and traditional team, tried just one that went for a TD but was called back for being inside the 25-yard line. The Tigers contended that it should have been the first-ever Cup TD pass. Afterwards, one reporter commented: "The pass is alright and serviceable in Canadian football. The CRU will legislate the pass into all series for next fall." The prediction turned out to be premature – forward passing was not allowed in the 1930 Grey Cup.

The final hurdle that the slow introduction of this new form of "aerial" attack had to endure came in the form of the initial passing rules and restrictions – for instance, any passes falling incomplete were treated as a live ball! Had that rule not changed later on, how much passing would there be in today's game?

And though they would lose close, heartbreaking championship games to the Montreal Alouettes in 2009 and 2010 (the phrase "13th man" will forever after have unpleasant connotations in Regina), the Roughriders were now a force to reckon with. Gone forever were the sacrificial lambs.

Saskatchewan is a big space with a sparse population – five times as many people live in Toronto and environs as in the entire province – and Regina is the smallest city in the country to have its own big-league team. Though football has been played there for more than a century and Regina clubs were among the first western teams to challenge for the Grey Cup, and though the 'Riders were part of the modern Canadian Football League from its inception, for long stretches of their history they were hopelessly out of contention.

All the same, any conversation about the culture and lore of Canadian football will very quickly turn to Saskatchewan. Any list of its most beloved players will be topped by the quarterback and running back tandem of "the Little General," Ron Lancaster, and George Reed – one from Pennsylvania, one from Washington – who are as firmly fixed in this country's sports pantheon as any homegrown hockey player.

Beyond that, as the sports world changes, and the larger world changes, there's a natural tendency to look towards Regina and see the game as it was, pure, simple, and unspoiled. The Roughriders are owned, figuratively and literally, by the community in which they make their home. They represent not just a city but an entire province. Their fans travel enormous distances, sometimes in awful prairie weather, just for the privilege of sitting in the stadium that was long known as Taylor Field.

In tough times – and there have been tough times – the people of Saskatchewan did whatever was necessary to keep the team alive. Those stories of season's tickets paid for with bushels of wheat can't all be apocryphal. Once, it took a telethon to cover the Roughriders' debts and keep the club solvent. People reached deep not just in Saskatchewan but all across the country, because a little, sentimental piece of every CFL fan's heart resided there, because Saskatchewan was everyone's second-favourite team (unless you lived in Winnipeg). Perpetual underdogs, passionately supported, the "national team" from a society as distinct as they come, the Green 'Riders are unlike anything else in Canadian sport. That's why, on the two occasions the Grey Cup has been staged in Regina, it was at least a little bit like bringing the big game to Brigadoon.

Regina's legendary Taylor Field.

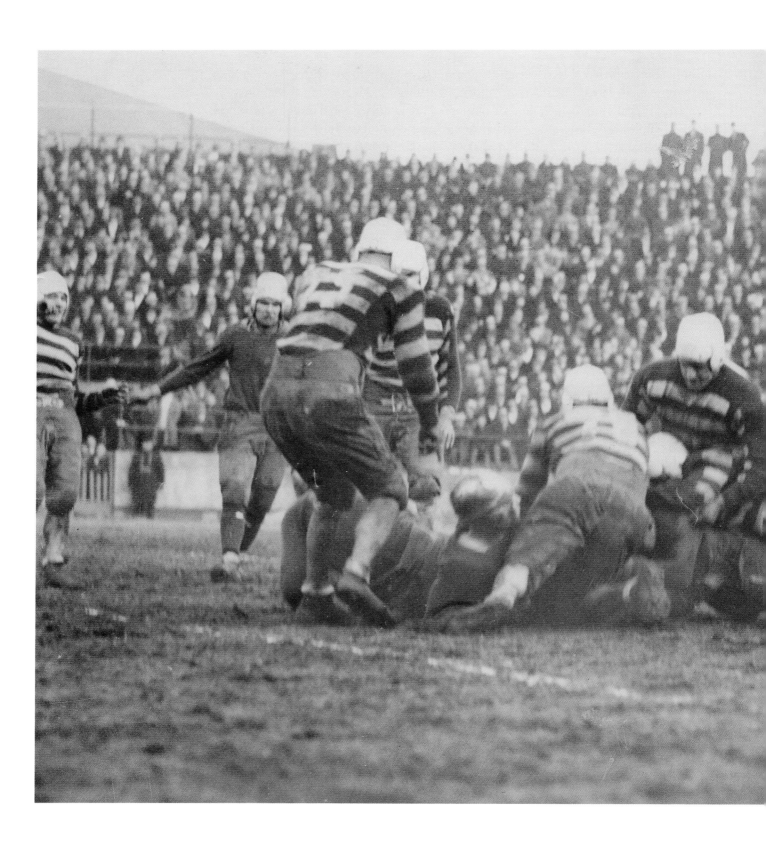

This is also true: though there have been precious few championships for 'Rider fans to celebrate, on the occasions when their teams got to the big game, something dramatic has invariably happened. That was the case even with the first Regina Grey Cup team in 1923, which suffered that 54–0 beating.

The eastern sports press was unsparing in its contempt.

"Regina Drubbed in Farcical Final" was the headline in *The Globe*.

"They were dazed, dumfounded and drubbed without being able to raise their hands in self defence. Outclassed in every position . . . they gave a woeful exhibition . . . the visitors appeared to have a lot of natural ability, but lacked plays, strategy and experience."

Another newspaper report was made up simply of short, sarcastic stabs at the visitors. Among the more choice items: "Next year's dominion final should be a handicap affair. . . The eastern champions should be compelled to spot the western representatives at least twenty points. . . . Saturday's game looked like a herd of elephants playing cross-tag with a flock of jack rabbits. . . . Western football tactics, as exemplified by the Regina team, are prehistoric. . . . That Regina team certainly took a swell photo."

Amid the snarkiness, it was noted in press reports that the crowd in Toronto actually got behind the 'Riders, even as the hopelessness of their cause became apparent. It's the first recorded example of what would become a continuing theme: Saskatchewan as sentimental favourites.

Undaunted, the men from the prairies kept right on accepting the challenge – and kept right on losing. Six times between 1928 and 1934, the Roughriders emerged as the dominant team in the west, and six times they failed to win the Grey Cup – by a cumulative score of 122–27.

Though the results were consistent, those games were hardly uneventful. The 1929 Grey Cup, for instance, in which the 'Riders played the Hamilton Tigers on a day

The Argos take on the Roughriders in 1933.

Between 1928–34 the Roughriders would fail to make the Grey Cup game only once, though they lost every time. Seen here playing in 1930 against Toronto's Balmy Beach.

so terrible that only a hundred or so fans were in the stands at the HAAA Grounds for kickoff, marked the occasion of the first forward pass ever thrown in the championship game. The rule book was rather fluid in those days, as the game was quickly evolving. The newly legalized forward pass first caught on in the west, and it would be the Roughriders' best hope against a powerful Hamilton team.

"While Regina gave a fine exhibition of the art of forward-passing, probably the best yet seen in Eastern Canada, it could not be said that their gains made up for their losses," M. J. Rodden of *The Globe* reported. "Most of the Regina passes were short ones, and they were scientifically made by [Jersey Jack] Campbell. Tigers had practiced the play for only three days, and hadn't taken it seriously at any time. Much confusion seemed to exist among players and officials regarding

uniform interpretation." (In fact, Hamilton's only forward pass of the game went for a touchdown, but it was called back because the officials ruled that it had been thrown inside the Regina 25-yard line – thus violating the existing rules. Problem was, because of all the snow, no one really knew for sure where the yard lines were.)

"Tigers were (confused) when Campbell, a southpaw, dropped back from snap in the last thirty minutes of the game and commenced to hurl the ball far and wide," Lou Marsh wrote in the *Toronto Star*, describing what would come to be known as zone and man-to-man defence. "The Bengals had absolutely no defence for the play. Instead of working an area defence for the forward pass they tried to cover up the men they thought were going to receive the ball, and the result was that Prairie Patrol made ground on every pass they tried. Out of twelve or fifteen forward passes the boys from the Saskatchewan Capital completed at least ten without a bobble – and on the others they held the Big Cats for a substantial gain. It is hard to believe that story which came out of the west to the effect that the Roughriders had only used the forward pass twice before this season. It looked like a great play – against Tigers. It certainly was spectacular."

For all of the new play's shock value, the Tigers won relatively comfortably, 14–3.

In the 1931 game, it was the 'Riders' opponents, the Montreal Winged Wheelers, who completed the first touchdown pass in Grey Cup history, en route to a 22–0

DYNASTIES AND DROUGHTS

EACH ERA OF CANADIAN football has had its stars, those whose talents reflected the most admired skills of their day. Over the years these standouts have ranged from the rough-and-tumble "inside wing" plungers of the 1930s, such as Brian Timmis and Dave Sprague, and the talented two-way players of the 1950s, like Jackie Parker and Hal Patterson, to the more recent passing heroes, including Doug Flutie and Anthony Calvillo. In 1909, the premier gridiron hero was Hugh Gall, renowned for his "aerial" skills.

Today, the concept of an "aerial attack" is easily understood as referring to the passing game. But in 1909, the forward pass was not yet legal. Instead, punting ability was prized over all other skills – even above running with the ball. In Hugh Gall's era, then, the aerial attack meant the kicking game, and it was his forte. He could kick well with either foot, and would kick on any down in an attempt to gain valuable field position. Scores

in football were low in those days, and the "single," or "rouge," was more common than any other scoring method.

As a halfback for the University of Toronto and later for Parkdale, Gall played in three Grey Cups and was twice on the winning team. He was the first player to score a point in a Grey Cup game (after a 65-yard punt and rouge) and added that day's first touchdown as well on a five-yard end run. Gall's eight singles in 1909 remain the record to this day. So the game we recognize as the first to award the ancient trophy featured a man who – despite the appearance of being much older than his years – probably could not be outkicked by any player of any age or era.

The best way to describe Gall's "game" and persona may be found in 1910 Grey Cup accounts: "As Simpson was the main works on the Tiger back line, so was Gall for Varsity. The young player, with the old man's face . . . booted the pig-skin in the style that has given him the reputation of being Canada's greatest." In 1913, after Gall's final Grey Cup appearance, *The Hamilton Spectator* assessed him as follows: "Parkdale was Hugh Gall and a dozen Hugh Galls couldn't beat this team."

No discussion of this great Hall of Famer would be complete without pausing to consider an oddity of the Canadian game: the average distance that punts travel has changed little, if any, since Gall's day.

The Edmonton Eskimos won five consecutive Grey Cups between 1978 and 1982.

win over the western champions. The 1934 game saw the last drop kicks for points in a Grey Cup – by the Sarnia Imperials, who beat the Riders 20–12.

In 1951, Saskatchewan made their first Grey Cup appearance in the modern era of Canadian football, and their first wearing the now-famous green and white. The team's colours had at different times been gold and purple, blue and white, and, for most of its early history, red and black. The first green uniforms arrived in 1948, after one of the club's executives found them at a bargain price in a Chicago surplus store. That was the same year that the Regina Roughriders were rechristened the Saskatchewan Roughriders.

DYNASTIES	FROM	TO	YEARS	GAMES	WON	OF NOTE
Edmonton Eskimos	1973	1982	10	9	6	Won five in a row, 1978–82
Hamilton Tiger-Cats	1957	1967	11	9	4	Played in five in a row, 1961–65
Montreal Alouettes	2000	2010	11	8	3	Five games in six years, 2005–10
Winnipeg Blue Bombers	1957	1965	9	6	4	Bud Grant era
Toronto Argonauts	1945	1952	8	5	5	Undefeated in five games
Calgary Stampeders	1991	2001	11	6	3	Wally Buono era

APPEARANCE DROUGHTS	FROM	TO	YEARS	GAMES	WON	OF NOTE
Ottawa Rough Riders/Renegades	1982	Today	19	0	0	Last game in 1981, vs. Edmonton
Calgary Stampeders	1950	1967	18	0	0	Lost in 1949 and 1968
Toronto Argonauts	1953	1970	18	0	0	Won in 1952, lost in 1971
British Columbia Lions	1965	1982	18	0	0	Won in 1964, lost in 1983
Winnipeg Blue Bombers	1966	1983	18	0	0	Lost in 1965, won in 1984
Regina/Saskatchewan Roughriders	1935	1950	16	0	0	Lost in 1934, lost in 1951

Historical notes:

Hamilton teams during war years of 1942–44 not included.

Edmonton did not appear in the Grey Cup from 1923 to 1951, but operated in only 12 of those seasons.

The CFL had a team based in Ottawa from 1958 until 1996, and from 2002 to 2005.

WIN DROUGHTS	FROM	TO	YEARS	GAMES	WON	OF NOTE
Regina/Saskatchewan Roughriders	1921	1965	45	8	0	First franchise win in 1966
Toronto Argonauts	1953	1982	30	2	0	Lost 1971,1982; won 1983
Ottawa Rough Riders/Renegades	1976	Today	24	1	0	Lost in 1981, last win 1976
Calgary Stampeders	1949	1970	22	3	0	Lost in 1949, 1968, 1970
Winnipeg Blue Bombers	1963	1983	21	1	0	Lost in 1965, won in 1984

Historical notes:

Wartime years of 1942–44 not included.

For Regina/Saskatchewan, 1921 was chosen as the start of this range because it was the first year in which western clubs were invited to play in the Grey Cup.

What was to that point the best-ever Saskatchewan team lost in crushing fashion, 21–14 to the Ottawa Rough Riders, in part because much of their squad – including star quarterback Glenn "Dobber" Dobbs – was hobbled by injury.

"We'll be back next year," Dobbs said to his centre, Red Ettinger, who needed painkilling shots around his injured ribs just to play in the game. "We'll be back and it'll be different."

They would be back – but not for a long, long time.

The 1951 game was also notable for the beginning of another great Grey Cup tradition. In 1948, the Calgary Stampeders and their travelling band of fans had turned the atmosphere of staid old Toronto upside down when they arrived to watch their team win its first Canadian championship. In 1951, the Saskatchewan fans followed suit.

"An indication of the great love of football in the west is the safari of Saskatchewan citizens which reached its eastern destination yesterday," Jim Vipond wrote in *The Globe and Mail.* "The long trainloads of gaily bedecked supporters complete with chuck wagons, horses, pretty gals, 15,000 loaves of bread and a special green ink edition of the Regina *Leader-Post.*"

Go to the Grey Cup now, and whichever teams are competing, you can bet that the streets will be filled with people dressed in green. They may not bring the loaves of bread anymore – but the Rider Nation brings the party.

The great 'Rider teams of the 1960s and 1970s made five trips to the Grey Cup, and again, even when they lost. In 1967, they were shut down entirely by a Hamilton defence that may have been the best of all time, 24–1. In 1969, it was the final game of Russ Jackson's stellar career, and his Ottawa Rough Riders prevailed. In 1972, Ian Sunter of the Tiger-Cats hit a field goal on the final play to clinch a dramatic victory for the home team at Ivor Wynne Stadium. And after what happened in the 1976 Grey Cup, Saskatchewanians would be haunted by "The Catch." Everyone knew that Ottawa's Tom Clements was going to throw the ball to Tony Gabriel in the game's final minute, but still the western 'Riders couldn't stop it.

Bookending those games, were two epic victories that will live on in Saskatchewan sporting lore.

Returning to the championship for the first time since 1951, the 1966 'Riders were a powerhouse on both sides of the ball, with Reed, a season removed from being named the league's most outstanding player, very close to his peak.

Back in 1963, the Roughriders had announced their renaissance by beating the

Calgary Stampeders in a two-game, total-points semifinal after losing the first game 35–9 in Calgary. So despondent were 'Riders fans that few showed up for the second game on a frosty winter day. But as the miracle unfolded, they left their houses and headed en masse for Taylor Field. By the time the teams came out for the third quarter, the stadium was packed, and the 'Riders rolled to an unlikely victory, taking the game 39–12, and the two-game set 48–47 (they went on to lose two out of three games to the B.C Lions in the western final).

Three years later, facing Jackson and the Rough Riders at Empire Stadium in Vancouver, they were finally ready to accomplish what no Saskatchewan team had done before. After playing a close, back-and-forth first half, the Roughriders took control after the break. A touchdown pass from Lancaster to Hugh Campbell put them ahead, and fittingly Reed sealed the victory with a 31-yard touchdown run straight up the middle. The victory celebration that followed, and the weeks during which the Cup visited what seemed like every crossroads village in every corner of the vast province, made that one long prairie winter a little bit easier to endure.

After Lancaster and Reed retired, the Roughriders fell on hard times. During one stretch lasting into the 1980s, they missed the playoffs eleven years in a row. Lancaster returned as head coach, but the magic that he possessed as a quarterback simply didn't translate. (It would, eventually, but not until he moved on to coaching jobs in Edmonton and Hamilton.) Those were the years of near bankruptcy, of

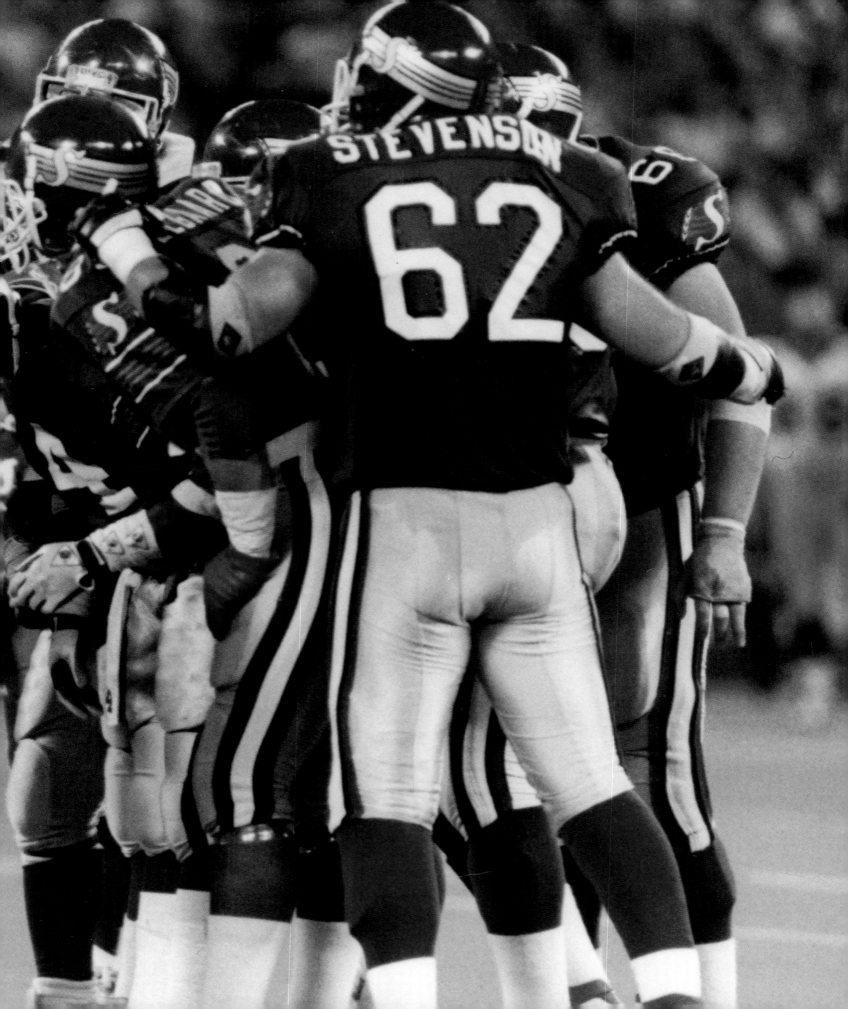

telethons, and of faint hopes. With no wealthy private owner to pay the bills, the community that owned the club had to dig into its own pockets to keep it alive.

The team that finally emerged at the end of that dark era was one of the best in 'Riders history, with Austin as its star quarterback, receiver Don Narcisse as his favourite target, and a kicker named Dave Ridgway – "Robokicker," they nicknamed him, for his great consistency, because he seemed to almost never miss.

In 1989, the 'Riders finished third in the west, with just a 9–9 record, and then beat both Calgary and heavily favoured Edmonton – a 16–2 team that year – on the road in the playoffs to advance to the first Grey Cup played at Toronto's then brand-new SkyDome. The opponents were familiar, from 1972 and 1967, and from all the way back in 1928, 1929 and 1932: the Hamilton Tiger-Cats, champions of the east, Grey Cup winners three years earlier, an experienced and explosive squad quarterbacked by Mike Kerrigan.

Both teams had terrific defences, but you wouldn't have known it that day under the dome. On the fast indoor field, offensive records fell by the wayside. As it soon became clear that whichever team had the ball last would probably win.

Forty-four seconds before the finish, it looked like the Ticats had forced overtime, when Tony Champion made a spectacular touchdown catch while falling backwards. But Austin had other ideas. Following the kickoff, he calmly and precisely marched the Roughriders into field goal range, setting Ridgway up for a 35-yard attempt on the second to last play of the fourth quarter. Of course he wouldn't miss. Final score: Saskatchewan 43, Hamilton 40.

"It's funny how it works out," Ridgway said afterward. "They played a great football game and it comes down to a skinny little guy with a clean uniform. But that's what they pay me for."

Was it the best Grey Cup ever?

Through ninety-nine often-spectacular games, that bar has been set very high. But you know that in one football-loving province of this country, there isn't even a debate.

George Reed (right) played his entire career with the 'Riders and is considered the greatest running back in CFL history. Pictured here with Hugh Campbell.

EPILOGUE

INTO THE FUTURE

Through more than a century, through two world wars, through changing times and changing tastes and in an evolving nation, the Grey Cup has been a constant, Canada's great autumn ritual.

Once, it was just a football game – and not even the biggest one of the year. Once, it belonged only to central Canada. Once, before the fans from Calgary took things into their own hands, it came and went and was defined only by what happened between kickoff and the final whistle. And for a short while, the truth is that its continuity, its future, seemed anything but secure.

But now, as the 100th Grey Cup is played in Toronto in 2012 – amid the largest, most ambitious, most spectacular festival ever staged around the championship game – it is clearer than ever that we have come to value, to cherish, and to celebrate that which is uniquely ours.

Canadian football is a pure product of our country and of our culture. It is *our* game, not someone else's, played under our rules on our field. Somehow, across the decades, for more than a century, it has retained its special character, even as so much in sport and elsewhere has become homogenized.

Hockey gets most of the attention as our "national" sport, but the Swedes and Finns and Czechs and Russians and more than a few Americans embrace it with nearly equal passion. And though the Stanley Cup and the Grey Cup share much in terms of their origins, the hockey championship long ago became the property of the National Hockey League, a business operated out of the United States, with the vast majority of its franchises located outside of our borders.

But for the brief American expansion in the early 1990s, dictated by necessity, the Canadian Football League has been ours and ours alone; nowhere else on the planet do they play three-down, twelve-man, 110-yard football. And nowhere else is there the true equivalent of the Grey Cup game, with its long history, its homey, small-town character, its status as an unofficial national holiday.

It is organic. It wasn't invented in a boardroom. It wasn't the product of marketing research. It's not a *brand*. Like the trophy itself, it has been through highs and lows, has accumulated a few dents along the way, but every year, with a little polish and elbow grease, it shines anew.

Not everyone in Canada is a football fan. But on Grey Cup Sunday, so many of us sit back, find a rooting interest, and revel – even if only for that one day of the calendar year – in the same game our parents and grandparents and great-grandparents enjoyed.

And what does all of that mean in an era in which the entire planet, including every sporting event from everywhere at any time, is instantly accessible through one gadget or another?

Well, it could be that it means more than it ever did.

There was a time when it was easy to take the Grey Cup for granted. It came along every fall, always right on schedule, so comfortable, so familiar, that it might get lost in all that was new and different and novel and of the moment. Yesterday's news, in other words.

But something interesting has been happening as so many of those familiar lines of demarcation between countries and cultures have become blurred or erased altogether. We Canadians seem to want and need those things that remind us of their Canadian-ness – those touchstones, those traditions, those opportunities to wrap ourselves in the flag and celebrate what is ours and ours alone. Looking back at the 2010 Winter Olympics in Vancouver and Whistler, it's clear that that longing is what so much of the ecstatic, patriotic celebration was all about.

And that's why the Grey Cup not only endures but thrives as we head deeper into the twenty-first century. That's why it doesn't just have a glorious, colourful, idiosyncratic past, but also a bright future. This sport, invented more than 150 years ago, and this game, about to be played for the 100th time, are part of what makes us us, what defines on this ever-shrinking planet. It's part of what links our Canadian tribe. Whether our families have been in this country for generations or arrived yesterday, the Grey Cup is one of the answers to the ever-tricky question: "So, what is it that makes you a Canadian?"

Which isn't to say that everyone who piles into the Spirit of Edmonton room or Riderville – who knows what "Oskee Wee Wee" means – who can holler a mournful "Arrrrrr-goooos" or belt out "Green Is the Colour" – who loves their Stamps or their Lions or their Bombers or their Als – will be thinking about profound issues of cultural autonomy when this year's Grey Cup kicks off at Rogers Centre.

No – they'll just be there for the game, and for the party.

But that's the beauty of ritual, isn't it? A grand coming together, a powerful collective experience, a pillar of national identity, and a heck of a good time – all rolled into one.

Yes, that's the Grey Cup.

APPENDICES

THE GREY CUP - 1909 TO 2011
YEAR-BY-YEAR RESULTS

YEAR	NO	DATE	SITE	STADIUM	ATTEND	CHAMPION	PTS	RUNNER-UP	PTS	WINNING COACH	LOSING COACH
2011	99	Nov 27	Vancouver	B.C. Place	54,313	B.C. Lions	34	Winnipeg	23	Wally Buono	Paul LaPolice
2010	98	Nov 28	Edmonton	Commonwealth	63,317	Montreal	21	Saskatch'n	18	Marc Trestman	Ken Miller
2009	97	Nov 29	Calgary	McMahon	46,020	Montreal	28	Saskatch'n	27	Marc Trestman	Ken Miller
2008	96	Nov 23	Montreal	Olympic	66,308	Calgary	22	Montreal	14	John Hufnagel	Marc Trestman
2007	95	Nov 25	Toronto	Rogers Centre	52,230	Saskatch'n	23	Winnipeg	19	Kent Austin	Doug Berry
2006	94	Nov 19	Winnipeg	Canad Inns	44,786	B.C. Lions	25	Montreal	14	Wally Buono	Jim Popp
2005	93	Nov 27	Vancouver	B.C. Place	59,157	Edmonton	38	Montreal	35	Dan Maciocia	Don Matthews
2004	92	Nov 21	Ottawa	Frank Clair	51,242	Toronto	27	B.C. Lions	19	Mike Clemons	Wally Buono
2003	91	Nov 16	Regina	Taylor Field	50,909	Edmonton	34	Montreal	22	Tom Higgins	Don Matthews
2002	90	Nov 24	Edmonton	Commonwealth	62,531	Montreal	25	Edmonton	16	Don Matthews	Tom Higgins
2001	89	Nov 25	Montreal	Olympic	65,255	Calgary	27	Winnipeg	19	Wally Buono	Dave Ritchie
2000	88	Nov 26	Calgary	McMahon	43,822	B.C. Lions	28	Montreal	26	Steve Buratto	Charlie Taaffe
1999	87	Nov 28	Vancouver	B.C. Place	45,118	Hamilton	32	Calgary	21	Ron Lancaster	Wally Buono
1998	86	Nov 22	Winnipeg	Winnipeg	34,157	Calgary	26	Hamilton	24	Wally Buono	Ron Lancaster
1997	85	Nov 16	Edmonton	Commonwealth	60,431	Toronto	47	Saskatch'n	23	Don Matthews	Jim Daley
1996	84	Nov 24	Hamilton	Ivor Wynne	38,595	Toronto	43	Edmonton	37	Don Matthews	Ron Lancaster
1995	83	Nov 19	Regina	Taylor Field	52,564	Baltimore	37	Calgary	20	Don Matthews	Wally Buono
1994	82	Nov 27	Vancouver	B.C. Place	55,097	B.C. Lions	26	Baltimore	23	Dave Ritchie	Don Matthews
1993	81	Nov 28	Calgary	McMahon	50,035	Edmonton	33	Winnipeg	23	Ron Lancaster	Cal Murphy
1992	80	Nov 29	Toronto	SkyDome	45,863	Calgary	24	Winnipeg	10	Wally Buono	Urban Bowman
1991	79	Nov 24	Winnipeg	Winnipeg	51,985	Toronto	36	Calgary	21	Adam Rita	Wally Buono
1990	78	Nov 25	Vancouver	B.C. Place	46,968	Winnipeg	50	Edmonton	11	Mike Riley	Joe Faragalli
1989	77	Nov 26	Toronto	SkyDome	54,088	Saskatch'n	43	Hamilton	40	John Gregory	Al Bruno
1988	76	Nov 27	Ottawa	Landsdowne	50,604	Winnipeg	22	B.C. Lions	21	Mike Riley	Larry Donovan
1987	75	Nov 29	Vancouver	B.C. Place	59,478	Edmonton	38	Toronto	36	Joe Faragalli	Bob O'Billovich
1986	74	Nov 30	Vancouver	B.C. Place	59,579	Hamilton	39	Edmonton	15	Al Bruno	Jack Parker
1985	73	Nov 24	Montreal	Olympic	56,723	B.C. Lions	37	Hamilton	24	Don Matthews	Al Bruno
1984	72	Nov 18	Edmonton	Commonwealth	60,081	Winnipeg	47	Hamilton	17	Cal Murphy	Al Bruno

YEAR	NO	DATE	SITE	STADIUM	ATTEND	CHAMPION	PTS	RUNNER-UP	PTS	WINNING COACH	LOSING COACH
1983	71	Nov 27	Vancouver	B.C. Place	59,345	Toronto	18	B.C. Lions	17	Bob O'Billovich	Don Matthews
1982	70	Nov 28	Toronto	Exhibition	54,741	Edmonton	32	Toronto	16	Hugh Campbell	Bob O'Billovich
1981	69	Nov 22	Montreal	Olympic	52,478	Edmonton	26	Ottawa	23	Hugh Campbell	George Brancato
1980	68	Nov 23	Toronto	Exhibition	54,661	Edmonton	48	Hamilton	10	Hugh Campbell	John Payne
1979	67	Nov 25	Montreal	Olympic	65,113	Edmonton	17	Montreal	9	Hugh Campbell	Joe Scannella
1978	66	Nov 26	Toronto	Exhibition	54,695	Edmonton	20	Montreal	13	Hugh Campbell	Joe Scannella
1977	65	Nov 27	Montreal	Olympic	68,205	Montreal	41	Edmonton	6	Marv Levy	Hugh Campbell
1976	64	Nov 28	Toronto	Exhibition	53,389	Ottawa	23	Saskatch'n	20	George Brancato	John Payne
1975	63	Nov 23	Calgary	McMahon	32,454	Edmonton	9	Montreal	8	Ray Jauch	Marv Levy
1974	62	Nov 24	Vancouver	Empire	34,450	Montreal	20	Edmonton	7	Marv Levy	Ray Jauch
1973	61	Nov 25	Toronto	Exhibition	36,475	Ottawa	22	Edmonton	18	Jack Gotta	Ray Jauch
1972	60	Dec 3	Hamilton	Ivor Wynne	35,950	Hamilton	13	Saskatch'n	10	Jerry Williams	Dave Skrien
1971	59	Nov 28	Vancouver	Empire	34,584	Calgary	14	Toronto	11	Jim Duncan	Leo Cahill
1970	58	Nov 28	Toronto	Exhibition	32,669	Montreal	23	Calgary	10	Sam Etcheverry	Jim Duncan
1969	57	Nov 30	Montreal	Autostade	33,172	Ottawa	29	Saskatch'n	11	Frank Clair	Eagle Keys
1968	56	Nov 30	Toronto	Exhibition	33,185	Ottawa	24	Calgary	21	Frank Clair	Jerry Williams
1967	55	Dec 2	Ottawa	Landsdowne	31,407	Hamilton	24	Saskatch'n	1	Ralph Sazio	Eagle Keys
1966	54	Nov 26	Vancouver	Empire	32,344	Saskatch'n	29	Ottawa	14	Eagle Keys	Frank Clair
1965	53	Nov 27	Toronto	Exhibition	32,655	Hamilton	22	Winnipeg	16	Ralph Sazio	Bud Grant
1964	52	Nov 28	Toronto	Exhibition	32,655	B.C. Lions	34	Hamilton	24	Dave Skrien	Ralph Sazio
1963	51	Nov 30	Vancouver	Empire	36,465	Hamilton	21	B.C. Lions	10	Ralph Sazio	Dave Skrien
1962	50	Dec 1	Toronto	Exhibition	32,655	Winnipeg	28	Hamilton	27	Bud Grant	Jim Trimble
		Dec 2	(Completion of final 9:29)		(approx. attendance for Dec 2 was 15,000; no scoring final 9:29)						
1961	49	Dec 2	Toronto	Exhibition	36,592	Winnipeg	21	Hamilton	14	Bud Grant	Jim Trimble
1960	48	Nov 26	Vancouver	Empire	33,133	Ottawa	16	Edmonton	6	Frank Clair	Eagle Keys
1959	47	Nov 28	Toronto	Exhibition	34,426	Winnipeg	21	Hamilton	7	Bud Grant	Jim Trimble
1958	46	Nov 29	Vancouver	Empire	27,391	Winnipeg	35	Hamilton	28	Bud Grant	Jim Trimble
1957	45	Nov 30	Toronto	Varsity	27,425	Hamilton	32	Winnipeg	7	Jim Trimble	Bud Grant
1956	44	Nov 24	Toronto	Varsity	39,417	Edmonton	50	Montreal	27	Frank Ivy	Doug Walker
1955	43	Nov 26	Vancouver	Empire	27,301	Edmonton	34	Montreal	19	Frank Ivy	Doug Walker
1954	42	Nov 27	Toronto	Varsity	27,328	Edmonton	26	Montreal	25	Frank Ivy	Doug Walker
1953	41	Nov 28	Toronto	Varsity	27,313	Hamilton	12	Winnipeg	6	Carl Voyles	George Trafton
1952	40	Nov 29	Toronto	Varsity	27,391	Toronto	21	Edmonton	11	Frank Clair	Frank Filchock
1951	39	Nov 24	Toronto	Varsity	27,341	Ottawa	21	Saskatch'n	14	Clem Crowe	Harry Smith
1950	38	Nov 25	Toronto	Varsity	27,101	Toronto	13	Winnipeg	0	Frank Clair	Frank Larson
1949	37	Nov 26	Toronto	Varsity	20,087	Montreal	28	Calgary	15	Lew Hayman	Les Lear
1948	36	Nov 27	Toronto	Varsity	20,013	Calgary	12	Ottawa	7	Les Lear	Wally Masters
1947	35	Nov 29	Toronto	Varsity	18,885	Toronto	10	Winnipeg	9	Ted Morris	Jack West
1946	34	Nov 30	Toronto	Varsity	18,960	Toronto	28	Winnipeg	6	Ted Morris	Jack West
1945	33	Dec 1	Toronto	Varsity	18,660	Toronto	35	Winnipeg	0	Ted Morris	Bert Warwick
1944	32	Nov 25	Hamilton	HAAA Civic	3,871	Mtl Navy	7	Ham FWC	6	Glen Brown	Eddie McLean
1943	31	Nov 27	Toronto	Varsity	16,423	Ham FWC	23	Wpg RCAF	14	Brian Timmis	Reg Threlfall
1942	30	Dec 5	Toronto	Varsity	12,455	Tor RCAF	8	Wpg RCAF	5	Lew Hayman	Reg Threlfall
1941	29	Nov 29	Toronto	Varsity	19,065	Winnipeg	18	Ottawa	16	Reg Threlfall	Ross Trimble
1940	28	Nov 30	Toronto	Varsity	4,998	Ottawa	12	Balmy Bch	5	Ross Trimble	Alex Ponton
		Dec 7	Ottawa	Landsdowne	1,700	Ottawa	8	Balmy Bch	2		
1939	27	Dec 9	Ottawa	Landsdowne	11,737	Winnipeg	8	Ottawa	7	Reg Threlfall	Ross Trimble
1938	26	Dec 10	Toronto	Varsity	18,778	Toronto	30	Winnipeg	7	Lew Hayman	Reg Threlfall
1937	25	Dec 11	Toronto	Varsity	11,522	Toronto	4	Winnipeg	3	Lew Hayman	Bob Fritz
1936	24	Dec 5	Toronto	Varsity	5,883	Sarnia	26	Ottawa	20	Art Massucci	Billy Hughes
1935	23	Dec 7	Hamilton	HAAA Cricket G	6,405	Wpg 'Pegs	18	Hamilton T	12	Bob Fritz	Fred Veale

YEAR	NO	DATE	SITE	STADIUM	ATTEND	CHAMPION	PTS	RUNNER-UP	PTS	WINNING COACH	LOSING COACH
1934	22	Nov 24	Toronto	Varsity	8,900	Sarnia	20	Regina	12	Art Massucci	Greg Grassick
1933	21	Dec 9	Sarnia	Davis Field	2,751	Toronto	4	Sarnia	3	Lew Hayman	Pat Ouelette
1932	20	Dec 3	Hamilton	HAAA Cricket G	4,806	Hamilton T	25	Regina	6	Billy Hughes	Al Ritchie
1931	19	Dec 5	Montreal	Molson	5,112	Mtl AAA	22	Regina	0	Clary Foran	Al Ritchie
1930	18	Dec 6	Toronto	Varsity	3,914	Balmy Bch	11	Regina	6	Alex Ponton	Al Ritchie
1929	17	Nov 30	Hamilton	HAAA Cricket G	1,906	Hamilton T	14	Regina	3	Mike Rodden	Al Ritchie
1928	16	Dec 1	Hamilton	HAAA Cricket G	4,767	Hamilton T	30	Regina	0	Mike Rodden	Howie Milne
1927	15	Nov 26	Toronto	Varsity	13,676	Balmy Bch	9	Hamilton T	6	Dr. Harry Hobbs	Mike Rodden
1926	14	Dec 4	Toronto	Varsity	8,276	Ottawa	10	U of Tor	7	Dave McCann	Ron McPherson
1925	13	Dec 5	Ottawa	Landsdowne	6,900	Ottawa	24	Wpg TT	1	Dave McCann	Harold Roth
1924	12	Nov 29	Toronto	Varsity	5,978	Queen's U	11	Balmy Bch	3	Billy Hughes	M.Rodden/A.Buett
1923	11	Dec 1	Toronto	Varsity	8,629	Queen's U	54	Regina	0	Billy Hughes	Jack Ellis
1922	10	Dec 2	Kingston	Richardson	4,700	Queen's U	13	Edm Elks	1	Billy Hughes	Deacon White
1921	9	Dec 3	Toronto	Varsity	9,558	Toronto	23	Edm Esks	0	Sinc McEvenue	Deacon White
1920	8	Dec 4	Toronto	Varsity	10,088	U of Tor	16	Toronto	3	Laddie Cassels	Mike Rodden
1919		No playoff or Grey Cup game due to a rules dispute									
1916		No games were played due to WW I (1916-1918)									
1915	7	Nov 20	Toronto	Varsity	2,808	Hamilton T	13	Toronto RC	7	Liz Marriott	Ed Livingstone
1914	6	Dec 5	Toronto	Varsity	10,500	Toronto	14	U of Tor	2	Billy Foulds	Hugh Gall
1913	5	Nov 29	Hamilton	HAAA Cricket G	2,100	Hamilton T	44	Tor Park	2	Liz Marriott	Ed Livingstone
1912	4	Nov 30	Hamilton	HAAA Cricket G	5,337	Hamilton A	11	Toronto	4	Liz Marriott	Jack Newton
1911	3	Nov 25	Toronto	Varsity	13,687	U of T	14	Toronto	7	Dr. A.B. Wright	Billy Foulds
1910	2	Nov 26	Hamilton	HAAA Cricket G	12,000	U of T	16	Hamilton T	7	Harry Griffith	Seppi Dumoulin
1909	1	Dec 4	Toronto	Rosedale Fld	3,807	U of T	26	Tor Park	6	Harry Griffith	Ed Livingstone

(The 1940 Grey Cup was played as a two-game total points series)

ALL-TIME GREY CUP STANDINGS TO 2011

TEAM	G	W	L	LAST GAME	LAST WIN
Toronto Argonauts	21	15	6	2004	2004
Edmonton Eskimos-Elks	24	13	11	2005	2005
Winnipeg Blue Bombers/'Pegs	24	10	14	2011	1990
Ottawa Rough Riders-Senators	15	9	6	1981	1976
Hamilton Tiger-Cats	18	8	10	1999	1999
Montreal Alouettes	18	7	11	2010	2010
B.C. Lions	10	6	4	2011	2011
Calgary Stampeders	12	6	6	2008	2008
Regina-Saskatchewan Roughriders	18	3	15	2010	2007

TEAM	G	W	L	LAST GAME	LAST WIN
OTHER TEAMS:					
Hamilton Tigers	8	5	3	1932	1932
University of Toronto	6	4	2	1926	1920
Queen's University	3	3	0	1924	1924
Sarnia Imperials	3	2	1	1936	1936
Toronto Balmy Beach	4	2	2	1940	1930
Hamilton Alerts	1	1	0	1912	1912
Montreal AAA Winged Wheelers	1	1	0	1931	1931
Toronto RCAF Hurricanes	1	1	0	1942	1942
Montreal St. Hyacinthe-Don Navy	1	1	0	1944	1944
Hamilton Flying Wildcats	2	1	1	1944	1943
Baltimore CFL Stallions	2	1	1	1995	1995
Toronto Rowing Club	1	0	1	1915	
Winnipeg Tammany Tigers	1	0	1	1925	
Toronto Parkdale Canoe Club	2	0	2	1913	
Winnipeg RCAF Bombers	2	0	2	1943	

GREY CUP AWARDS

YEAR	MOST VALUABLE PLAYER	MOST VALUABLE CANADIAN
2011	Travis Lulay, QB, British Columbia	Andrew Harris, RB, British Columbia
2010	Jamel Richardson, WR, Montreal	Keith Shologan, DT, Saskatchewan
2009	Avon Cobourne, RB, Montreal	Ben Cahoon, SB, Montreal
2008	Henry Burris, QB, Calgary	Sandro DeAngelis, K, Calgary
2007	James Johnson, DB, Saskatchewan	Andy Fantuz, WR, Saskatchewan
2006	Dave Dickenson, QB, British Columbia	Paul McCallum, K/P, British Columbia
2005	Ricky Ray, QB, Edmonton	Mike Maurer, FB, Edmonton
2004	Damon Allen, QB, Toronto	Jason Clermont, SB, British Columbia
2003	Jason Tucker, WR, Edmonton	Ben Cahoon, SB, Montreal
2002	Anthony Calvillo, QB, Montreal	Pat Woodcock, WR, Montreal
2001	Marcus Crandell, QB, Calgary	Aldi Henry, DB, Calgary
2000	Robert Drummond, RB, British Columbia	Sean Millington, RB, British Columbia
1999	Danny McManus, QB, Hamilton	Mike Morreale, WR, Hamilton
1998	Jeff Garcia, QB, Calgary	Vince Danielsen, SB, Calgary
1997	Doug Flutie, QB, Toronto	Paul Masotti, WR, Toronto
1996	Doug Flutie, QB, Toronto	Mike Vanderjagt, K/P, Toronto
1995	Tracy Ham, QB, Baltimore	Dave Sapunjis, SB, Calgary
1994	Karl Anthony, DB, Baltimore	Lui Passaglia, K/P, British Columbia
1993	Damon Allen, QB, Edmonton	Sean Fleming, K, Edmonton
1992	Doug Flutie, QB, Calgary	Dave Sapunjis, SB, Calgary
1991	Raghib Ismail, RB, Toronto	Dave Sapunjis, SB, Calgary
1990	Tom Burgess, QB, Winnipeg (offence) Greg Battle, LB, Winnipeg (defence)	Warren Hudson, FB, Winnipeg
1989	Kent Austin, QB, Saskatchewan (offence) Chuck Klingbeil, DT, Saskatchewan (defence)	Dave Ridgway, K, Saskatchewan
1988	James Murphy, WR, Winnipeg (offence) Mike Gray, DT, Winnipeg (defence)	Bob Cameron, P, Winnipeg
1987	Damon Allen, QB, Edmonton (offence) Stewart Hill, DE, Edmonton (defence)	Mislon Jones, RB, Edmonton
1986	Mike Kerrigan, QB, Hamilton (offence) Grover Covington, DE, Hamilton (defence)	Paul Osbaldiston, K/P, Hamilton
1985	Roy Dwealt, QB, British Columbia (offence) James Parker, DE, British Columbia (defence)	Lui Passaglia, K/P, British Columbia
1984	Tom Clements, QB, Winnipeg (offence) Tyrone Jones, LB, Winnipeg (defence)	Sean Kehoe, RB, Winnipeg
1983	Joe Barnes, QB, Toronto (offence) Carl Brazley, DB, Toronto (defence)	Rick Klassen, DT, British Columbia
1982	Warren Moon, QB, Edmonton (offence) Dave Fennell, DT, Edmonton (defence)	Dave Fennell, DT, Edmonton
1981	J.C. Watts, QB, Ottawa (offence) John Glassford, LB, Ottawa (defence)	Neil Lumsden, RB, Edmonton
1980	Warren Moon, QB, Edmonton (offence) Dale Potter, LB, Edmonton (defence)	Dale Potter, LB, Edmonton
1979	David Green, RB, Montreal (offence) Tom Cousineau, LB, Montreal (defence)	Don Sweet, K, Montreal
1978	Tom Wilkinson, QB, Edmonton (offence) Dave Fennell, DT, Edmonton (defence)	Angelo Santucci, RB, Edmonton
1977	Sonny Wade, QB, Montreal (offence) Glen Weir, DT, Montreal (defence)	Don Sweet, K, Montreal

cont'd next page

GREY CUP COACHES

HEAD COACH	GAMES	WINS
Don Matthews	9	5
Wally Buono	9	5
Bud Grant	6	4
Frank Clair	6	5
Hugh Campbell	6	5
Mike Rodden	5	2
Billy Hughes	5	4
Reg Threlfall	5	2
Lew Hayman	5	5
Jim Trimble	5	1
Al Ritchie	4	0
Ralph Sazio	4	3
Eagle Keys	4	1
Al Bruno	4	1
Ron Lancaster	4	2

YEAR	MOST VALUABLE PLAYER	MOST VALUABLE CANADIAN
1976	Tom Clements, QB, Ottawa (offence) Cleveland Vann, LB, Saskatchewan (defence)	Tony Gabriel, TE, Ottawa
1975	Steve Ferrughelli, RB, Montreal (offence) Lewis Cook, DB, Montreal (defence)	Dave Cutler, K, Edmonton
1974	Sonny Wade, QB, Montreal (offence) Junior Ah You, DE, Montreal (defence)	Don Sweet, K, Montreal
1973	Charlie Brandon, DT, Ottawa	Garry Lefebvre, WR/P, Edmonton
1972	Chuck Ealey, QB, Hamilton	Ian Sunter, K, Hamilton
1971	Wayne Harris, LB, Calgary	Dick Suderman, DE, Calgary
1970	Sonny Wade, QB, Montreal	
1969	Russ Jackson, QB, Ottawa	
1968	Vic Washington, RB, Ottawa	
1967	Joe Zuger, QB, Hamilton	
1966	None selected	
1965	None selected	
1964	None selected	
1963	None selected	
1962	Leo Lewis, RB, Winnipeg	
1961	Ken Ploen, QB, Winnipeg	
1960	Ron Stewart, RB, Ottawa	
1959	Charlie Shepard, RB, Winnipeg	

GREY CUP OFFICIALS 1909 TO 2011

REFEREES	
Jake Ireland	12
Hec Crighton	9
Paul Dojack	8
Dave Yule	7
Seymour Wilson	6
Don Barker	6
Joe O'Brien	5
Harry Ross	3
Glen Johnson	3
Phil Mackenzie	2
W.B. Hendry	2
Ben Simpson	2
Hal De Gruchy	2
Reg De Gruchy	2
John McKelvey	2
Cliff Roseborough	2
Harry Bowden	2
Ray Boucher	2
Bill Fry	2
Bill Dell	2
Lorne Woods	2
Ken Lazaruk	2
Andre Proulx	2

JUDGES AND UMPIRES	
Bill Nairn	13
Seymour Wilson	12
Jacques Decarie	10
Al McColman	10
Cliff Roseborough	8
Chuck Paul	8
Ken Picot	8
Bill Hagans	8
Hap Shouldice	7
Art McAvoy	7
Taylor Patterson	6
Dave Hutton	6
Brent Buchko	6
Kim Murphy	6
Don Cousens	6
Reg De Gruchy	5
Eddie Grant	5
Johnny Munro	5
Paul Dojack	5
Ray Boucher	5
Bernie Prusko	5
Heinz Brademann	5

TOTAL GREY CUPS	
Seymour Wilson	18
Hec Crighton	13
Bill Nairn	13
Paul Dojack	13
Jake Ireland	12
Cliff Roseborough	10
Jacques Decarie	10
Dave Yule	10
Al McColman	10
Five tied with	8

(Does not include games assigned as alternate or observer)

GREY CUP TEAM RECORDS, 1909–2011

MOST GAMES
24 — Edmonton Eskimos
24 — Winnipeg Blue Bombers/'Pegs
21 — Toronto Argonauts

MOST CONSECUTIVE APPEARANCES
6 — Edmonton Eskimos (1977–82)
5 — Regina Roughriders (1928–32)
5 — Hamilton Tiger-Cats (1961–65)

MOST WINS
15 — Toronto Argonauts
13 — Edmonton Eskimos
10 — Winnipeg Blue Bombers/'Pegs

MOST LOSSES
15 — Regina/Saskatchewan Roughriders
14 — Winnipeg Blue Bombers/'Pegs
11 — Edmonton Eskimos/Elks
11 — Montreal Alouettes

MOST POINTS, ALL-TIME
533 — Edmonton Eskimos/Elks (24 games)
430 — Toronto Argonauts (21 games)
416 — Winnipeg Blue Bombers/'Pegs (24 games)

MOST POINTS, ONE TEAM
54 — Queen's University, 1923, vs. Regina (0)
50 — Edmonton, 1956, vs. Montreal (27)
50 — Winnipeg, 1990, vs. Edmonton (11)

MOST POINTS, BOTH TEAMS
83 — Saskatchewan vs. Hamilton, 1989 (43–40)
80 — Toronto vs. Edmonton, 1996 (43–37)
77 — Edmonton vs. Montreal, 1956 (50–27)

FEWEST POINTS, BOTH TEAMS
7 — Toronto vs. Sarnia, 1933 (4–3)
7 — Toronto vs. Winnipeg, 1937 (4–3)
13 — Toronto RCAF vs. Winnipeg RCAF, 1942 (8–5)
13 — St. Hyacinthe/Donnacona Navy vs. Hamilton Flying Wildcats, 1944 (7–6)
13 — Toronto vs. Winnipeg, 1950 (13–0)

FEWEST POINTS, WINNING TEAM
4 — Toronto, 1933, vs. Sarnia (3)
4 — Toronto, 1937, vs. Winnipeg (3)
7 — St. Hyacinthe/Donnacona Navy Combines, 1944, vs. Hamilton Flying Wildcats (6)

MOST POINTS, LOSING TEAM
40 — Hamilton, 1989, vs. Saskatchewan (43)
37 — Edmonton, 1996, vs. Toronto (43)
36 — Toronto, 1987, vs. Edmonton (38)

MOST TOUCHDOWNS, ONE TEAM
9 — Queen's University, 1923, vs. Regina
7 — Hamilton Tigers, 1913, vs. Toronto Parkdale
7 — Edmonton, 1956, vs. Montreal

MOST TOUCHDOWNS, BOTH TEAMS
11 — Edmonton (7) vs. Montreal (4), 1956
9 — Queen's University (9) vs. Regina (0), 1923
9 — Toronto (4) vs. Edmonton (5), 1996

MOST FIELD GOALS, ONE TEAM
6 — Montreal, 1977, vs. Edmonton
6 — Hamilton, 1986, vs. Edmonton
6 — Edmonton, 1993, vs. Winnipeg
6 — British Columbia, 2006, vs. Montreal

MOST FIELD GOALS, BOTH TEAMS
9 — Edmonton (6) vs. Winnipeg (3), 1993
8 — Montreal (6) vs. Edmonton (2), 1977
8 — Saskatchewan (4) vs. Hamilton (4), 1989

FIRST DOWNS, OFFENCE & POSSESSION (SINCE 1952)

MOST FIRST DOWNS, ONE TEAM
38 — Edmonton, 1956, vs. Montreal
36 — Edmonton, 1955, vs. Montreal
35 — Montreal, 1954, vs. Edmonton

FEWEST FIRST DOWNS, ONE TEAM
6 — Hamilton, 1965, vs. Winnipeg
7 — Montreal, 1991, vs. Calgary
7 — Toronto, 2002, vs. Edmonton

MOST FIRST DOWNS, BOTH TEAMS
66 — Edmonton (36) vs. Montreal (30), 1955
63 — Edmonton (38) vs. Montreal (25), 1956

MOST FIRST DOWNS RUSHING, ONE TEAM
34 — Edmonton, 1956, vs. Montreal
29 — Edmonton, 1955, vs. Montreal

MOST FIRST DOWNS PASSING, ONE TEAM
24 — Saskatchewan, 1989, vs. Hamilton
23 — Montreal, 1955, vs. Edmonton

MOST FIRST DOWNS BY PENALTY, ONE TEAM
5 — British Columbia, 1988, vs. Winnipeg
5 — Edmonton, 2003, vs. Montreal

MOST YARDS NET OFFENCE, ONE TEAM
651 — Montreal, 1954, vs. Edmonton
606 — Edmonton, 1980, vs. Hamilton
566 — Edmonton, 1955, vs. Montreal

MOST YARDS NET OFFENCE, BOTH TEAMS
1,115 — Edmonton (566) vs. Montreal (549), 1955
1,076 — Edmonton (425) vs. Montreal (651), 1954
1,023 — Edmonton (557) vs. Montreal (466), 1956

FEWEST YARDS NET OFFENCE, ONE TEAM
102 — Edmonton, 1977, vs. Montreal
150 — Edmonton, 1974, vs. Montreal
170 — Calgary, 1970, vs. Montreal

FEWEST YARDS NET OFFENCE, BOTH TEAMS
384 — Montreal (234) vs. Edmonton (150), 1974
386 — Hamilton (207) vs. Winnipeg (179), 1965

LONGEST SCORING DRIVE (YARDS)
101 — Montreal (12 plays), 1954, vs. Edmonton
101 — Montreal (7 plays), 1956, vs. Edmonton
100 — Edmonton (3 plays), 1980, vs. Hamilton

MOST PLAYS FROM SCRIMMAGE
116 — Edmonton, 1956, vs. Montreal
100 — Winnipeg, 1961, vs. Hamilton

RUSHING (SINCE 1952)

MOST RUSHING ATTEMPTS, ONE TEAM
82 — Edmonton, 1956, vs. Montreal
62 — Edmonton, 1955, vs. Montreal
57 — Winnipeg, 1961, vs. Hamilton

FEWEST RUSHING ATTEMPTS, ONE TEAM
8 — Toronto, 1982, vs. Edmonton
8 — Montreal, 2008, vs. Calgary

MOST RUSHING ATTEMPTS, BOTH TEAMS
116 — Edmonton (82) vs. Montreal (34), 1956

MOST RUSHING YARDS, ONE TEAM
457 — Edmonton, 1956, vs. Montreal
438 — Edmonton, 1955, vs. Montreal
291 — Montreal, 1954, vs. Edmonton

FEWEST RUSHING YARDS, ONE TEAM
24 — Hamilton, 1984, vs. Winnipeg
36 — Winnipeg, 1992, vs. Calgary

MOST RUSHING YARDS, BOTH TEAMS
643 — Edmonton (457) vs. Montreal (186),
 1956
556 — Edmonton (265) vs. Montreal (291),
 1954

FEWEST RUSHING YARDS, BOTH TEAMS
84 — Calgary (48) vs. Winnipeg (36), 1992

MOST RUSHING TOUCHDOWNS, ONE TEAM
6 — Queen's University, 1923, vs. Regina
6 — Edmonton, 1956, vs. Montreal
5 — Hamilton Tigers, 1913, vs. Toronto
 Parkdale

MOST RUSHING TOUCHDOWNS, BOTH TEAMS
9 — Edmonton (6) vs. Montreal (3), 1956
6 — Queens University (6) vs. Regina (0), 1923

PASSING (SINCE 1952, EXCEPT *SINCE 1909)

MOST PASS ATTEMPTS, ONE TEAM
58 — Calgary, 1991, vs. Toronto
49 — Calgary, 1992, vs. Winnipeg
48 — Calgary, 1995, vs. Baltimore
48 — Winnipeg, 1953, vs. Hamilton

FEWEST PASS ATTEMPTS, ONE TEAM
5 — Hamilton, 1965, vs. Winnipeg

MOST PASS COMPLETIONS, ONE TEAM
35 — Edmonton, 2005, vs. Montreal (OT)
34 — Calgary, 1991, vs. Toronto
33 — Calgary, 1992, vs. Winnipeg

FEWEST PASS COMPLETIONS, ONE TEAM
2 — Hamilton, 1965, vs. Winnipeg

MOST PASSING YARDS, ONE TEAM
508 — Montreal, 1955, vs. Edmonton
480 — Calgary, 1992, vs. Winnipeg
474 — Saskatchewan, 1989, vs. Hamilton

FEWEST PASSING YARDS, ONE TEAM
65 — Winnipeg, 1965, vs. Hamilton
67 — Hamilton, 1957, vs. Winnipeg
71 — Hamilton, 1965, vs. Winnipeg

MOST PASSING TOUCHDOWNS, ONE TEAM*
4 — Toronto, 1946, vs. Winnipeg
4 — Ottawa, 1969, vs. Saskatchewan
4 — Edmonton, 1980, vs. Hamilton
4 — Winnipeg, 1990, vs. Edmonton

KICKING (SINCE 1952, EXCEPT *SINCE 1909)

MOST PUNTS, ONE TEAM
19 — Hamilton, 1961, vs. Winnipeg
17 — Winnipeg, 1959, vs. Hamilton
17 — Hamilton, 1967, vs. Saskatchewan
(Note: Toronto punted 29 times vs. Sarnia in 1933)

MOST PUNTS, BOTH TEAMS
33 — Winnipeg (17) vs. Hamilton (16), 1959
33 — Winnipeg (14) vs. Hamilton (19), 1961

MOST PUNTING YARDS, ONE TEAM
782 — Winnipeg, 1959, vs. Hamilton
760 — Hamilton, 1967, vs. Saskatchewan
749 — Hamilton, 1961, vs. Winnipeg
(Note: Punting yards only — does not include yardage on unsuc-
cessful field goal attempts)

MOST PUNTING YARDS, BOTH TEAMS
1,417 — Winnipeg (782) vs. Hamilton (635), 1959
1,316 — Winnipeg (613) vs. Hamilton (703), 1961

MOST FIELD GOAL ATTEMPTS, ONE TEAM
7 — Montreal, 1977, vs. Edmonton
7 — Edmonton, 1993, vs. Winnipeg

MOST FIELD GOALS MADE, ONE TEAM*
6 — Montreal (7 attempts), 1977, vs. Edmonton
6 — Hamilton (6 attempts), 1986, vs. Edmonton
6 — Edmonton (7 attempts), 1993, vs. Winnipeg
6 — British Columbia (6 attempts), 2006, vs.
 Montreal

MOST FIELD GOAL ATTEMPTS, BOTH TEAMS
11 — British Columbia (6) vs. Baltimore (5), 1994
10 — Edmonton (7) vs. Winnipeg (3), 1993

MOST FIELD GOAL ATTEMPTS, BOTH TEAMS*
9 — Edmonton (6) vs. Winnipeg (3), 1993
8 — Montreal (6) vs. Edmonton (2), 1977
8 — Saskatchewan (4) vs. Hamilton (4), 1989

MOST KICKOFFS, ONE TEAM
10 — Winnipeg, 1984, vs. Hamilton
10 — Hamilton, 1989, vs. Saskatchewan

MOST KICKOFFS, BOTH TEAMS
18 — Hamilton (10) vs. Saskatchewan (8), 1989

MOST KICKOFF YARDS, ONE TEAM
662 — Hamilton, 1969, vs. Saskatchewan
551 — Winnipeg, 1984, vs. Hamilton

KICK RETURNS
(SINCE 1952, EXCEPT *SINCE 1909)

MOST PUNT RETURNS, ONE TEAM
17 — Winnipeg, 1961, vs. Hamilton
15 — Winnipeg, 1957, vs. Hamilton
15 — Winnipeg, 1959, vs. Hamilton
15 — Saskatchewan, 1967, vs. Hamilton
15 — Montreal, 1970, vs. Calgary

MOST PUNT RETURN YARDS, ONE TEAM
118 — Winnipeg, 2011, vs. British Columbia
117 — Montreal, 1977, vs. Edmonton
114 — Ottawa, 1976, vs. Saskatchewan

PUNT RETURN TOUCHDOWNS, ONE TEAM*
1 — Winnipeg, 1935, vs. Hamilton Tigers
1 — Ottawa, 1976, vs. Saskatchewan
1 — Baltimore, 1995, vs. Calgary
1 — Toronto, 1996, vs. Edmonton

MOST KICKOFF RETURNS, ONE TEAM
10 — Saskatchewan, 1989, vs. Hamilton
10 — Hamilton, 1984, vs. Winnipeg

MOST KICKOFF RETURN YARDS, ONE TEAM
296 — Saskatchewan, 1989, vs. Hamilton
244 — Toronto, 1991, vs. Calgary

PENALTIES AND TURNOVERS (SINCE 1952)

MOST PENALTIES, ONE TEAM
19 — Montreal, 1977, vs. Edmonton
15 — Edmonton, 1979, vs. Montreal
14 — Edmonton, 2003, vs. Montreal

MOST PENALTIES, BOTH TEAMS
27 — Montreal (19) vs. Edmonton (8), 1977
27 — Edmonton (14) vs. Montreal (13), 2003
23 — Winnipeg (12) vs. British Columbia (11), 1988
23 — Edmonton (12) vs. Montreal (11), 2005

MOST PENALTY YARDS, BOTH TEAMS
189 — Edmonton (67) vs. Montreal (122), 2003
181 — Winnipeg (86) vs. British Columbia (95), 1988
178 — Edmonton (108) vs. Montreal (70), 2002

MOST TURNOVERS, ONE TEAM
11 — Edmonton, 1986, vs. Hamilton
10 — Montreal, 1956, vs. Edmonton
10 — Winnipeg, 1957, vs. Hamilton
10 — Edmonton, 1977, vs. Montreal

MOST TURNOVERS, BOTH TEAMS
16 — Edmonton (11) vs. Hamilton (5), 1986
14 — Edmonton (5) vs. Montreal (9), 1954
14 — Edmonton (10) vs. Montreal (4), 1977

FEWEST TURNOVERS, BOTH TEAMS
1 — Toronto (0) vs. Edmonton (1), 1996
1 — Toronto (0) vs. British Columbia (1), 2004
1 — Montreal (0) vs. Saskatchewan (1), 2010
1 — British Columbia (0) vs. Winnipeg (1), 2011

MOST FUMBLES, ONE TEAM
8 — Montreal, 1954, vs. Edmonton
8 — Winnipeg, 1957, vs. Hamilton
8 — Edmonton, 1973, vs. Ottawa
8 — Edmonton, 1986, vs. Hamilton

MOST FUMBLES, BOTH TEAMS
14 — Edmonton (6) vs. Montreal (8), 1954
12 — Hamilton (4) vs. Winnipeg (8), 1957

MOST FUMBLES LOST, ONE TEAM
7 — Edmonton, 1986, vs. Hamilton
6 — Montreal, 1954, vs. Edmonton
6 — Winnipeg, 1957, vs. Hamilton

MOST INTERCEPTIONS THROWN, ONE TEAM
4 — Montreal, 1956, vs. Edmonton
4 — Edmonton, 1977, vs. Montreal
4 — Hamilton, 1980, vs. Edmonton

MOST INTERCEPTIONS THROWN, BOTH TEAMS
6 — Edmonton (2) vs. Montreal (4), 1956
6 — Edmonton (3) vs. Ottawa (3), 1981

DEFENSIVE STATISTICS (SINCE 1952)

MOST QUARTERBACK SACKS, ONE TEAM
13 — Hamilton, 1986, vs. Edmonton
8 — British Columbia, 1985, vs. Hamilton
7 — Edmonton, 1956, vs. Montreal
7 — Edmonton, 1979, vs. Montreal
7 — Edmonton, 1982, vs. Toronto
7 — British Columbia, 1983, vs. Toronto
7 — Toronto, 1991, vs. Calgary

MOST QUARTERBACK SACKS, BOTH TEAMS
15 — Hamilton (13) vs. Edmonton (2), 1986
10 — Edmonton (6) vs. Hamilton (4), 1980
10 — British Columbia (8) vs. Hamilton (2), 1985

MOST FUMBLE RETURNS, ONE TEAM
6 — Hamilton, 1957, vs. Winnipeg
6 — Hamilton, 1986, vs. Edmonton

MOST FUMBLE RETURN YARDS, ONE TEAM
90 — Edmonton, 1954, vs. Montreal
84 — British Columbia, 1964, vs. Hamilton

MOST INTERCEPTION RETURN YARDS, ONE TEAM
88 — Winnipeg, 1990, vs. Edmonton
88 — Montreal, 1977, vs. Edmonton

MOST DEFENSIVE TACKLES, ONE TEAM
88 — Montreal, 1956, vs. Edmonton
67 — Montreal, 1955, vs. Edmonton
64 — Hamilton, 1961, vs. Winnipeg

MOST SPECIAL-TEAM TACKLES, ONE TEAM
20 — Hamilton, 1957, vs. Winnipeg
18 — Hamilton, 1967, vs. Saskatchewan
17 — Hamilton, 1961, vs. Winnipeg

MISCELLANEOUS

HIGHEST ATTENDANCE
68,318 — Nov. 27, 1977, Olympic Stadium, Montreal (Montreal 41, Edmonton 6)
66,308 — Nov. 23, 2008, Olympic Stadium, Montreal (Calgary 22, Montreal 14)
65,255 — Nov. 25, 2001, Olympic Stadium, Montreal (Calgary 27, Winnipeg 19)
65,113 — Nov. 25, 1979, Olympic Stadium, Montreal (Edmonton 17, Montreal 9)
63,317 — Nov. 28, 2010, Commonwealth Stadium, Edmonton (Montreal 21, Saskatchewan 18)

MOST FREQUENT HOST STADIUMS
30 — Varsity Stadium, Toronto†
12 — Exhibition Stadium, Toronto
8 — B.C. Place, Vancouver
7 — Empire Stadium, Vancouver
7 — Hamilton AAA Grounds, Hamilton
†Includes first leg of home-and-home series, 1940

STADIUMS HOSTING ONLY ONE GAME
Rosedale Field, Toronto (1909)
Richardson Stadium, Kingston (1922)
Percival Molson Memorial Stadium, Montreal (1931)
Davis Field, Sarnia (1933)
Autostade, Montreal (1969)

COLDEST GREY CUP GAMES
−17°C — Winnipeg, 1991
−11°C — Montreal, 1931
−10°C — Sarnia, 1933
−10°C — Calgary, 1975
−10°C — Edmonton, 1984

TEAMS THAT HAVE WON AT HOME (SINCE 1945)
2011 — British Columbia
1994 — British Columbia
1977 — Montreal
1972 — Hamilton
1952 — Toronto
1950 — Toronto
1947 — Toronto
1946 — Toronto
1945 — Toronto

GREY CUP HOST CITIES

46 — Toronto
15 — Vancouver
10 — Hamilton
8 — Montreal
6 — Ottawa
4 — Calgary
4 — Edmonton
3 — Winnipeg
2 — Regina
1 — Kingston
1 — Sarnia

(Note: In 2012, Toronto hosts the Grey Cup for the 47th time. In 2013, Regina will host for the third time.)

GREY CUP INDIVIDUAL RECORDS

MOST APPEARANCES

9   Mel Wilson, Winnipeg, Winnipeg RCAF, Calgary
9   John Barrow, Hamilton
9   Tommy Grant, Hamilton
9   Angelo Mosca, Hamilton, Ottawa
9   Dave Cutler, Edmonton
9   Larry Highbaugh, Edmonton
9   Hank Ilesic, Edmonton, Toronto

MOST GAMES PLAYED FOR WINNING TEAM

7   Jack Wedley, Toronto, St. Hyacinthe/Donnacona Navy
7   Bill Stevenson, Edmonton
7   Hank Ilesic, Edmonton, Toronto

SCORING

MOST POINTS, ONE GAME

23   Don Sweet, Montreal, 1977
22   Jim Van Pelt, Winnipeg, 1958
21   Paul Osbaldiston, Hamilton, 1986
21   Sean Fleming, Edmonton, 1993

MOST POINTS, CAREER

72   Dave Cutler, Edmonton (9 games)
63   Paul Osbaldiston, Hamilton (4 games)
61   Don Sweet, Montreal (5 games)

MOST TOUCHDOWNS SCORED, ONE GAME

4   Art Wilson, Hamilton Tigers, 1913
3   Red Storey, Toronto, 1938
3   Jackie Parker, Edmonton, 1956
3   Tom Scott, Edmonton, 1980

MOST TOUCHDOWNS SCORED, CAREER

6   Damon Allen, Edmonton, British Columbia, Toronto (5 games)
5   Hal Patterson, Montreal, Hamilton (7 games)
5   Brian Kelly, Edmonton (6 games)

MOST CONVERTS, ONE GAME

6   Dave Cutler, Edmonton, 1980
6   Trevor Kennerd, Winnipeg, 1990

MOST CONVERTS, CAREER

17   Don Sutherin, Hamilton, Ottawa (8 games)
16   Dave Cutler, Edmonton (9 games)
15   Sean Fleming, Edmonton (6 games)

MOST CONVERT ATTEMPTS, CAREER

21   Don Sutherin, Hamilton, Ottawa (8 games)
17   Dave Cutler, Edmonton (9 games)
15   Sean Fleming, Edmonton (6 games)

LONGEST FIELD GOAL (YARDS)

53   Carlos Huerta, Baltimore, 1995
52   Dave Cutler, Edmonton, 1975
51   Bob Macoritti, Saskatchewan, 1976
51   Terry Baker, Montreal, 2000

MOST FIELD GOALS MADE, ONE GAME

6   Don Sweet, Montreal, 1977
6   Paul Osbaldiston, Hamilton, 1986
6   Sean Fleming, Edmonton, 1993
6   Paul McCallum, British Columbia, 2006

MOST FIELD GOALS MADE, CAREER

18   Dave Cutler, Edmonton (9 games)
17   Don Sweet, Montreal (5 games)
16   Paul Osbaldiston, Hamilton (4 games)

MOST FIELD GOAL ATTEMPTS, ONE GAME

7   Don Sweet, Montreal, 1977
7   Sean Fleming, Edmonton, 1993

MOST FIELD GOAL ATTEMPTS, CAREER

22   Don Sweet, Montreal (5 games)
21   Dave Cutler, Edmonton (9 games)
21   Lui Passaglia, British Columbia (5 games)

HIGHEST FIELD GOAL PERCENTAGE, CAREER (AT LEAST 8 ATTEMPTS)

100.0   Mike Vanderjagt, Toronto, 1996–97 (9/9)
91.7   Paul McCallum, British Columbia, 1997, 2006 (11/12)
90.9   Trevor Kennerd, Winnipeg, 1984, 1988, 1990 (10/11)

MOST CONSECUTIVE FIELD GOALS MADE

13   Paul Osbaldiston, Hamilton (over 3 games)
9   Mike Vanderjagt, Toronto (over 2 games)
9   Paul McCallum, British Columbia (over 2 games)

MOST SINGLES, ONE GAME

8   Hugh Gall, University of Toronto, 1909
6   Huck Welch, Hamilton Tigers, 1929

MOST SINGLES, CAREER

12   Hugh Gall, University of Toronto, Toronto Parkdale (3 games)
12   Pep Leadlay, Queen's University, Hamilton Tigers (6 games)
10   Huck Welch, Hamilton Tigers, Montreal AAA (4 games)

RUSHING

MOST RUSHING ATTEMPTS, ONE GAME

30   Norm Kwong, Edmonton, 1955
28   Johnny Bright, Edmonton, 1956
23   George Reed, Saskatchewan, 1966

MOST RUSHING ATTEMPTS, CAREER

77   George Reed, Saskatchewan (4 games)
76   Mike Pringle, Baltimore, Montreal, Edmonton (4 games)
76   Norm Kwong, Calgary, Edmonton (7 games)

LONGEST RUSH (YARDS)

80   Vic Washington, Ottawa, 1968
74   Garney Henley, Hamilton, 1962
61   Ken Hobart, Hamilton, 1985 (QB record)

MOST RUSHING YARDS, ONE GAME

169   Johnny Bright, Edmonton, 1956
159   Antonio Warren, British Columbia, 2004
145   Norm Kwong, Edmonton, 1955

MOST RUSHING YARDS, CAREER
393   Mike Pringle, Baltimore, Montreal, Edmonton (4 games)
358   Leo Lewis, Winnipeg (6 games)
346   George Reed, Saskatchewan (4 games)

MOST RUSHING TOUCHDOWNS, ONE GAME
4   Art Wilson, Hamilton Tigers, 1913
3   Red Storey, Toronto, 1938

MOST RUSHING TOUCHDOWNS, CAREER
6   Damon Allen, Edmonton, British Columbia, Toronto (5 games)
4   Art Wilson, Hamilton Tigers (1 game)
4   Johnny Bright, Edmonton (4 games)
4   Avon Cobourne, Montreal (4 games)
4   Jim Germany, Edmonton (6 games)
4   Norm Kwong, Calgary, Edmonton (7 games)

PASS RECEIVING

MOST PASS RECEPTIONS, ONE GAME
12   Red O'Quinn, Montreal, 1954
12   Tom Scott, Edmonton, 1980
11   Ben Cahoon, Montreal, 2006
11   Nik Lewis, Calgary, 2008

MOST PASS RECEPTIONS, CAREER
46   Ben Cahoon, Montreal (8 games)
29   Hal Patterson, Montreal, Hamilton (7 games)
26   Tom Scott, Edmonton (5 games)

LONGEST PASS RECEPTION (YARDS)
99   Pat Woodcock, Montreal, 2002 (from Anthony Calvillo)
90   Red O'Quinn, Montreal, 1954 (from Sam Etcheverry)
90   Paul Dekker, Hamilton, 1961 (from Bernie Faloney)

MOST PASS RECEIVING YARDS, ONE GAME
290   Red O'Quinn, 1954, Montreal
174   Whit Tucker, 1966, Ottawa
174   Tom Scott, 1980, Edmonton

MOST PASS RECEIVING YARDS, CAREER
658   Ben Cahoon, Montreal (8 games)
575   Hal Patterson, Montreal, Hamilton (7 games)
465   Red O'Quinn, Montreal (3 games)

MOST PASS RECEIVING TOUCHDOWNS, ONE GAME
3   Tom Scott, Edmonton, 1980

MOST PASS RECEIVING TOUCHDOWNS, CAREER
5   Brian Kelly, Edmonton (6 games)
4   Hal Patterson, Montreal, Hamilton (7 games)
4   Tom Scott, Edmonton (5 games)

PASSING

MOST PASS ATTEMPTS, ONE GAME
58   Danny Barrett, Calgary, 1991
49   Doug Flutie, Calgary, 1992
48   Doug Flutie, Calgary, 1995
48   Jack Jacobs, Winnipeg, 1953

MOST PASS ATTEMPTS, CAREER
298   Anthony Calvillo, Montreal (8 games)
170   Doug Flutie, Calgary, Toronto (4 games)

MOST PASS COMPLETIONS, ONE GAME
35   Ricky Ray, Edmonton, 2005
34   Danny Barrett, Calgary, 1991
33   Doug Flutie, Calgary, 1992

MOST PASS COMPLETIONS, CAREER
179   Anthony Calvillo, Montreal (8 games)
108   Doug Flutie, Calgary, Toronto (4 games)
85   Bernie Faloney, Edmonton, Hamilton (7 games)

HIGHEST COMPLETION PERCENTAGE, ONE GAME
78.9   Doug Flutie, Toronto, 1997
77.8   Ricky Ray, Edmonton, 2005
76.3   Anthony Calvillo, Montreal, 2008

HIGHEST COMPLETION PERCENTAGE, CAREER
65.9   Ricky Ray, Edmonton
64.6   Jack Jacobs, Winnipeg

MOST PASSING YARDS, ONE GAME
508   Sam Etcheverry, Montreal, 1955
480   Doug Flutie, Calgary, 1992
474   Kent Austin, Saskatchewan, 1989

MOST PASSING YARDS, CAREER
2,470   Anthony Calvillo, Montreal (8 games)
1,420   Doug Flutie, Calgary, Toronto (4 games)
1,357   Danny McManus, Winnipeg, British Columbia, Edmonton, Hamilton (6 games)

MOST TOUCHDOWN PASSES, ONE GAME
4   Russ Jackson, Ottawa, 1966
3   11 players (Joe Krol, Tor., 1946; Sam Etcheverry, Mtl., 1954; Ron Lancaster, Sask., 1966; Sonny Wade, Mtl., 1977; Warren Moon, Edm., 1980; Roy Dewalt, B.C., 1985; Mike Kerrigan, Ham., 1989; Kent Austin, Sask., 1989; Tom Burgess, Wpg., 1990; Danny McManus, Edm., 1996; Doug Flutie, Tor., 1997)

MOST TOUCHDOWN PASSES, CAREER
9   Anthony Calvillo, Montreal (8 games)
8   Russ Jackson, Ottawa (4 games)
8   Danny McManus, Winnipeg, British Columbia, Edmonton, Hamilton (6 games)
8   Bernie Faloney, Edmonton, Hamilton (7 games)

MOST INTERCEPTIONS THROWN, CAREER
8   Sam Etcheverry, Montreal (3 games)
6   Bruce Lemmerman, Edmonton (4 games)
6   Ron Lancaster, Ottawa, Saskatchewan (6 games)

COMBINED YARDS AND KICK RETURNS

MOST COMBINED YARDS, ONE GAME
290   Red O'Quinn, Montreal, 1954
279   Antonio Warren, British Columbia, 2004
260   Raghib Ismail, Toronto, 1991

MOST COMBINED YARDS, CAREER
770   Leo Lewis, Winnipeg (6 games)
698   Hal Patterson, Montreal, Hamilton (7 games)
666   Ben Cahoon, Montreal (8 games)

MOST PUNT RETURNS, ONE GAME
13   Ron Latourelle, Winnipeg, 1961
12   Darnell Clash, British Columbia, 1985

MOST PUNT RETURNS, CAREER
38   Ron Latourelle, Winnipeg (5 games)
23   Keith Stokes, Montreal, Winnipeg (3 games)
22   Gregg Butler, Edmonton (4 games)

MOST PUNT RETURN YARDS, ONE GAME
118   Jovon Johnson, Winnipeg, 2011
105   Darnell Clash, British Columbia, 1985
93   Chris Wright, Baltimore, 1995

MOST PUNT RETURN YARDS, CAREER
237 Keith Stokes, Montreal, Winnipeg (3 games)
232 Ron Latourelle, Winnipeg (5 games)
223 Henry Williams, Edmonton (4 games)

LONGEST PUNT RETURN (YARDS)
82 Chris Wright, Baltimore, 1995
80 Jimmy Cunningham, Toronto, 1996
79 Bill Hatanaka, Ottawa, 1976

MOST KICKOFF RETURNS, ONE GAME
8 Dwight Edwards, Toronto, 1997
7 Obie Graves, Hamilton, 1980
7 Rufus Crawford, Hamilton, 1984

MOST KICKOFF RETURNS, CAREER
11 Rufus Crawford, Hamilton (2 games)
9 Tom Richards, Edmonton (2 games)
9 Leo Lewis, Winnipeg (6 games)

MOST KICKOFF RETURN YARDS, ONE GAME
183 Raghib Ismail, Toronto, 1991
169 Tim McCray, Saskatchewan, 1989
143 Tony Tompkins, Edmonton, 2005

MOST KICKOFF RETURN YARDS, CAREER
311 Leo Lewis, Winnipeg (6 games)
218 Henry Williams, Edmonton (4 games)
187 Tom Richards, Edmonton (2 games)

LONGEST KICKOFF RETURN (YARDS)
96 Tony Tompkins, Edmonton, 2005 (TD)
95 Adrion Smith, Toronto, 1997 (TD)
91 Henry Williams, Edmonton, 1996 (TD)

LONGEST UNSUCCESSFUL FIELD GOAL RETURN (YARDS)
115 Henry Williams, Edmonton, 1987 (TD)

PUNTING AND KICKOFFS

MOST PUNTS, ONE GAME
17 Charlie Shepard, Winnipeg, 1959
17 Joe Zuger, Hamilton, 1967

MOST PUNTS, CAREER
64 Hank Ilesic, Edmonton, Toronto (9 games)
53 Joe Zuger, Hamilton (5 games)
51 Cam Fraser, Hamilton (4 games)

MOST PUNTING YARDS, ONE GAME
782 Charlie Shepard, Winnipeg, 1959
760 Joe Zuger, Hamilton, 1967

MOST PUNTING YARDS, CAREER
2,735 Hank Ilesic, Edmonton, Toronto (9 games)
2,171 Joe Zuger, Hamilton (5 games)
2,166 Cam Fraser, Hamilton (4 games)

LONGEST PUNT (YARDS)
87 Alan Ford, Saskatchewan, 1967
85 Garry Lefebvre, Edmonton, 1973
84 Lui Passaglia, British Columbia, 1988

MOST KICKOFFS, ONE GAME
10 Trevor Kennerd, Winnipeg, 1984
10 Paul Osbaldiston, Hamilton, 1989

MOST KICKOFFS, CAREER
31 Dave Cutler, Edmonton (9 games)
29 Don Sutherin, Hamilton, Ottawa (8 games)
27 Sean Fleming, Edmonton (6 games)

MOST KICKOFF YARDS, ONE GAME
622 Paul Osbaldiston, Hamilton, 1989
551 Trevor Kennerd, Winnipeg, 1984

MOST KICKOFF YARDS, CAREER
1,623 Don Sutherin, Hamilton, Ottawa (8 games)
1,478 Paul Osbaldiston, Hamilton (4 games)

LONGEST KICKOFF (YARDS)
100 Dave Cutler, Edmonton, 1982

DEFENSIVE STATISTICS

MOST INTERCEPTION RETURNS, ONE GAME
3 James Johnson, Saskatchewan, 2007

MOST INTERCEPTION RETURNS, CAREER
4 Joe Hollimon, Edmonton (6 games)

MOST INTERCEPTION RETURN YARDS, ONE GAME
88 Vernon Perry, Montreal, 1977
88 Greg Battle, Winnipeg, 1990
54 Dick Thornton, Toronto, 1971

LONGEST INTERCEPTION RETURN (YARDS)
74 Vernon Perry, Montreal, 1977
56 Greg Battle, Winnipeg, 1990
54 Dick Thornton, Toronto, 1971

MOST FUMBLE RETURNS, ONE GAME
3 Phil Minnick, Winnipeg, 1965

LONGEST FUMBLE RETURN (YARDS)
90 Jackie Parker, Montreal, 1954
72 Ralph Goldston, 1958
70 Dick Fouts (5) and Bill Munsey (65), British Columbia, 1964

INTERCEPTIONS RETURNED FOR TOUCHDOWNS
In Grey Cup history, eight interceptions have been returned for touchdowns:
James Johnson, Saskatchewan, 2007
Adrion Smith, Toronto, 1996
Karl Anthony, Baltimore, 1994
Charles Gordon, British Columbia, 1994
Ed Berry, Toronto, 1991
Greg Battle, Winnipeg, 1990
Joe Krol, Toronto, 1945
Ike Sutton, Hamilton, 1932

MOST QUARTERBACK SACKS, ONE GAME
5 Grover Covington, Hamilton, 1986
4 Tyrone Jones, Winnipeg, 1984
3 Junior Ah You, Montreal, 1977
3 Dave Fennell, Edmonton, 1982
3 Rick Klassen, British Columbia, 1983
3 James Parker, British Columbia, 1985

MOST QUARTERBACK SACKS, CAREER
9 Dave Fennell, Edmonton (8 games)
7 John Barrow, Hamilton (9 games)
7 James Parker, Edmonton, British Columbia (5 games)

MOST DEFENSIVE TACKLES, ONE GAME (SINCE 1954)
16 Juan Sheridan, Montreal, 1955
13 Jackie Parker, Edmonton, 1955
12 Vince Scott, Hamilton, 1957

MOST DEFENSIVE TACKLES, CAREER
48 John Barrow, Hamilton (9 games)
42 Dan Kepley, Edmonton (7 games)
34 Juan Sheridan, Montreal (3 games)

INDEX

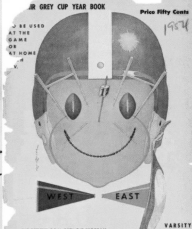

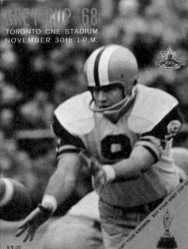

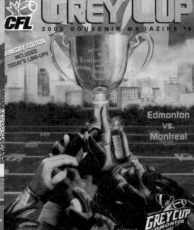
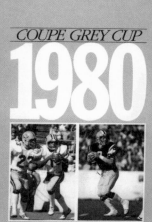